CLASHING TIDES OF COLOR

A Vivid Depiction and Analysis of a World in Competitive Disintegration and in Danger of Complex Chaos

T LOTHROP STODDARD

Ostara Publications

CLASHING TIDES OF COLOR

A Vivid Depiction and Analysis of a World in Competitive Disintegration and in Danger of Complex Chaos

T LOTHROP STODDARD

First published 1935.

This edition 2019

Ostara Publications

ostarapublications.com

ISBN 9781646066445

Contents

PROLOGUE
A WORLD IN DISINTEGRATION

OUR troubled times present an amazing paradox: a gigantic interplay of building up and tearing down; a simultaneous process of synthesis and disintegration. The contemporary world is being mastered, yet is becoming masterless. The new master is Western machine civilization. Having established its supremacy over those Western peoples who were its creators, it is now conquering the entire earth. From a material standpoint, its triumphant march athwart the globe cannot seemingly be stayed.

This civilization is unique. Nothing like it has ever happened before. Hence there are no precedents enabling us to foretell its ultimate effects. We simply do not know how mankind in general or particular races will adapt to the machine. But, judging by what is now going on in the world, this adaptation will be very difficult. We realize the profound transformations which machine civilization has already brought to us Occidentals among whom it arose. So, when we ponder what it has already done to us, we may well ask what it will do to peoples of widely different blood and temperament on whom it is breaking suddenly, without warning or preparation.

Suddenness is indeed the outstanding feature of the mechanizing process in which man is today involved. This machine civilization is supremely dynamic. Its distinctive characteristic is change—constant, rapid, and with no visible bounds. This accounts for the ever-quickening *tempo* of our times, wherein successive phases follow one another with bewildering speed and are sometimes literally telescoped—with the most disconcerting results.

The upshot is the downright chaotic state of contemporary world-affairs. And how appallingly swift has been the rise of the present world-situation! Because of recent developments, the previous balance between East and West has been virtually destroyed. Yet no new balance is as yet in sight, chiefly because Orient and Occident alike are ceasing to be their old selves. Both are losing their former coherence through internal disruption. This gives rise to a veritable welter of cross-purposes. All is provisional. It is most emphatically a transition period. Furthermore, there seems to be no way of estimating how long this transitional epoch will endure.

The transitory nature of our time is so obvious that forward-looking minds everywhere strive to glimpse a better and more stable era. What should it be like?

The machine clearly tends to unify the planet, in an economic sense. The practical benefits of an economically united and efficiently run world would be enormous. Science already makes theoretically possible a high general level of economic well-being. Surely an alluring prospect to a war-racked and depression-ridden age!

It certainly allures all those who see our troubles solved by a close-knit world-unity transcending not merely economic barriers but also national and racial lines. Whatever immediate concessions such international planners may feel obliged to make, the ultimate goal of most internationalist thinking is a planet-wide federation powerful enough to impose its decisions. Although we usually call this "internationalism," such a world-order could hardly fail to evolve into something beyond a federation of nations; into a World-State of truly *cosmopolitan* character.

Yet, right here bobs up the other side of our paradox: despite all this planning, few signs of such a world-order are today visible. On the contrary, never have national and racial divisions been more pronounced.

We get the contradictory spectacle of men talking one way and acting in quite another. The most eloquent appeals to self-interest seem to have no real effect upon conduct.

Why? Internationalists are wont to lay it on ignorance, crass conservatism, and so forth. Yet, making due allowance—for such matters, do they fully explain the world-wide scope of the stubborn resistance to anything like a genuine world-order? May there not exist other factors left out of the reckoning?

Perchance we may get a clue to the dilemma when we consider the character of the cosmopolitan internationalism which prevails today. Concentrating, as it does, upon the economic aspects of a mechanistic civilization, it is essentially materialistic in its aims and views mankind almost wholly in a materialistic way. Most internationalists incline toward the doctrine known as "economic determinism." This theory asserts that human motives and actions are basically due to economic causes.

But is this true? When present-day internationalists cite economic determinism, are they not making much the same mistake as the *laissez-faire* liberals of a century ago with their idea of an "economic man" guided by shrewd and calculating self-interest?

We certainly know today that the Economic Man is a myth. We are likewise assured by psychology and other sciences that mankind is primarily not rationalistic but emotional; also, that man's emotional nature cannot be described solely in terms of passion and prejudice but, in addition, as idealistic and spiritual.

Convictions move men to action more profoundly than does mere self-interest. 'When ideals and economics really clash, economics is apt to get the worst of it. And that is just what seems to be happening today.

Furthermore, men differ profoundly from one another in blood and temperament. These differences are reflected in their various groupings. And men tend instinctively to react against the sort of unification implied in a cosmopolitan world-order. Deep emotions are aroused. Cherished idealistic and racial values are involved.

All this reveals the profounder aspects of the query Can Man adapt himself to the Machine No one will seriously deny that our mechanistic civilization logically implies an increasing degree of human co-operation; that *some* sort of world-order is needed if our civilization is to endure.

Yet can it be a world-order which puts economic considerations ahead of everything else? At such a price, may not men refuse even the boon of material prosperity?

With these basic considerations in mind, we shall attempt a survey of the outstanding problems in contemporary world-affairs. But let us first consider certain broad phases that influence them all.

The Thunderbolt of Armageddon

The cataclysm of 1914 was no malign accident. Its causes, deep-rooted in the past, made tragedy inevitable. Long before that fateful year, some far-sighted observers began to fear that stormy times were at hand. But such misgivings were exceptional. The average European or American professed a robust faith in the nineteenth-century gospel of automatic progress. As Georg Brandes aptly put it: "We entered the twentieth century devoted to illusions."

Thus, wedded to illusion, the sudden outburst of the Great War caught the mass of mankind mentally unprepared. There is a peculiar poignancy to memories of that last pre-war June of 1914. Below the thin crust of tranquility, volcanic forces were seething. Yet no perception of those lethal forces was in the minds of ordinary men.

"An age was dying, but it was not conscious of its own decease What was it, in a word, that was dying during those gentle days of June Security, perhaps So the age of progress made no bow to posterity, composed no last will and testament It did not know that it was about to die."[1]

No More Certitudes!

The mental and spiritual shock of the Great War, coming unheralded like a bolt from the blue, was terrible. Only today do we begin to realize the range and depth of Armageddon's shattering effects in the realms of mind and soul.

The hardest spiritual blow which the war dealt our Western world was the smashing of its faith in progress. Though already suspect before the war in certain circles, it had remained the central idea in the world-outlook of the average European and American. This assurance the war effectively destroyed throughout Europe. In America it lingered on in the guise of an irrational optimism

---

1 R. L. Duffus, "Just Before the Great War," *New York Times Magazine*, June 17, 1934.

until the Great Depression completed the devastating work begun by the Great War. We may safely say that today belief in automatic progress is pretty well extirpated.

But this loss of faith entails grave spiritual consequences. Along with the vanished idea of progress has gone much of that sense of security and optimistic certainty which did so much to energize the Western world throughout the nineteenth century. Ever since 1914 we have been oppressed by a deepening pall of insecurity. As for the old-time certainty—where is it to be discovered in our current affairs? War and revolution have assailed our entire political, economic, and social order. No institution, no ideal has been immune.

The grim truth is that today, humanly speaking, *there are no more certitudes.* I say "humanly speaking" because, beyond the material world, beyond even the ethical relationships of man to man, there lies the spiritual borderland where finite man reaches out towards the Infinite. Religion is of transcendent importance, and its effects upon every phase of human life are as profound as they are manifold.

Yet religion, *as such,* cannot properly form a part of our present survey, because religion lies on a different plane. All true religious experience is essentially personal, arrived at subjectively, not through reason, but by faith. There is thus no common denominator enabling us to evaluate purely religious problems with those of this world.

The war enormously aggravated problems of adaptation to a machine civilization which would have arisen even if Armageddon had never been. The chaotic confusion of the Western spirit produced both by the war itself and by the hollowness of the post-war settlement explains the existence of vast multitudes yearning for security; homesick for lost certitudes.

And that, in turn, accounts for much of the current drift to political extremes like Communism or Fascism in its various forms. For each of these movements offers the believer new certainties in place of the old. Both are, in the last analysis, militant creeds. Both command allegiance, silence criticism, proclaim finalities. On either of their martial bosoms the sincere convert can find peace of mind.

The Decline of Western-White Supremacy

To the shattering impact of the Great War and its aftermath is due in large measure the amazingly rapid shifts in world-affairs during the last fifteen years. For the preceding four centuries the basis of world-politics had been the ever-waxing ascendancy of the white peoples of Europe and their offshoots in America. By the year 1900, Western world-supremacy had attained its climax. At that date, Western man stood the indisputable master of the planet.

Then came a swift turn of fortune. The first real challenge to white world-supremacy was the Russo-Japanese War of 1904. It showed that an Oriental people had adopted Western machine civilization—enough of it, at any rate, to beat a European Great Power both on land and sea. The shock to Western prestige was prodigious and far-reaching. Throughout Asia and even in Africa, races hitherto resigned or sullenly submissive began to dream of throwing off white control.

Japan's transformation was merely a sign of the Westernizing trend throughout the world. Western machine civilization had ceased to be the monopoly of its creators. Not merely Western technique but Western ideas were undermining the whole fabric of ancient societies in the most distant parts of the globe.

The inevitable result must be a readjustment in the relations of the white and non-white races which would necessarily imply a lessening of white world-supremacy. This would have come even without the Russo-Japanese War. But the readjustment would have been much more gradual—a process of devolution rather than spasms of revolt. Even the shock of that war left the West powerful enough to discourage sudden overturns by violent methods.

The Great War upset the wavering balance of world politics. Throughout Asia, at least, white supremacy was clearly foredoomed. The chief uncertainty was whether the West would be strong enough to beat an orderly retreat; whether the process of retirement could be so arranged as to avert catastrophic wars and the almost equally catastrophic sundering of economic ties which, in the form of trade and investment, had been close-knit during the long period of Western control Unfortunately, Europe's failure to close the Great War with a constructive peace, together with its chronic internal broils, further weakened its effective strength, and hastened the decline of its prestige and authority in the outer world. And, of course, this correspondingly encouraged all those bent on overthrowing white supremacy by war or revolution.

"The Rising Tide of Color"

Such was the ominous situation toward the close of 1919. The peace treaties just signed were obviously mere pacts of power imposed upon defeated nations who would never reconcile themselves to such humiliating inferiority. The so-called peace was thus no peace; it was a mere truce, big with the threat of future internecine wars.

The "New Europe" was, therefore, erected on rotten foundations. Also, by building on those same foundations, the experimental League of Nations was badly compromised.

This was not all. Bleeding, ulcerated, semi-bankrupt Europe was menaced with red revolution. Bolshevik Russia had thrown down the gauntlet to the "bourgeois" world, and Communism was spreading like wildfire through starving, war-crazed peoples. In that gloomy autumn of 1919, there was a very real danger that most of Europe would either go Communist or sink into downright chaos.

Such was the moment when the author of this, present book undertook a survey of the relations between the white and non-white worlds.

He called it *The Rising Tide of Color Against White World-Supremacy.* And he believes the title fitted a condition which then existed. At that time, the racial world-situation possessed a certain epic simplicity.

On one side stood the West, gravely weakened morally as well as materially, but retaining great military and economic power. In opposition stood an awakened Orient.

All Asia had become conscious of deep antagonism to a Western supremacy still strong enough to call for joint efforts by Asiatics if they hoped to throw off Western control. The scales almost balanced. As the West grew weaker, a crucial hour might arrive when the East would strike for decisive victory.

This the writer realized. What he did not then sufficiently realize was the rate at which Western machine civilization was sweeping over the world. He failed to note that the effects of Western technique, methods, and ideas upon the Orient were more disruptive there than in the West itself. That fact, however, the ensuing fifteen years have amply proved.

We thus observe the following paradox: The very factor which quickened the Orient, armed Japan, and undermined Western supremacy has at the same time so disintegrated the old Orient that united action against the West becomes virtually impossible. The Homeric duel between an embattled East and West is apparently adjourned, *sine die*.

That does not mean that Asia's desire to end Western supremacy has abated. It merely means that the struggle has become much more complex. "The Rising Tide" has risen portentously, these past fifteen years. Only, instead of roaring in like a tidal bore up an estuary, it has become more like a rip-tide—a confused welter of swirling eddies and choppy waves dashing against one another as well as against the confining shores.

In short, East and West are today subject to the same process of disintegration, though at different *tempos* and in different ways. If the West has almost lost its former sense of solidarity, the East is being literally Balkanized by the impact of Western civilization and by novel ideas such as Nationalism and Communism.

True, the basic contrast between Orient and Occident still persists. Their relations must be readjusted, and it is unlikely that this will be done peacefully.

The coming decades in world-affairs will almost certainly be turbulent and full of trouble. Yet the likelihood of a clean-cut racial world-war grows ever more remote. We are much more apt to see a tangled series of local or regional wars, uprisings, and revolutions, not merely between Eastern and Western peoples, but also between Orientals themselves.

Nationalism Rampant

Nationalism is today aflame throughout the world. It is unquestionably the great dynamic of our time. Deplored and condemned alike by idealists and economists, the nationalistic ferment goes on without resistance. Every attempt to establish a "world—order" transcending national lines has come to naught. Indeed, these very attempts at international action seem to quicken the ferment and stir up nationalist passions.

Why is this? Why have all those eloquent exhortations, those solemn warnings, those logical appeals to self-interest failed to reverse the current trend? Explanations are legion.

Some champions of internationalist ideals tell us that nationalism is a disease—a sort of group-madness today afflicting mankind in a peculiarly virulent form. Others ascribe it to the persistence of primitive instincts; to the call of clan and tribe, ringing down the ages and setting strict emotional bounds to the extent of human association. Still others ascribe present-day nationalism chiefly to the sinister propaganda of munition-makers and other brands of "patrioteers."

Now, all these explanations may contain a deal of truth. But they do not fully account for a movement of such intensity and world-wide scope. Let us try to dig a little deeper below the surface of events.

What is nationalism, anyway? There is nothing really mysterious about it. Nationalism is a state *of mind;* a *belief,* held by a large number of individuals, that they constitute a "nationality." In short, it is a sense of *belonging together* as a nation.

This "nation," as visualized by its believers, is a people or community associated together and organized under one government, and dwelling together in a distinct territory.

When the nationalist ideal is realized, we have what is known as a state. But we must not forget that this "state" is the coming to pass of an ideal which may have pre-existed for generations as a mere pious hope, with no outward signs like state sovereignty or physical frontiers.

On the other hand, a state need not be a nation. Witness the defunct Hapsburg Empire of Austria-Hungary—a mere assemblage of discordant nationalities, which flew to pieces under the shock of war.

So much for nationalism, *per se*. The next query is: Why should it be the dominant trend of our time? It was not always thus. At certain past epochs the nationalistic spirit was almost unknown. Of course, we must realize that nationalism is no recent invention. Even in its modern phase it is more than a century old, and it was busily remaking the map of Europe before our machine civilization had fairly got under way. Yet only since this civilization matured has nationalism attained its present intensity and spread throughout the globe. Hence, we may infer that, though nationalism is not a product of the machine, the machine has powerfully affected nationalism. And may we not also infer that the effect has been highly stimulating?

At first blush that sounds absurd, because the logical trend of our machine civilization would seem to be toward world unification. Science, the supreme expression of our age, is rapidly knitting the world together in a material sense. The airplane and the radio have virtually abolished distance. Nations and races once remote from one another are now being literally jostled together. Economically, countries have become interdependent, especially for raw materials. All this apparently implies the speedy emergence of a genuine world-organization. Internationalists of various shades unite in asserting that unless we humans learn to co-operate and devise effective controls on nationalistic rivalries and passions, we are headed for a grand smash in which our civilization will presumably perish.

This line of argument certainly sounds logical. Only—it doesn't seem to have much practical effect on human conduct. Science has effectively shrunk the globe, but it has not solidified mankind. All peoples may, in a sense, be neighbors, yet closer contacts do not necessarily promote friendship and mutual understanding. In many cases, quite the contrary! The more peoples are compressed, jostled together, economically standardized, the more they seem to rebel; to assert their independence and individuality. This is not primarily due to any doctrine or propaganda. It appears to be an instinctive reflex, springing from profound psychological causes.

The upshot is that, throughout the world, instead of drawing together, the peoples draw apart. Almost everywhere we see at work a process of nationalistic fragmentation.

The southern Irish prepare to bolt the British Empire, while Ulster refuses to merge its identity in a United Ireland. Flemings and Walloons may presently split up Belgium. Central Europe is decidedly Balkanized. Throughout Asia nationalism flames, and parts of Africa likewise smolder. Latin America grows more and more nationalistic; even the five tiny republics of Central America, after talking federation for a hundred years, are still jealously separatist. Most ironical of all, Soviet Russia, founded on the internationalism of the proletariat, is undoubtedly evolving a distinct nationalism of its own!

These nationalisms are not merely political and cultural, they are economic as well The old-fashioned ideal of free trade has everywhere gone into the discard. Frontiers nowadays are tariff walls to boot. Each people seeks "a well-balanced national life." This, in practice, implies a large measure of "autarchy"—economic self-sufficiency

And, curiously enough, the very perfecting of our mechanistic civilization aids autarchy—at least, on the industrial side. Machines, automatic or semi-automatic, which can be set up anywhere and do not need a large class of skilled operatives, have outmoded the former world-wide division of labor that made certain countries hives of industry and other lands producers of raw materials. For that matter, chemistry holds out the prospect of a radically new scientific agriculture, so intensive and so enormously productive that even small, highly industrialized countries can easily feed themselves.

Such developments upset traditional notions about world-commerce and finance. In the future, it may be that world-trade will be largely confined to an exchange of raw materials unevenly distributed by nature, and to luxury goods of various kinds. That seems to be the logical outcome of the doctrine of "economic nationalism" so widely held today.

The peoples protect and foster their individualities by raising nationalistic barriers, much as apartment-house dwellers in big cities raise psychological barriers which isolate them from their neighbors much more effectively than is the case with the physically scattered inhabitants of a thinly populated countryside.

Such protective measures are taken even though they may entail heavy economic sacrifices and the risk of desolating wars. This is largely because nations sense the logical consequences of present-day internationalism. They see that such a world-order logically implies a super-state vested not only with authority to decide all disputes between peoples, but also to establish universal controls over trade, industry, finance, immigration, and other vital matters. We can thus visualize the scope of a cosmopolitan world-organization: The abolition of nations, or at least their subordination to local units in a world-federation; the leveling of economic as well as of political frontiers; the pooling of natural resources; the averaging of living-standards.

One more implication of a world thus cosmopolitanised should be noted: the eventual disappearance of racial differences. This ultimate possibility is set forth by the eminent British scientist, Sir Arthur Keith. "If," he points out, "all mankind is to sleep under a common tribal blanket, black, yellow, brown, and white must give and take in marriage, and distribute in common progeny the inheritance which each has come by in their uphill struggle through the ages of prehistoric time toward the present day." [2]

Now, whether an internationalized world would, or would not, bring mankind lasting peace and prosperity, certain it is that peoples today so treasure their national and racial identities that they refuse to pay the price of this internationalism. Why? Is it because of special material advantages or expansive desires; because of racial snobbery, pride, and prejudice? In part, yes. But also because of the creative energy, social cohesion, internal sympathies, and patriotic devotion evoked by national and racial sentiments.

These vital matters have been so ably analyzed by an American thinker that we cannot do better than quote him. Says Professor Josey: "The problem presented by the existence of racial and national

2 From his rectorial address at the University of Aberdeen, Scotland, in 1931.

groups, often hostile to each other, should be approached through a consideration of questions such as these: Is the destruction of all group-consciousness possible? Will the destruction of race and national consciousness eliminate group feelings and antagonisms? Will its destruction make for the good of mankind? Is it probable that loyalty to groups based on economic interest or on feelings of caste will make for greater good than loyalty to groups based on race and nationality?"[3]

His answer in each case is an emphatic: *No!* He holds that, despite their defects and exaggerations, groups animated by such emotions are so energized that they produce the confidence, enterprise, and efficiency needed for progress; the personal inspiration and enthusiasm which normally flower in a creative culture, and the altruistic loyalty that prevents disruptive internal feuds. He therefore asks: "Will not the destruction of national and race loyalty merely serve as the signal for the breaking apart of men and the formation of new groups, based perhaps on economic interests, between which the struggle is to continue in a form more bitter and disastrous than the present struggles between nations and races?"[4]

This is just what the Communist has in mind when he condemns nationalist wars, only to preach the "class war." And it is precisely by exalting nationality and race that Fascism has discovered a highly effective antidote to Communist propaganda.

Perhaps equally effective against the spread of Communism are the new nationalisms of the Orient. In China, for example, a rapidly growing national consciousness is the chief bulwark against the Reds, as well as the main hope that China will ultimately emerge from its present chaos.

The sympathetic loyalties evoked by nationalism have likewise a special interest for awakening Asia. Callous indifference to all men outside a narrow circle of family, caste, or clan has characterized the Orient from time immemorial.

The Chinese are proverbial for this unlovely trait, while in India caste sunders men more absolutely than the most extreme nationalistic or racial feeling has ever done The high-caste Brahmin

3 Charles Conant Josey, *Race and National Solidarity*, p. v (New York, 1923).
4 *Ibid.*, p. 522.

regards the no-caste Pariah as an unclean beast whose very shadow spells pollution. Recent relaxations of caste rigors, slight though they may be, are due almost wholly to the appearance of nationalism in India, where previously it was unknown.

We therefore see that nationalism, so often condemned as a barrier to human impulses, frequently widens the circle of sympathy even though it does not include all mankind.

Such considerations as these help to explain the trend toward nationalism which sweeps the world today.

Race and Racialism

We are now prepared to consider intelligently the factor of race, which we have already seen to be closely interwoven with that of nationalism.

Strictly speaking, there is no logical connection between the two. Nationalism is a state of mind. Race is a physiological fact, which may be accurately determined by scientific tests such as skull-measurement, hair-formation, and color of eyes and skin. In other words, race is what people anthropologically *really* are; nationalism is what people politically *think* they are.

Actually, however, race and nationalism are apt to reinforce each other. True nation-building (as distinguished from mere polyglot states like the old Hapsburg Empire), is powerfully aided when a population is made up of similar racial strains and thus displays those temperamental qualities which tend to be associated with physical traits. Conversely, strong national feeling, by keeping a population distinct and relatively isolated, favors racial uniformity.

To be sure, the process of race-building is usually a long one. To evolve a relatively stable breed may take many centuries. Indeed, if the original racial elements be too diverse, fusion may never really take place. Yet, under favorable circumstances, it can occur within a few generations. Aleš Hrdlička, by his numerous studies of the Old American stock, has proved this conclusively. Originating as they mostly do from closely related North European strains, the present-day descendants of Colonial forebears show a distinct racial type, despite the fact that for two or three centuries the stock has been exposed to wide differences in climate and living conditions throughout the United States. This Old American type is naturally very similar to contemporary North European stocks. Yet it is distinctively itself—a new blend of the white branch of mankind.

A well-marked racial group is strongly conscious of its kinship, prizes it, and instinctively protects its race-identity by avoiding intermarriage with widely different types. What is often dubbed "race-prejudice" springs from very deep psychological causes. It arises instinctively from the primitive emotion known as the "consciousness of kind," and therefore cannot be attributed primarily to any theory or doctrine of race-superiority. Behind all questions of relative racial value there stands the obvious and stubborn fact of *race-difference.*

What is the significance of these racial units? Consider first the biological aspect. While there are today no absolutely pure racial groups, mankind has for untold ages been divided into several main branches which differ widely one from another and which, despite much local crossing, have never really fused. The white man, the Negro, the yellow-skinned Mongoloid have varied little in either appearance or temperament since the dawn of history. They are basic factors in the racial situation. And, of course, within each of these main branches are sub-varieties, clearly distinct from one another.

Now, when a given population is mainly of one racial type, it possesses a notable degree of biological harmony. Through ages of natural selection, both physical and psychological traits have been smoothed into an easy-running whole. In highly specialized stocks the range of possible variation is quite limited, so that you can get a good general notion of how a particular individual will look and even how he will probably react to given situations. A racially uniform population is a stable population which tends to think and act alike.

The greater the racial diversity of a people, the wider the range of physical and temperamental variation among the individuals who compose it. Hence, a proportional lessening of political and social stability. Here we touch the question, endlessly debated, of the good or bad effects of crossbreeding. Its strictly biological results are not merely beclouded by emotion, they are also obscured by the interplay of social factors. The balance of scientific evidence, however, seems clearly to show that while the crossing of sub varieties is either not unfavorable or may even be stimulatingly beneficial, the crossing of primary racial groups such as whites, Negroes, and Mongoloids is, *on the average,* distinctly unfortunate.

This *average* factor is vitally important. The plant or animal breeder absolutely controls his experiment. It paid Luther Burbank, for instance, to make a thousand crosses to get one fine, new variety, because he could instantly destroy all the bad ones.

We, however, cannot thus summarily rid ourselves of our human waste-products. They remain to plague us by *disorganizing* our established stocks.

For that is just what wide cross-breeding does. Heredity is a very complicated matter. Each individual carries in his germ-plasm thousands of genetic units which normally are transmitted in compact blocks, harmonious with one another. When widely different races interbreed, however, this harmonized hereditary fabric is disrupted. And the disruptive process, once begun, goes rapidly on.

"This needs to be especially emphasized from our knowledge of Mendelian segregation. Formerly, inheritance was considered to be typically blending, and the subsequent generations of a racial cross were thought to be very much like the first. This is now known to be far from correct.

"Characters that appear to blend in the first generation of the cross segregate out in various combinations in the second and subsequent generations, and in wide crosses we get a motley array of the most diverse forms. The more different factors there are, the larger the number of different combinations that can be made of them. And however harmonious the blend made in the first cross, even the second generation is apt to produce many unfortunate combinations of traits."[5]

Madison Grant sums up the matter when he says that the inevitable result of mixture between diverse races is "disharmony

5 S. J. Holmes, *Studies in Evolution and Eugenics, pp.* 223–24 (New York, 1923).

in the offspring, and the more widely separated the parent stocks, the greater is this lack of harmony likely to be in both mental and physical characters."[6]

Surely, there can be no reasonable doubt that, since we cannot destroy our biological mistakes, cross-breeding beyond relatively narrow limits is a highly dangerous proceeding. A widely cross-bred population will necessarily be biologically chaotic, and this biological chaos will inevitably be reflected in its political and social life. That is no mere theory. We see melancholy examples of it in peoples to the south of us, especially in the Caribbean area, where mixtures of whites, Negroes, and Indians are most common. The disastrous consequences on the national life of those peoples are only too clear.

We can now appreciate not only how race and nationalism reinforce one another but also how both factors tend to combine in the growing revolt against the cosmopolitan aspects of our mechanistic civilization. The establishment of a world-organization with authoritative political and economic controls would not merely override the independence and initiative of peoples; it would likewise disintegrate their national consciousness, would tend to replace patriotism with class loyalties, and would ultimately promote race-mixture by blurring political, economic, and even cultural lines.

A close-knit, federated world is, of course, the internationalist goal. Yet we have seen that many serious thinkers believe such a world-order would involve evils which might well outweigh its material advantages. And, alongside this intellectual opposition, the current wave of nationalistic and racial passions reveals a stirring of emotions deep and powerful.

It is interesting to note that racial as distinguished from nationalistic self-consciousness is rapidly gaining ground. During the past decade, what we may call full-fledged *racialism* has become a major factor in world-affairs. The significance of race as proved by the biological sciences has impressed public opinion in many lands. The practical effects of this are, today, visible both in their domestic and foreign policies. Racial considerations undoubtedly reinforced

6 Madison Grant, *The Conquest of a Continent, p.* 9 (New York, 1933).

economic and social motives for the stringent Asiatic immigration-exclusion laws passed by America and all the British Dominions. Likewise, scientific discoveries concerning the disruptive effects of wide cross-breeding have strengthened traditional objections to the intermingling of primary races and have thus strengthened "color lines."

Alongside these more or less random effects there has developed a trend of thought which emphasizes race as a basic factor in human affairs.

Though largely concerned with internal problems like eugenics and birth-control, it also enters the field of world-politics by emphasizing racial ties or differences in the grouping of nations. Of this trend, the *Norden* movement, which stresses the close blood-kinship of the Scandinavian peoples, is a good example.

Racialist ideas are, of course, most strikingly prominent in the Nazi Germany of today. These ideas, however, are so mixed up with an ulcerated nationalism and are so surcharged with mere emotion that the resulting compound is hard to evaluate. Ever since the war, Germany has been highly abnormal in almost every respect. She is obviously in rapid transition, and just how she will evolve is at present highly uncertain.

The racialist theory underlying current German thought is perhaps best summarized in a well-known book by Doctor Hans Guenther, one of the most scholarly members of the National-Socialist party.

He says that, while the traditional idea of a nation is little more than "the sum of the now-living citizens of a given state . . . racial and eugenic insight brings a different idea of the true nature of a people. A people is then looked upon as a fellowship with a common destiny of the past, the living, and the coming generations—a fellowship with one destiny, rooted in responsibility toward the nation's past, and looking toward its responsibility to the nation's future; to the coming generations. . .

Thus the Nordic ideal becomes for us an ideal of unity. That which is common to all the divisions of the German people is the Nordic strain. The question is not so much whether we men now living are more or less Nordic; the question put to us is whether we have the courage to make ready for future generations a world cleansing itself racially and eugenically."[7]

An American writer, in a recent work, sets forth the broader aspects of the racialist point of view. Confronting the problem of a world so transformed by our mechanistic civilization that extensive readjustments are needed, he sees the solution, not in a cosmopolitan world-state, but in vast politico-economic unions founded on racial realities:

"Here alone, in this resurgent sense of racial identities, do we find something more profound and fundamental than the nationalistic spirit. . . . In the last analysis, nationalism is only the aboriginal instinct for identity with the tribe or herd. But the tribe itself is only a fragment of the race, and once old quarrels, local jealousies are forgotten, identity with the main body of the race satisfies every impulse toward group-solidarity. The race absorbs, but does not destroy, the individuality of its group components. Once complete identity with the race is attained, the perpetuity of tribal dialects, tribal customs, tribal creeds and traditions, is assured. They are assimilated into the general heritage of the race."[8]

Is Adjustment Possible?

Our exploratory survey has led us far. Yet, at its close, we get the oft-recurring query: *Can Man adapt himself to the Machine?* That is the sphinx-riddle, whereof the answer will determine the fate of our times. And the verdict is in suspense, because the situation is at once so confused and so unpredictable that prophecy becomes a vain thing.

In certain ways, the triumph of our civilization is complete. Its most stubborn rivals, the old civilizations of the Orient, have been beaten; broken. On this battleground, no real adversary remains. Western civilization has literally conquered the world. The world—but *not Man!* Our civilization is pre-eminently a mechanistic

7 Hans F. K. Guenther, *The Racial Elements of European History*, pp. 263–67 (from the English translation).

8 Woodbern E. Remington, *World States and the Machine Age*, pp. 23–24 (Columbus, Ga., 1932).

civilization. Its triumphs have been over the forces of nature. From nature modern civilization has wrested innumerable secrets, has harnessed illimitable powers, and has thereby so transformed the scheme of things that we, today, live in a new material world.

Yet, in this transformed world, Man remains practically unchanged. That is true even of the advanced races who have lived through the whole transformative cycle produced by the new techniques they themselves created. It is truer still of other races on whom those changes have burst like a tornado, uprooting their established order and strewing the ground with wreckage which must be cleared away before new construction is possible. Superficial Westernization of Oriental lands should not deceive us. The deeper effects of the process are as yet barely visible. The task of genuine adaptation in a fresh synthesis has scarcely begun

Will it succeed? We do not yet know, for throughout the East there are many disquieting portents. Even Japan, our star pupil, has not yet qualified for her graduation diploma. There is something very wrong with this semi-Westernized Japan; something that cuts deeper than cramped acres and a redundant birth-rate. Modern Japan is sick in mind and soul.

China is in far worse plight. The old China has been literally torpedoed by the explosive impact of Western civilization. A whole social order is shattered, apparently beyond repair. A civilization older than the pyramids is foundering before our eyes like a great ship going down at sea. And the crew of that huge derelict numbers more than one-fourth of all mankind!

India is another portentous question-mark. Then, there is the problem of the backward races, especially those of Africa. Unlike the Orientals, these folk had no well-developed civilizations to shatter.

Yet this very absence of creative achievement renders them dubious candidates for true Westernization. Thus far, our mechanistic civilization seems to have exerted an almost wholly destructive influence upon them, breaking down their primitive codes and cultures, but giving little in return.

Thus, neither in Asia nor in Africa is there any immediate likelihood of a new synthesis of native and Western elements.

But the West itself is not unified, save, perchance, in a mechanistic sense. And the present trends of our machine technic—standardizing, hybridizing, vulgarizing, have aroused a growing revolt of idealistic and cultural factors threatened with disintegration. They refuse to subordinate, to efface themselves. Why? In the last analysis, because our mechanistic civilization has not yet shown that it has commensurate values to offer.

All this throws grave doubt upon internationalist programs, as they are framed today. What seems to be needed is a fresher, wider approach to the problem; a clear realization that no genuine solution can be formulated until all its elements are duly taken into account.

To establish a world-order which will harmonies such diverse factors may, to many persons, sound like a utopian dream. Yet all attempts to found a world-order based upon economic motives and urged by arguments addressed chiefly to the sentiments of fear or material self-interest have thus far failed.

At present, the idealism of the world is a house divided against itself Cosmopolitan internationalism tends to antagonize traditional loyalties to nation, race, and culture. A broader, better-balanced world-vision is needed in order to harmonies idealisms today divergent, thereby uniting them behind a truly constructive program for common ends.

PART I: THE LOST COMITY OF THE WEST

CHAPTER I
THE DISRUPTION OF EUROPEAN—WHITE SOLIDARITY

FROM the vast bulk of Asia a deeply indented peninsula juts far to the westward. This is Europe, the nucleus of the white race and the center of Western civilization. Europe's colonial offshoots, however powerful they may have become, were until recently mere marginal fringes of the great central nucleus which decisively dominated the fortunes of the whole.

Europe was then a real entity; the outgrowth of an age-long process of organic evolution, with a distinct life of its own. In short, it was a true *comity* of peoples, kindred in blood and sharing basic ideals. This intimate European comity is one of the great constants of history. The joint heritage of Greece, Rome, Medieval Christendom, and the Industrial Revolution, it was a complex of ideals, culture, institutions, and technology which long rendered Europe the mistress of the world.

Yet this majestic fabric, slow-woven through many centuries, is today rent and tattered. Why is this well-knit fabric thus maltreated? How has a master-product of Time's loom been so swiftly and harshly unraveled?

The comity of modern Europe rested upon deep spiritual and cultural foundations. Its character was predetermined by long-past episodes like the Persian Wars and Caesar's conquest of Gaul; by ancient achievements such as the Parthenon and the Roman Law.

The Greeks created a marvelous civilization whose art, literature, and ideas live and inspire us today. Political disunion prevented the Greeks from achieving world-supremacy. This political shortcoming Rome supplied. Taking over Greek culture, the Romans brought most of Europe under the unifying discipline of the *Pax Romana.* The result was an organic unity, held together not so much by force or statecraft as by a common civilization and attitude of mind.

When Greco-Roman civilization decayed, the Classic world was saved from spiritual disruption and moral anarchy by a new unifying principle—Christianity. Having assimilated into itself much of the old Classic culture and tradition, Christianity was the cement which held Europe together through the turbulence of the Dark Age after the fall of Rome, and which presently engendered another European comity—that of the Middle Ages. Though Medieval Europe was an intricate mosaic of Feudal principalities, these political divisions were all subordinated to certain paramount principles and institutions. "Christendom" was a close-knit spiritual whole, and however widely the Christian might wander within its borders he felt himself, in a sense, at home. Furthermore, all educated men had a common culture and actually spoke a common (Latin) learned tongue. The prevailing tendency was, therefore, to lay stress on the likenesses rather than on the differences of the various European peoples.

By the fifteenth century this Medieval comity had declined. Its civilization was either ossified or decadent. The unearthing of Classic culture by the Renaissance gave men a new outlook on life; the rise of sovereign States broke the Feudal political mosaic, and Church unity was shattered by the Reformation. Modern Europe was born.

This Europe differed profoundly from that of the Middle Ages. Nevertheless, it also was a true comity. Europe had ceased to be Catholic, but it was still Christian. Educated men continued to share a common culture, this time humanistic in quality, sprung from the Renaissance. Lastly, despite the disruptive theory of unlimited State sovereignty formulated by Machiavelli and his successors, State action was, in fact, limited by effective restraints. Modern Europe, right down to 1914, was run on a principle known as the Balance of Power. And, despite all the epithets hurled at it of late years, it *was* a principle, with distinct merits of its own. It certainly implied that a European comity existed, that stability was its normal condition, and that the common benefits derived from an orderly balance were paramount. Thus, down to 1914, Europe's many wars retained a certain limited character. The balance of power in Europe might be altered, but the comity of Europe would not thereby be destroyed.

Perhaps national rivalries would sooner have overstepped these implied limits had it not been that all of Europe was, directly or indirectly, engaged in a great common enterprise.

The epoch-making voyages of Columbus and Da Gama at the close of the fifteenth century transformed Europe from a dead-end peninsula of Asia into the potential overlord of the planet. The ensuing four hundred years of discovery, conquest, and scientific achievement resulted in that world-supremacy of the white peoples which reached its climax at the end of the nineteenth century.

Now a four-hundred-year cycle of planet-wide expansion not only gave Europeans a joint objective; it also inspired them with a sense of superiority and a consciousness of their common heritage.

Though they fought one another strenuously over the spoils of empire, the European peoples tended to close ranks against a common foe—as in the international expedition to Peking in 1900, when the Chinese Boxers started a general anti-white revolt.

By this time the United States had become a Great Power; the first colonial offshoot of Europe to attain that status. Yet, despite her political isolation from the European motherland, America was then regarded as an outlying member of the family.

The essentially "Pan-European" sentiment underlying white supremacy is stressed by a noted British thinker of those days. Condemning Europe's internal rivalries and broils, Charles H. Pearson wrote, about 1890:

"It would be well if European statesmen could understand that the wars which carry desolation into civilized countries are allowing the lower races to recruit their numbers and strength.

"Two centuries hence it may be matter of serious concern to the world if Russia has been displaced by China on the Amoor, if France has not been able to colonize North Africa, or if England is not holding India. For civilized men there can be only one fatherland, and whatever extends the influence of those races that have taken their faith from Palestine, their canons of beauty from Greece, and their civil law from Rome, ought to be a matter of rejoicing to Russian, German, Anglo-Saxon, and Frenchmen alike."[1]

Throughout the nineteenth century the sentiment of white-Western solidarity was strong. The great explorers and empire-builders who spread white ascendancy to the ends of the earth felt that they were apostles of their race and civilization as well as of a particular nation. Rivalries might be keen and colonial boundary questions acute; nevertheless, in their calmer moments, the white peoples felt that the expansion of one buttressed the expansion of all.

Furthermore, this world-wide expansion was not pursued out of mere lust for self-aggrandizement. It was largely infused with a sense of duty and high destiny. Kipling uttered the popular version of this feeling when he coined his famous phrase: "The White Man's Burden." Yet this slogan only faintly conveys the almost religious spirit of consecration with which many of the great European empire-builders undertook their task. This is especially true of the builders of Britain's colonial empire. Men like Havelock, Nicholson, and Gordon, the martyr of Khartoum, felt themselves engaged in something very like a divine mission. This belief in themselves and in their cause was a source of immense spiritual power. It likewise promoted mutual understanding and kept colonial rivalries within bounds.

Though Western solidarity was being undermined by disruptive forces long before 1914, its sustaining sentiment survived strongly right down to the Great War. A good illustration of instinctive white solidarity in the pre-war decade is a French journalist's description of the attitude of white spectators (of various nationalities) gathered to watch the landing in Japan of the first Russian prisoners taken in the Russo-Japanese War.

He depicts in moving language the literally horrifying effect of the spectacle upon himself and his fellows. "The humiliation of these whites," he says, "was solemn, frightful. I completely forgot that these captives were Russians, and I would add that the other Europeans there, though anti-Russian, felt the same *malaise*. They also were forced to admit that these captives were their own kind.

1 Charles H. Pearson, *National Life and Character*, pp. 14–15 (London, 1893).

When we took the train for Kobé, an instinctive solidarity drove us huddling into the same compartment."[2]

The old faith in the white man's mission and the need for effective unity in its accomplishment are strongly stressed by one of Britain's later empire-builders on the very eve of Armageddon. Surveying the political problems of his prewar world in a volume of essays published in 1913, Sir Harry Johnston stated:

"The main object of my book is a plea for the promotion of peace and good-will among white nations, to start with; and when the ambitions and the allotment of spheres of influence amongst the Caucasian peoples have been nicely adjusted, then to see that the educational task of the Caucasian is carried out in a right, a Christian, a practical and sympathetic fashion towards the other races and sub-species of humanity . . . Of course it would be fatuous to count on the Millennium setting in after the next Round Table Conference at the Hague . . . But when, after a time, we find that a war between white nations does not profit, we shall learn to reserve our armaments for constraining the recalcitrant peoples to keep the peace, and finally devote all our fierceness, all our courage, vigor, and ingeniousness to attacking and subduing to our will the forces of Nature."[3]

We thus see that, down to the Great War, the comity of the West was a vital reality. Our survey shows that for ages the white peoples had possessed a true "symbiosis" or common life, ceaselessly mingling their bloods and exchanging their ideas. Accordingly, the various white nations which are the race's political expression might be regarded as so many planets gravitating about the sun of a common civilization. No such sustained and intimate comity of peoples has elsewhere prevailed. Not even the cultural solidarity of the Far Eastern peoples is comparable in scope.

The Great War shattered the comity of the West. The political and economic dislocations inflicted by the war and intensified during the post-war period are merely the material evidence of spiritual dislocations equally acute and far more serious. That a single war, however terrible, should have shattered an age-old fabric which had

---

2 René Pinon, 1.4 *Lutte pour le Pacifique, p.* i6 (Paris, 1905).

3 Sir Harry Johnston, *Common Sense in Foreign Policy, pp.* v–vi (London, 1913).

stood the strains and stresses of a thousand previous conflicts may at first sight seem incredible. We cannot grasp the true inwardness of what transpired unless we realize that the Great War was itself a symptom rather than a cause; that it was an upheaval due to disruptive forces which had been gathering for a very long time.

The spiritual origins of this disruptive trend run far back—certainly into the eighteenth century. They are there revealed in the literature of the Romantic movement typified by Rousseau, and they find their political expression in the increasingly unbridled nationalisms of the nineteenth century.

Many of these movements disclosed a singular lack of balance; a fanatical preoccupation with one factor to the exclusion of aught else; finally, in a contemptuous disregard of the historic Western comity. All this meant that the European peoples were reversing their traditional attitude, and that instead of realizing their basic likenesses they were laying more and more stress upon particularistic differences.

In some cases the trend went to truly absurd lengths. Remnants of peoples long submerged suddenly reasserted themselves—with very little to get assertive about. Nevertheless, they busied themselves by frantically trying to resurrect such of their primitive speech and culture as had not been lost in time's oblivion. They were resolved at all costs to be *different,* and in this virtual obsession the sense of what they had in common with their European fellows became well-nigh obliterated.

Furthermore, this hyper-nationalism, obviously abnormal in character, joined forces with the old doctrine of unlimited State sovereignty which had appeared at the Renaissance, and the twain formed a new intellectual and emotional compound with highly explosive possibilities.

These disruptive factors were the root-cause of the furious rivalries which chronically endangered the peace of Europe during the decade before the Great War All the European Powers displayed a reckless absorption in their special ambitions and showed a callous disregard of common interests which portended approaching catastrophe. The rapid undermining of Europe's basic solidarity was only too clear. The mine was laid for an earth-shaking explosion.

Thus, when the explosion did take place in 1914, it was bound to be very different in character from any that had occurred before. The Great War was, in truth, the Armageddon of the Western world. And the first shots of Armageddon saw the comity of the West literally blown from the muzzles of the guns. An eruption of internecine hatreds burst forth more intense and general than war-passions had ever been. Both sets of combatants proclaimed a duel to the death; both sides vowed the enemy to something near annihilation; while even scientists and *littérateurs,* disrupting the ancient commonwealths of wisdom and beauty, put one another furiously to the ban.

In their savage death-grapple neither side hesitated for an instant to grasp at any weapon, whatever the ultimate consequences to the race. The Allies poured into white Europe colored hordes of every pigment under the sun; the Teutonic Powers wielded Pan-Islam as a besom of wrath to sweep clean every white foothold in Hither Asia and North Africa; while far and wide over the Dark Continent black armies fought for their respective masters—and learned the hidden weaknesses of the white man's power. Every day the tide of intestine hatred within the white world rose higher, until the very concept of a common blood and culture seemed in danger of being blotted out.

As the war dragged interminably on, reflective persons began to fear that Europe might be headed for chaotic dissolution. In 1916, Lord Loreburn expressed apprehension lest the war entail general bankruptcy and "such a destruction of the male youth of Europe as will break the thin crust of civilization which has been built up since the Dark Ages."[4] And toward the close of 1917, Lord Lansdowne uttered his despairing cry: "We are not going to lose this war, but its prolongation will spell ruin for the civilized world."

In November, 1918, after four and one-half years of unremitting slaughter, the Great War ended with a decisive victory for the Allies and America, leaving Europe bled white, semi-bankrupt, and spiritually shattered. The hopes of a war-sick world were now centered on the Peace Conference. But these hopes were vain, for the mountain labored and brought forth—the Versailles Treaty!

4 *The Economist* (London), June 17, 1916, p. 1134.

There is no need here to castigate in detail that notorious "settlement." The ink of the signatures was barely dry when its most glaring faults were denounced by numerous competent critics, including some who had taken part in the Peace Conference itself, such as the South African statesman, General Smuts, and the British economist, John Maynard Keynes. After the lapse of sixteen years, few informed persons can honestly maintain that this precious document is a sound basis for Europe's future. Indeed, the dragon's teeth of new wars so effectively sown at Versailles are already beginning visibly to sprout.

The unsoundness of the peace-settlements coupled with a growing apprehension of the logical consequences caused profound disillusionment throughout Europe, thus aggravating the inevitable post-war demoralization. But how could it have been otherwise? Lacking a sound basis for reconstruction, the war-shattered comity of Europe has remained a wreck. Instead of bending their energies to restoring their lost comity, the European peoples have spent most of their diminished resources on bigger and better armaments, stepping on one another's economic toes with tariffs and embargoes, and getting generally primed up for a "next war," which would presumably spell their common ruin.

Indeed, why speak of a "next" war when Europe's status ever since Versailles has hardly been one of "peace" in the normal sense of the word. May it not be possible that the Great War really did not end with the Armistice, but that it merely went into a new phase waged with economic instead of military weapons?

We need not here discuss the complex tensions which have agitated Europe since 1918. What we desire to stress is their disastrous effects upon the life of Europe itself and upon the general world-situation.

So deep-going has been post-war Europe's *malaise* that some qualified observers fear lest, if it be not soon relieved, the European peoples are in danger of intellectual and spiritual disintegration. The Italian historian Ferrero believes that this would produce consequences graver even than those arising from the decay of Greco-Roman civilization in the third century A.D. In similar vein, a well-known British thinker, Christopher Dawson, writes: "Ever since the war, Europe has been fighting a losing battle with the forces of dissolution. The world-supremacy that European civilization possessed in the last century is a thing of the past, and today its very existence is threatened. It is not merely that Western industry and finance have lost their old monopoly in the world-market, or that Oriental nationalism is challenging European political supremacy. Far more serious is the disappearance of the moral prestige of Western civilization and the denial of its spiritual and intellectual standards of value."[5]

The noted Spanish philosopher, Ortega y Gasset, acutely analyses these wider implications when he says: "The world today is suffering from a grave demoralization which has its origin in the demoralization of Europe. One of the main causes for this is the displacement of the power formerly exercised by our Continent over the rest of the world and over itself . . . No one knows towards what center human things are going to gravitate in the near future; hence the life of the world has become scandalously provisional."[6]

The shattered comity of Europe is indeed a disaster of incredible magnitude. This lost comity was, as already remarked, the greatest and most enduring constant of all human history. When it functioned normally, we compared the European peoples to a system of planets moving rhythmically about the sun of a common civilization.[7]

Well, that central sun, like some strange variable star, has not only waned suddenly in light and heat; it has also lost much of its gravitational pull. Accordingly, its attendant planets, the Western peoples (including those of the Americas and elsewhere) tend to fly off at tangents, and the whole system is threatened with permanent disruption. What this signifies we shall observe in succeeding chapters.

---

5 Christopher Dawson, "The New Decline and Fall," *The Commonweal,* June 20, 1932.

6 José Ortega y Gasset, *The Revolt of the Masers,* p. 195 (New York, 1932–English translation).

7 Here using the term in its cultural and spiritual sense rather than with reference to its mechanistic technique or other material aspects.

PART I
CHAPTER II
THE SECESSION OF RUSSIA

IN the disaggregation of Europe's comity, outlying members were earliest affected by the disruptive trend. This is notably true of Russia, which broke off at a sharp tangent and is now pursuing a course peculiarly its own.

In order to estimate what this violent secession means both to the West and to the world at large, we should understand the basic facts of the Russian situation.

Russia is the historic borderland between Europe and Asia. Sprawled across the illimitable plains that stretch almost uninterruptedly from Central Germany to the Pacific Ocean, Russia was predestined to be a battleground of East and West. For ages, races and ideas have alike swept across its vast expanse, clashing and mingling. Sometimes Europe has predominated; at other times Asia. And the upshot of it all has been the emergence of qualities neither quite Eastern nor Western but smacking of Russia itself.

The pendulum between East and West in Russia has swung with a certain rhythm. Our first historic glimpse of what is now Russia reveals a land inhabited by many small tribes, primitive in culture but distinctly European in blood. Yet already this unorganized folk were being cruelly assailed by Mongoloid nomads ranging in from the eastward. Unable to cope with these fierce foes, the primitive Russians besought the aid of Scandinavian adventurers passing by on the waterways which led athwart the land, from the Baltic to the Black Sea. A Viking chief named Rurik took charge. He and his bold Norsemen repelled the Asiatic raiders and organized an effective state centering at Kiev in southwestern Russia. Thus Russia began under distinctly Western auspices and the rule of a Nordic aristocracy.

Presently this early Russia was modified by semi-Oriental influences coming up the waterways from the south. Kiev was converted to Christianity in its Byzantine form, and whatever hailed from Constantinople had an Eastern flavor. However, the new cultural blend was still European rather than Asiatic. And farther north were independent Russian statelets even more Western in character. This was notably true of the commercial Free Cities, Novgorod and Pskov, which were closely affiliated with the German Hanseatic League.

Russia was predominantly Western down to the great Mongol-Tartar invasion of the thirteenth century. This terrible visitation swung Russia violently towards Asia. Kiev was destroyed, almost all of Russia was conquered, and quantities of Mongoloid blood were injected into the Russian stock. As time passed, a new political nucleus arose at Moscow in central Russia. The Muscovite rulers, who took the title of Czar threw off the Mongol yoke and unified the Russian folk. But the Czardom of Muscovy was in almost every respect an Oriental land, virtually closed to the West.

With the advent of Peter the Great at the end of the seventeenth century, the pendulum again gave a violent swing—this time westward. Czar Peter vowed to Europeanize Russia, and he went at it by the same strong-arm methods that his modern prototype, Mustapha Kemal of Turkey, is using today.

Peter shaved off the sacrosanct beards of his *Boyars* just as Kemal makes all Turks wear Western-style hats or caps. Abandoning Moscow, the masterful Czar built a brand-new capital on the Baltic, appropriately naming it Saint Petersburg and calling it Russia's "window to the West." In order to hasten the Westernizing process, Peter (and his successors) staffed the government with Europeans, mostly Germans and Scandinavians. These formed the nucleus of a new ruling class, largely Western in origin. It "prided itself upon its freedom from Asiatic blood. Here and there a few noble families admitted or even boasted descent from one of Tamerlane's commanders, but otherwise the surface of foreign culture, ideas, methods, and even language which radiated over the country from the Romanov court was wholly European."[1]

1 Walter Duranty in *The New York Times* of December 20, 1931.

On its economic side, Czarist Russia was a sort of European colony; commercial or industrial progress was almost wholly due to Western capital and management.

Russia thus *looked* European and was generally deemed an organic part of the Western world right down to the Great War. However, all this was little more than a veneer. The Orthodox Church and the Mongol conquest had set their Oriental imprints upon Russia too deeply for even Czar Peter to rub them out. The government remained a despotism on the Asiatic pattern, dominating peasant masses virtually untouched by Western influences. Between rulers and ruled lay an unbridged gulf.

This deep rift within the Russian nation was reflected in the unharmonized character of its culture and ideas. The intellectual class was sharply divided between Westernizers and haters of the West who called themselves "Slavophils." One of their leading lights, Danilevski, proclaimed that "the Russian genius is the exact opposite of the European genius, and Russia fell into a trap when she became European." In similar vein, another prominent Slavophil, Prince Ukhtornski, asserted: "Asiatic blood is strongest within us. And Asia knows that, while there is a deep chasm between her and Western Europe, there is not even a ditch between her and Russia."

These cultural antagonisms were cross-cut by political antagonisms equally intense, ranging from die-hard up-holders of autocracy to anarchistic Nihilists and the pioneers of Communism.

Thus divided against itself, Russian national life became increasingly perturbed and confused. Two centuries of Westernization had obviously not sufficed to bind Russia mentally and spiritually to Europe. Peter's work remained a veneer.

It is thus not strange that under the terrific stress of the Great War this veneer began to crack and split. In 1917, Czarist Russia collapsed, and in the chaotic interregnum which ensued, a ruthless, purposeful Communist minority rode to power on the revolutionary whirlwind. The tremendous portent of Red Russia had come into being.

What did Red Russia portend? Several momentous things. First, it meant that the Western veneer imposed by Czar Peter had been savagely ripped off and that the semi-Oriental Russia of the masses was exposed to full view. Also, Russia's new rulers promptly declared war, not merely upon the previous order in Russia itself but on the whole "bourgeois" world; on the very social and spiritual bases of Western civilization. The secession of Russia from the European-Western comity was complete.

Whither had Red Russia gone? Towards Asia? Had the historic pendulum swung back violently, as of yore? In a sense, yes. But not quite as in the past, because new factors were now present which before had been unknown.

Under Communism, Russia has obviously become more Asiatic in many ways. The extirpation of its most European upper-class stock was paralleled by the loss of its European borderlands (Poland, Finland, the Baltic Provinces) which took advantage of the revolutionary chaos to declare their independence. Red Russia is thereby thrown clear out of historic Europe. Its western borders are once more those of old Muscovy—an Oriental land. Recognizing the logic of the situation, Lenin resolutely scrapped Peter's fiat capital on the Baltic, the treasured "window to the West," and made Moscow once more the center of Russian life.

Russia's foreign policy has been consistently based on friendly relations with the peoples of Asia. Indeed, its present rulers are themselves largely Asiatic in blood. Stalin is a Georgian; other prominent figures are likewise from the Caucasus or Armenia, while the numerous Jewish leaders are all of Asiatic derivation. Communism, opposed as it is on principle to racial distinctions, has systematically striven to break down the ethnic consciousness of Russia's diverse elements. These efforts have borne fruit. Intermarriage has become much more frequent, especially among the younger generation. The cities, in particular, are vast melting-pots. As a result, Asiatic strains are being diffused rapidly through the population. Lastly, the gigantic industrial projects under the Five-Year Plan, which lie mainly towards the Urals or in Siberia, are shifting Russia's economic center of gravity eastward, towards Asia.

Red Russia is thus obviously moving towards Asia. But does this imply that it is likewise moving towards *Asiaticism,* in the historic sense of the term? The East's traditional attitude has been one of easy-going timelessness and mystical contemplation, interspersed with brief fits of frantic energy due usually to the spur of some religious idea. This Oriental spirit certainly characterized the Russian masses and indicated their strong Asiatic trend. When the Russian pendulum swung eastward in the past, these Asiatic tendencies were accentuated; as when, after the Mongol conquest, Russian princelets aped the manners of Tartar Khans.

But surely this is not so today. Russia's Communist rulers are doing their utmost to root out such Asiatic traits from the masses. They seek to mold a people which shall be instinctively practical, punctual, efficient, and capable of sustained, highly disciplined effort. No Asiaticism there! Besides, as Lobanov-Rostovsky acutely remarks, "What is this 'Asia' which Russia is supposed to yearn for? Asia in the days of Muscovy meant glittering, gigantic empires full of dreamland wonders and deep, elaborate cultures . . . Today, save for a highly industrialized island-empire (Japan) itself largely Westernized, we have in Asia only a nebulous, cosmic mass of humanity fermenting under the inoculation of alien conceptions. Venerable native institutions are crumbling or degenerating, and we cannot yet say whether this galvanizing of Asiatic life by European influences will lead to the creation of a new synthesis of values or, on the contrary, to anarchy and decay. Thus, pro-Asiatic Russians must either take that which Asia herself is renouncing or wait for that which is still unborn and therefore uncertain."[2]

If Russia has seceded from the comity of Europe and disdains the discredited comity of Asia, whither is she headed and what is she trying to do? The answer appears to be that the Russian Communists aim at the same goal which many Asiatics today have in mind. They want to take over the purely material aspects of our mechanistic civilization while rejecting the cultural and spiritual basis from which it has sprung.

A glance at the nature of Russian Communism will make this clear. Doctrinally, Communism is a hard, dialectic materialism, scorning whatever savors of religious mysticism. Yet, in its Russian manifestation at least, Communism has engendered a group-mysticism inspiring a fanatical fervor distinctly religious in character. The Russian Communist Party is a sort of militant

2 A. Lobanov-Rostovsky, "Russia at the Crossroads," *Slavonic Review*, April, 1928.

religious order blindly obedient to a body of doctrine every jot and tittle of which is an article of faith. The bible of Marx, the glosses of Lenin, and Stalin's pronouncements *ex cathedra* are infallible; not to be argued or disputed—on pain of heresy. The Supreme Pontiff of this new dispensation naturally acquires an aura of quasi-divinity. The embalmed corpse of Lenin has become an object of mass-pilgrimage, while the adulation accorded his successor, Stalin, suggests a cross between a Byzantine Emperor and the Grand Lama of Tibet. These are obviously religious phenomena. Whatever the theory, in practice, Russia is today ruled by a materialistic theocracy. That sounds like a contradiction of terms, yet it is just what Red Russia has produced. Keynes has shrewdly analyzed the seeming paradox when he says: "We shall not be able to understand Russian Communism unless we view it as, at one and the same time, a persecuting, missionary religion and an experimental economic technique."[3]

Communism's militant religious aspect accounts for its relentless hostility to other faiths. For Communism is not merely anti-Christian; it is against *all* religion as hitherto conceived. Within Red Russia's borders, Islam, Judaism, Buddhism, even the shamanistic cults of Arctic nomads, are equally vowed to eventual extinction.

All the old gods being thus slated for "liquidation," what shall the orthodox Communist revere? There is, of course, the sacred fiat of the "Party Line" and its incarnation, the Party Head, enshrined in the Kremlin. Yet, behind this embodied abstraction there appear the outlines of something even more portentous: *The Machine.*

We have already remarked that Red Russia hankers after all the mechanistic aspects of our civilization, but wants to take them *minus* our ethical standards and spiritual ideals. Stalin himself typifies this attitude, and one of the best-qualified interpreters of Red Russia shows why. Says William Henry Chamberlin: "Brought up in a little town in a remote mountainous country which scarcely knew modern industry, Stalin has unlimited admiration for the machine. 'When we put the Soviet Union in an automobile and the *muzhik* on the tractor,' Stalin wrote on one occasion, 'let the worthy capitalists who boast so loudly of their "civilization" try to overtake

3 Quoted in the *Yale Review*, December, 1931, p. 233.

us.' This is a revealing sentence. For Stalin, 'civilization' is a matter of 'putting the Soviet Union in an automobile and the *muzhik* on a tractor.' Wholesale executions, arrests, deportations, and sentences of banishment without trial—these have nothing to do with the question of whether or not a country is to be regarded as civilized."[4]

The ultimate object of Communist reverence is, however, not the Machine, but Man himself; Man, not as an individual, but as an idealized collectivity. Red Russia's goal lies beyond a new social order. It implies a population cast in a correspondingly new temperamental mold. Walter Duranty portrays the Communist utopia as a society "very similar to the ant-heap, where each member of the community has his allotted function, which he performs, one might almost say, automatically, that is, the process of regimentation has been so thoroughly perfected as to make the idea of individual independence repugnant, or, as the Bolsheviki would term it, anti-social."[5]

This goal, Russia's Communist rulers have set out resolutely to attain. And they seem to be, at least temporarily, succeeding. Thanks to the unremitting pressure of a highly efficient propaganda system, a generation is growing up not merely devoid of religion as we know it, but also without that sense of individual personality which we so highly prize. The young Russian Communist lives a thorough-going group-life to which everything personal is supposed to be strictly subordinated. If such a communized existence seems to us well-nigh incomprehensible, he deems ours equally strange—and unnatural.

Will this colossal experiment succeed? We have no precedents to guide us in our judgment, because never before was anything like it essayed. Here, as elsewhere in our transitional world, we should carefully distinguish between immediate results and ultimate consequences. Again, temperamental differences should be considered. It may well be that what is feasible for certain stocks would, for others, prove unworkable. The one certain arbiter is the

---

4 From a series of special articles by William Henry Chamberlin, entitled: "Russia—Without Benefit of Censor," published in *The Christian Science Monitor.* The above quotation taken from the article in the issue of June 7, 1934.

5 Walter Duranty, "Picture of a Regimented Land," *New York Times Magazine,* June 10, 1934.

test of time. Perhaps the most surprising thing that has come out of Soviet Russia is a new brand of nationality. In theory, Communism denounces Nationalism as a mischievous "bourgeois" delusion. The class-conscious worker allegedly knows no country. *Proletarians of all nations, unite!*

Marx's famous slogan was the watchword of Lenin's new Communist commonwealth which, though established on Russian soil, was assumed to be the nucleus of a world-wide federation of Soviet states formed after the triumph of the approaching world-revolution. Indeed, *U.S.S.R.* means "Union of Soviet Socialist Republics." The very name, "Russia," has been expunged. In those early days the Third International rather than the Soviet Government tended to occupy the center of the stage.

But the world-revolution did not come off, and the U.S.S.R. continued to be a lone Communist state in a hostile bourgeois world. Red Russia's rulers were of two minds. One school, led by Trotsky, continued to pin its faith on the world-revolution; the other school of thought believed in concentrating upon the U.S.S.R. until it should become a Communist Gibraltar, invulnerable to attack, yet strong enough to deal the bourgeois world its death-blow whenever the opportunity should arise. With the advent of Stalin, this latter theory prevailed and was proclaimed the "Party Line." When Trotsky and his fellows demurred, they were incontinently cast forth into the limbo of heterodoxy.

Prolonged concentration upon things Russian inevitably engendered a Russian attitude of mind. This soon began to tell. A full decade ago, keen-eyed Sir Philip Gibbs saw which way the wind was blowing. Returning from a trip to the U.S.S.R., he reported that nationalism was in the air. "Leaders whom I interviewed in Moscow," he wrote, "were beginning to think again of Russia as a world-power. All their talk was of that. They are Russians before they are Communists."[6]

Ten years of Stalin's rule has greatly accentuated this nationalist trend. Recently, *Pravda*, the Communist Party organ (and therefore unimpeachably orthodox), carried an editorial with the truly amazing title: "For Native Land"; the Russian word used being the

6 Sir Philip Gibbs, *Ten Years After*, pp. 187–88 (London, 1924).

habitual term of pre-revolutionary times. The editorial called for a patriotic union of the "one hundred and seventy millions for whom the Soviet land is their own mother."[7] After this official benediction, what loyal Communist can further cavil at the nationalism of the U.S.S.R.?

Trotsky, of course, violently dissents. He accuses Stalin of having sabotaged the world-revolution, declares the Third International bankrupt, and tries to form a "Fourth International" chemically pure from the taint of nationalism. But Trotsky is in exile. He is growing old. His followers are few. Whatever the future may bring, his Fourth International will probably be just another minor schism in a movement prolific of heresies.

Red Russia thus offers us that strange phenomenon, *National Communism*. Illogical, yet fact. And what a fact! One-sixth of the entire land-surface of the globe and 170, 000,000 people increasing by fully 3,000,000 per year! At that rate, the population would number 300,000,000 within half a century. Here, indeed, is a factor to be reckoned with in world-affairs.

Yet the reckoning is difficult. As already remarked, Red Russia, sundered culturally and spiritually from both East and West, and engrossed in a unique social experiment, pursues a course peculiarly its own. The one apparent certainty is that its secession from the comity of Europe seems to be irreparable. True, Red Russia will probably sit into the game of European diplomacy—indeed, she has already taken a hand. Furthermore, she will doubtless continue to mechanize and industrialize herself on Western lines. But all that does not mean that the broken moral and spiritual links will be reforged.

Will Russia even desire to do so? It is more than doubtful. Bent on developing Siberia much as America did its Far West after the Civil War, Russia today turns her back on Europe and gazes eastward. Should a well-settled Siberia shift Russia's center of gravity beyond the Urals, Europe might soon come to be regarded with relative indifference as something past; something outworn.

One symptom of Russia's waxing nationalism is the fact that Europe's former cultural prestige has almost vanished. The Russian

---

7 *Moscow Pravda,* issue of June 9, 1934.

people are fast acquiring a robust self-assurance coupled with a correlative disdain for its former revered mentors. Duranty reports that "the Russian is beginning to lose his traditional respect for the Western foreigner as a superior being, compared to whom he himself is a 'dark' and backward creature. This is particularly noticeable among the younger generation . . . Unfortunately, it cannot be denied that the average Russian, although still friendly and on the whole respectful toward the Western stranger within his gates, is becoming *en masse* more and more xenophobic and nationally arrogant. Which may have dire consequences in the future and already cannot be viewed without disquietude."[8]

So we leave Red Russia—a vast uncertainty in an uncertain world.

8 Walter Duranty, "The Russian Looks at the World," *New York Times Magazine,* March 29, 1931.

PART I
CHAPTER III
THE ALOOFNESS OF THE U.S.A.

IN these crucial times the position of the United States in the white-Western world is of cardinal importance. We have seen that the historic comity of Europe is profoundly shaken and that Russia, its great eastern borderland, has seceded—apparently beyond recall.

But besides its Eastmark, Europe, during its four centuries of planet-wide expansion, founded white outposts in the Americas and elsewhere overseas. Of all these racial seedlings, the United States has grown the fastest until it has today attained a giant's stature and a giant's strength. What should be America's role in the white world, and what its relations with the European motherland?

These queries far transcend political or economic matters; they involve every aspect of Western civilization. Upon their answer the future of the race itself in large part depends. At present, the Giant of the West stands aloof from Europe's troubles while, conversely, Europe offers scant hope of collaboration in America's prospective task as the upholder of the white race in that vast arena of the Pacific Ocean where East meets West.

This lack of harmony between Europe and America arises not merely from conflicting material interests, but likewise from divergent aspects of a common civilization. How the present differences arose; how far they were inevitable; and how, if possible, they can be subordinated to larger ends are of deep concern to parent and offspring.

America originated as scattered colonial offshoots, planted along the Atlantic fringe of a savage continent and necessarily subordinated to the parental will. This dependence ended politically with the Revolution which threw off English rule. Since freedom had been won at the cost of a long and bloody war, the resultant bitterness produced a reaction not merely against things British, but also, in a sense, against Europe as a whole.

Engrossed in the arduous task of building a nation, the Fathers of the Republic emphasized America's uniqueness and stressed the break with the colonial past. Jefferson asserted that the American soil had evolved a new race of men, while Tom Paine stated: "We have it in our power to begin the world over again. A situation similar to the present hath not happened since the days of Noah. The birthday of a new world is at hand."

These sentiments were strengthened by the course of events. Hardly had America begun its national life when Europe plunged into the interminable cycle of the Napoleonic Wars. And during this prolonged death-grapple, America, the innocent bystander, was roughly knocked about. Both sides so flagrantly violated America's neutral rights that she was forced first to take hostile action against France and then to engage in a wretched war with England.

Such unpleasant experiences confirmed Americans in their belief that the less they had to do with Europe the better for them. Washington undoubtedly reflected the temper of his times when, in his Farewell Address, he thus warned his fellow-countrymen against Old World entanglements: "Europe has a set of primary interests which to us have none or a very remote relation. Hence she must be engaged in frequent controversies, the causes of which are essentially foreign to our concerns. Hence, therefore, it must be unwise in us to implicate ourselves by artificial ties in the ordinary vicissitudes of her politics or the ordinary combinations and collisions of her friendships or enmities."

George Washington's measured counsel formed the basis of that traditional policy of aloofness from European affairs which persisted, substantially unaltered, down to America's entry into the Great War. When the Napoleonic war-cycle ended in 1815, this policy became as easy to follow as it was obviously sound. Henceforth, until the very close of the nineteenth century, American foreign policy was idyllically simple. It consisted in keeping out of Europe and in keeping Europe out of the Americas.

Having turned its back upon the Old World, the young republic plunged zestfully into its chosen task—the taming of the wilderness and national expansion from sea to sea. In the process America grew by leaps and bounds until, in the closing years of the nineteenth century, it had attained the stature of a first-class Power. However, the wider implications of this new status were ignored by Europe and were barely grasped by Americans themselves. In European eyes, America was a hermit nation with scant interest in the outer world. To most Americans, their traditional isolation seemed not only highly desirable but also quite natural—something that would indefinitely endure.

The Spanish War of 1898 simultaneously awakened America to an interest in world-affairs and Europe to a realization of America's latent strength. The hermit nation of the West suddenly emerged from its isolation.

Despite its undeveloped military and naval power, it easily vanquished Spain and acquired a colonial empire in the Far East through its conquest of the Philippines. Furthermore, alongside these political developments went a rapid growth of American foreign trade.

All this produced in Europe feelings of astonishment tinged with resentment and even with alarm. At the moment, Europe still was what for centuries she had been—predominant in world-affairs. Her peoples might quarrel among themselves, but they did not dream that their collective world-supremacy could be seriously challenged. Indeed, Europe was then in a militantly expansionist mood. Having partitioned Africa, the European Powers were planning a partition of China. In fact, some of them had been tentatively eyeing Latin America despite the Monroe Doctrine. New outlets for Europe's surplus population and preferential markets for its surplus manufactures were the objectives of a fierce and unrelenting quest.

Suddenly, amidst these surging imperialisms, the United States appeared upon the scene. America's war with Spain, its vigorous "Open Door" stand in China, and the marvelous growth of its export trade disclosed to Europe the presence of a new Great Power, outside the European circle, which apparently intended to have a voice in world-politics, and in world-economics as well. The revelation of America's business and industrial efficiency was especially distasteful, because American goods had begun to invade

Europe itself—hitherto the world's undisputed workshop. Here, indeed, was a redoubtable competitor! The upshot of all this was a rapid growth of anti-American sentiment. Europe's traditional attitude towards America had been one of uninformed indifference. The average European had viewed America as a fabulous land still largely tenanted by buffaloes and redskins. Remote and imperfectly civilized, such a country did not enter seriously into Europe's calculations.

Having thus underrated America, Europe now went to the other extreme and tended to overrate the significance of America's entry into the arena of world-affairs. Taking at face-value the somewhat boastful exuberance of a young nation elated by a victorious war, European diplomats began to plan against American "imperialism" while European publicists gravely discoursed upon "The American Peril." This anti-American trend ran on into the opening years of the new century. A survey of those days reveals a striking similarity with the wave of anti-American feeling which swept Europe after the Great War. We find the same emotions and ideas, including pleas for tariff discrimination against American goods and even a projected "Pan-Europe" on an anti-American basis.[1]

The momentous shift in world-affairs precipitated by the Russo-Japanese War dimmed "The American Peril" in European eyes. Preoccupied, first with the Far East and then with the series of diplomatic crises preceding the Great War, Europeans ceased to worry overmuch about the young "Colossus of the West." Also, the meteoric rise of Japan helped to correct Europe's political perspective. Here was another Great Power which had arisen outside the European family circle. Perhaps after all, such things had to happen. So Europe accommodated itself to a revised balance of political and economic forces, which lasted down to 1914.

This tentative equilibrium the Great War promptly shattered. With Europe tearing itself asunder, America automatically tipped the international scales. Long before America entered the struggle, Europe was deeply indebted, and it was obvious that the end of the war would leave Europe collectively so weakened and impoverished that America would bulk much larger in world-affairs.

1 For a more detailed survey of this phase of European-American relations, see my book, *Lonely America*, pp. 109–115 (New York, 1932).

These political and economic shifts were, however, as nothing compared to the simultaneous change in attitudes and states of mind. Hitherto the question had been whether Europe was disposed to regard America as substantially a full-fledged member of its own comity; whether it was prepared to deal with America on terms of complete equality in fields of joint interest, such as China. At heart, Europe still tended to think of America as occupying a semi-colonial and therefore subordinate status. We have seen how irritating was the realization of America's rise in the world scale and how hard Europe found the readjustment to a different point of view.

Suddenly Europe found itself courting American sympathy, eager for American aid. From the very start of the Great War, Britain and her allies worked unceasingly to win America to their cause, basing their appeals on kindred ideals and the heritage of a common civilization. The New World was insistently "called in to redress the balance of the Old."[2]

These appeals profoundly stirred the American people. They played a major part in bringing America into the war on the Allies' side. But they logically implied a sweeping transformation of European-American relations; a broadening of the traditional comity of Europe into a real white Western comity, with reciprocal ties and duties between all its parts throughout the world.

Such a comity could come to pass only if both Europe and America were inspired by truly idealistic motives and were prepared to act in mutual good faith for genuinely constructive ends. The moral test of their sincerity would be the nature of the peace-settlement after the Allies and America had won a decisive victory which would give them a free hand to carry out their plans.

The Versailles Conference had barely convened when there began a process of disillusionment, swift and terrible. The American public soon learned that all those war-time appeals to its idealism were basically propaganda to enlist America, not in a crusade for a better world, but in a *partisan* intervention to help the Allies garner

2 This was the striking phrase coined by George Canning, the British Foreign Secretary, when he blocked the plans of the Holy Alliance to restore Spain's rule over its revolted American colonies by throwing the support of the British Government to the Monroe Doctrine.

their selfish war-aims. Tragedy reached its climax when President Wilson, striving desperately to ensure a better future through the establishment of a League of Nations, personally pledged his word that America would not only ratify the Allied brand of "peace," but would *underwrite* it into the bargain.

Then ensued the political revulsion in America which ended in the repudiation of President Wilson, of the Versailles Treaty, of the League, of anything savoring of further involvement with a Europe which most Americans deemed incapable of decently setting its house in order. From the generous idealism of the war days, America swung violently over to an ultra-nationalist reaction coupled with renewed allegiance to the traditional doctrine of isolation.

Europe's disillusionment was equally intense. Though their statesmen had been unwilling or unable to make a constructive settlement, the peoples of Europe had counted on American idealism and effective American aid. When the American people repudiated Wilson's promises and ostentatiously abandoned Europe to its own devices, this seemed like a cynical betrayal in European eyes.

What exacerbated the bitterness was the fact that, though deprived of American assistance in an official way, Europe remained so dependent economically that it was forced to seek American aid by other means. The post-war decade saw American investment capital flow into Europe, along with American goods, American methods, and floods of American tourists.

But all this merely intensified a wave of anti-American feeling that swept Europe from end to end. Europeans tended more and more to rationalize their grievances into a sort of moral issue; to inveigh against the "American peril" and preach the duty of resisting wholesale Americanization.

This emotional wave reached its crest in 1929. When Europeans saw America smitten by the Great Depression, the legend of American invincibility was shattered and fear was thereby allayed. Also, fresh political and economic crises within Europe itself took people's minds off everything beyond their own immediate problems. Yet the antagonism persists. Europe and America continue to be sundered by a gulf of reciprocal dislike and misunderstanding.

As matters now stand, there does not seem to be any way by which Europe and America can agree on a program of constructive action. Certainly, America ought to keep hands off Europe, because nothing that America could do would benefit Europe as a whole. Any intervention in Europe's affairs would necessarily be a partisan intervention for one or another set of special interests which do not concern America and which would inevitably end in fresh disillusionment and mutual recriminations. Before America can truly help, Europe must find a way to set its own house in order. And this means more than technical readjustments of border-lines or arms quotas. It implies a reawakening of a *European* spirit; a revival of that traditional European comity which was shattered by Armageddon.

When Europe once more becomes something more than a geographical expression; when it develops the *will* to mend its shattered comity, it will surely find the *way.* And a Europe thus spiritually restored can usefully co-operate with America, because they have so much in common. America can never be in Europe, but America is *of* Europe. Despite many divergences, America remains linked to Europe by basic ideals and by the intimate bond of blood. On these solid foundations the structure of a broader white-Western comity ought ultimately to be reared. The pressure of alien, hostile forces should bring it eventually to pass.

PART I
CHAPTER IV
DISRUPTING LATIN AMERICA

MORE than half of the Western Hemisphere is in profound flux. From the Rio Grande to the antipodean Land of Fire,[1] stretches a world still in the making; a world which, in a sense, is being unmade. Against a background of untamed nature, human forces, elemental, primitive, wage an obscure yet titanic struggle. And the keynote of that struggle is *race.*

To understand Latin America's significance we must realize that its very name is a misnomer The phrase "Latin America" suggests an offshoot of the white race's southern branch and thus essentially an overseas extension of the Mediterranean peoples, just as the United States and the British Dominions stem from the white stocks of the north.

This, however, is but partially true. Latin America has never wholly belonged to the white world. Its Latin character, culturally as well as racially, is rather a veneer spread unevenly over an underlying mass alien in temperament and in blood.

Furthermore this veneer, hastily applied centuries ago, has not worn well. In many places it cracks and peels; in some spots it has virtually disappeared. Over large areas of "Latin" America, long-repressed elements today threaten to submerge not only the white man but white civilization. In short, most of this sub-hemisphere is racially colored man's land which has been getting steadily more colored for the past hundred years.

Yet this colorward trend is neither uniform nor universal. Latin America's antipodean south has become as thoroughly white as Europe itself. Elsewhere, solid enclaves of white settlement rise out

1 Tierra del Fuego, the southernmost part of South America, ending with the tip of Cape Horn.

of surrounding colored regions, or white ruling castes dominate, more or less successfully, non-white populations. Elsewhere, again, racial distinctions have been confounded in a general miscegenation. And this race-mixture is indeed "general." For, be it noted, color in Latin America is itself heterogeneous. It is part Red Indian and part Negro—primary stocks which differ from one another fully as much as the white race does from them both.

These multi-colored peoples live under wide differences of climate and soil. They are likewise divided politically into independent states most of whom have acquired an intense national consciousness. Finally, into this bizarre medley new influences are today percolating; this time from Yellow Asia. The result is an almost chaotic complexity whose outcome cannot even dimly be foreseen.

The one thing certain is that the relative uniformity attained in Spanish colonial times is disrupted beyond recall. Latin America's foundations were rough-hewn by the Spanish Conquest.[2] That very word "conquest" tells the story. The United States was *settled* by colonists planning homes and bringing their women. It was thus a genuine migration, and resulted in a full transplanting of white stock to new soil.

The Indians encountered were wild nomads, fierce of temper and few in number. After sharp conflicts they were extirpated, leaving virtually no ethnic traces behind.

Very different is the tale of Latin-American colonization. The Spanish Conquistadores were bold adventurers descending upon vast regions inhabited by relatively dense Indian populations, some of which, as in Mexico and Peru, had attained distinctive cultures of their own.

The Spaniards, invincible in their shining armor, paralyzed with terror these people still dwelling in the age of bronze and polished

2 Of course we should keep in mind the simultaneous acquisition of Brazil by Portugal. This, however, was less a conquest than a process of settlement spreading gradually over a vast area thinly peopled by wild Indian tribes. Brazil's whole historic evolution has been very different, and in the main aloof from that of its Spanish-speaking neighbors. Despite its huge size (almost one-half the entire area of the South American Continent) Brazil has been a relatively passive factor in Latin-American history.

stone. With ridiculous ease mere handfuls of whites overthrew empires and lorded it like gods over servile and adoring multitudes.

No conquest could have been outwardly more complete. The Indians were helpless as sheep before the mail-clad Conquistadores. And military conquest was succeeded by complete political domination. The Indian even lost his cultural heritage and became a passive tool in the hands of his white masters.

Yet one vital factor was lacking; one which, in the long run, affects everything else. That factor was race. The Spaniard did not seal his title-deed with the indelible stamp of unmixed blood. Hence, Latin America was not acquired in fee-simple by the white world.

Though the fabulous treasures acquired by the first Conquistadores drew fresh swarms of bold adventurers from Spain, their numbers were infinitesimal compared with the vastness of the quarry, while the proportion of women immigrants always lagged far behind that of the men. The breeding of pure whites in Latin America was thus both scanty and slow.

By contrast, the breeding of mixed-bloods began at once and attained notable proportions. Having slaughtered the Indian males or brigaded them in slave-gangs, the Conquistadores took the likeliest Indian women to themselves. The humblest man-at-arms had several female attendants, while the leaders became veritable pashas with great harems of concubines. The result was a prodigious output of half-breed children, known as "mestizos" or "cholos."

And soon a new ethnic complication was added. The Indians having developed a melancholy trick of dying off under slavery, the Spaniards imported African Negroes to fill the servile ranks, and since they took Negresses as well as Indian women for concubines, other halfbreeds—mulattoes—appeared. Here and there Indians and Negroes mated on their own account, the offspring being known as "zambos." In time, these various hybrids bred amongst themselves, producing the most extraordinary ethnic combinations. As the Peruvian, Garcia-Calderon, well puts it: "Grotesque generations with every shade of complexion and every conformation of skull were born in America—a crucible continually agitated by unheard-of fusions of races . . . But there was little Latin blood to be found in the homes formed by the sensuality of the first conquerors of a desolated America."[3] To be sure, this mongrel population long remained politically and socially negligible. The whole colonial order was based on the idea of white superiority, and the colors were carefully graded. The Spaniards regarded themselves as a master-caste, and excluded all save pure whites from civic rights and social privileges. Indeed, the European-born Spaniards refused to recognize even their colonial-born kinsmen as their equals, and "Creoles"[4] could not aspire to the higher distinctions or offices.

This discrimination against her own blood proved to be the Nemesis of Spain's colonial empire. Jealous and embittered, the white creoles awaited their opportunity. It came when Spain's colonial grip, already weakening, was suddenly paralyzed. Napoleon's invasion of the Peninsula threw the Motherland into chaos. Her colonial governors were left, unsupported, to fend for themselves. Promptly the white creoles stirred, conspired, and finally broke into open rebellion. Latin America's interminable revolutionary cycle had begun.

It started as a white civil war. The heroes of the revolution were aristocrats of pure white blood. But the revolution presently developed new phases. In the first place, the struggle was very long. Beginning in 1809, it lasted almost twenty years. The whites were decimated by fratricidal fury, and when the Spanish cause was finally lost, multitudes of loyalists, mainly of the superior social classes, left the country.

Meanwhile, the half-castes, who had rallied wholesale to the revolutionary banner, were demanding their reward. The creoles wished to close the revolutionary cycle and establish a new society based, like the old, upon white supremacy, with themselves substituted for the Spaniards. But this was far from suiting the half-castes. For them the revolution had just begun. Raising the cry of "democracy," then become fashionable through the North American and French Revolutions, they proclaimed the doctrine of

---

3 Garcia-Calderon, *Latin America: its Rise and Progress, p. 49* (English translation, London, 1913).

4 Although loose usage has since obscured its true meaning, the term "Creole" has to do, not with race, but with birthplace. "Creole" originally meant "one born in the colonies." Down to recent times this was perfectly clear. Whites were classed as "Creole" or "European"; Negroes as "Creole" or "African."

"equality" regardless of skin. Disillusioned and full of foreboding, Bolivar, the master-spirit of the revolution, disappeared from the scene. With prophetic insight, he wrote from his place of exile: "South America is ungovernable. We who made the revolution have plowed the sea!"

Bolivar's lieutenants, like the generals of Alexander, quarreled among themselves, split Latin America into jarring fragments, and waged a long series of internecine wars. The flood-gates of anarchy were opened, the result being a steady weakening of the whites and a corresponding rise of the half-castes in the political and social scale. Everywhere ambitious soldiers led the mongrel mob against the white aristocracy, breaking its power and making themselves dictators.

The consequences of all this were lamentable in the extreme. Latin America's level of civilization fell far below that of colonial days. Spanish rule, though narrow and tyrannical, had maintained peace and social stability. Now all was a hideous chaos wherein frenzied castes and colors grappled to the death. Ignorant mestizos and brutal Negroes trampled the fine flowers of culture under foot, while as by a malignant inverse selection the most intelligent and the most cultivated perished.

These deplorable conditions prevailed in Latin America until well past the middle of the nineteenth century. Then began a process of variation which produced striking differences between the Latin-American republics, some attaining a high degree of progressive prosperity whilst others continued to writhe in the vicious circle of brutal dictatorship and revolutionary anarchy.

The high lights of Latin America shine in its extreme south. Here we find three nations—Argentina, Uruguay, and Chile, which are today at once politically sound and abreast of the times economically and socially in almost every respect. These remarkable achievements contrast so vividly with the backwardness of other portions of Latin America that the reasons are well worth finding out.

Argentina and Uruguay are so closely associated geographically and historically that they had best be surveyed together. Curiously enough, their beginnings were rather unpromising. Since they produced neither gold nor tropical luxuries, Spain had neglected them and at the close of the colonial period they consisted of little more than the port-towns of Buenos Aires and Montevideo with a few dependent river-settlements. Their vast hinterlands of fertile prairie then harbored only wandering tribes of nomad savages.

During the last half of the nineteenth century, however, the development of ocean transport gave these antipodean prairies value as stock-raising and grain-growing sources for congested Europe, and Europe promptly sent immigrants to supply her needs. This immigrant stream gradually swelled into a veritable flood. The human tide was, on the whole, of sound stock, mostly Spaniards and North Italians, with some Nordic elements. Thus Europe locked antipodean America securely to the white world. Whatever may be the fate of other regions, these will remain white man's land, in full cultural communion with the rest of our civilization.

Chile has followed a different line of development from Argentina and Uruguay, but the outcome has been much the same. A land of cool climate, no gold, and warlike Araucanian Indians, Chile attracted the pioneer settler rather than the swashbuckling seeker of treasure-trove. These pioneers, mostly of good North Spanish stock, came to found homes and therefore usually brought their womenfolk out with them. Some crossing with the natives occurred, but the fierce Araucanian aborigines clung to their wild freedom and kept up an intermittent frontier warfare in which the occasions for race-mixture were relatively few. Above the hardy peasantry arose a resident squirearchy of an almost English type. This ruling gentry jealously guarded its racial integrity.

In Chile, as elsewhere, the revolution against Spain provoked a cycle of disorder. But the cycle was short, and was more a political struggle between white factions than a social welter of caste and race. Furthermore, Chile was receiving fresh accessions of European blood. These were of high quality and were mostly of North European origin. Many English, Scotch, and Irish gentlemen-adventurers, enlisting in the War of Independence, settled down in a land so reminiscent of their own. Germans also came in considerable numbers, settling especially in the colder south. Thus, the Chilean upper classes, always pure white, became steadily more Nordic in ethnic character. The political and social results were unmistakable. Chile rapidly evolved a stable society, essentially oligarchic and consciously patterned on aristocratic England. Efficient, practical, and extremely patriotic, the Chilean oligarchs made their country at once the most stable and the most dynamic factor in Latin America.

During the last two decades, to be sure, Chile's political life has become more democratic. The oligarchic rule of the "Hundred Families" is becoming a thing of the past, and the broadening of political rights has involved considerable disturbance. Yet these clashes are essentially struggles between white parties; they have virtually no racial significance.

Chile indeed prides herself on her white blood and deems this the best guarantee of her future. A recent American observer emphasizes this in the following lines: "Ask any Chilean what best characterizes his country and the chances are that he will respond, 'Uniformity of race.' He will point out to you that while in most other South American countries the Spanish Conquistadores mingled with Indians and later with slaves, while later Mongolian immigration has added a yellow tinge to the race, in Chile the bars have been tightly placed across the ports . . . By the time immigration became a question in Chile, the policy had been laid down. As a result, the main additions to Chilean population have been of North European stock . . . This has made for a unity of purpose and activity which is helpful to the country."[5]

The reasons for the progressiveness of these three South American countries are now clear. Climate is of course an important contributing factor, but the basic cause is unquestionably race. An American biologist who has made exhaustive researches into Latin America's ethnic problems thus sums up the matter: "These nations are the best existing opportunities of observing what might have been the type of South American colonists' descendants if the Caucasian pioneers and their offspring had not mixed their blood with that of the Indians and Negroes. In other words, we may observe in these countries the effect of environment alone upon the European colonists."[6]

5 Special article in *The Christian Science Monitor,* June 53, 1934.

6 Reginald G. Harris, "Eugenics in South America," *Publications of the Eugenics Research Association,* March, 1922.

What, then, were the effects produced by the meeting of radically different human stocks upon Latin-American soil? There can be no reasonable doubt that the results were generally bad, not only for the white man but for the non-white elements as well. The sudden elevation of rough adventurers (often of humble social origin) to a pinnacle of irresponsible power over hordes of cringing servitors was ruinous to character. Most of the Conquistadores quickly sank into a life of idleness, luxury, and vice. This deplorable social pattern persisted throughout the colonial period. It especially injured the creole whites who, pampered from birth by obsequious slaves, usually led an idle and vapid (existence, disdaining work as servile and debarred from higher callings by their European-born superiors.

Though the revolution gave the creoles wider opportunities, it left the social system unaltered, so the white aristocrats did little except go in for politics and mismanage their great landed properties, known as haciendas. From Mexico to Peru, this hacienda system presented the aspect of a diseased feudalism, with inefficient (and often absentee) white landowners and equally inefficient, densely ignorant, physically decadent colored *peons*. Contrast the hacienda system with the upstanding squirearchy and peasantry of Chile, or with the self-respecting, well-to-do peasant-farmers of Costa Rica, upland Colombia, and other districts settled by a predominantly white population. In every instance, economic and social conditions closely parallel the racial situation.

The reason why the Indians of Latin America everywhere sank to the status of wretched serfs was due, not solely to Spanish cruelty and oppression but also to the racial characteristics of the Indian himself. While the Spaniard tends to be a rather extreme individualist, the Indian functions primarily as a member of a tribal group. This trait is common to all branches of the Indian race. In the United States, for example, we have been trying for generations to fit the Indian into the fabric of our civilization, but in most cases we have lamentably failed. When graduated from a reservation and presented with a farm of his own, "Poor Lo" has usually mortgaged or sold it to buy whiskey. Money literally burns a hole in the Indian's pocket. Even our "oil-rich" Indians have often ended up as paupers after a brief splurge of unlimited drinks and high-powered automobiles. The Wheeler-Howard Bill, now pending in Congress, aims to save the Indian from poverty and degradation by revivifying his tribal organizations and settling these organic groups on lands held in common and inalienable.

If we in the United States are only now awakening to the true nature of our Indian problem (thanks largely to the scientific researches of biological and sociological specialists) the Latin-American whites can hardly be saddled with entire blame for the decadence of their Indian populations. The root-cause of the trouble is the contact of two incompatible human types with widely different temperaments and outlook on life.

The Indian's instinctive social bent reached its logical fulfillment in the Inca Empire of Peru. This highest achievement of the Indian race was an extreme form of State Socialism, wherein individual initiative was virtually nonexistent, independence of thought and action being unknown among the masses. Yet this almost robot-like condition aroused no popular dissatisfaction. On the contrary, the Inca people seem to have led singularly contented lives, following blindly and willingly a routine existence carefully prescribed and hallowed by strong religious sanctions. Obviously, this social system must have accorded with the Inca Indians' natural propensities.

Such was the powerful, elaborately organized state which Pizarro and 310 followers overthrew at a single blow. The reason is obvious. Once Pizarro had seized the Divine Person of the Inca, the keystone of the political arch was removed and the whole social structure crashed down in ruins. The docile masses were mentally paralyzed. Their old social order had gone, while their inborn make-up stopped them from adapting themselves to the new white civilization. So they sank into a dull apathy, until today the Indians of the Andean plateaux are probably the most wretched, dispirited folk to be found anywhere on earth, drugging their misery with pisco and coca, and thus becoming more and more degenerate. That is what contact with an alien race and civilization did to the Inca Indian. And we have already seen how the Indian enervated and corrupted his white masters.

What happened in Peru typifies what went on all over Latin America, wherever the conquering whites imposed themselves as a ruling caste over a settled Indian population. The Indian's immense conservatism, his invincible inertia, rendered genuine adaptation to white civilization impossible. With incredible tenacity he clung to his ancestral ways and showed a dull indifference to alien innovations.

Only where the Church gathered the Indians into communal groups, as the Jesuits did in Paraguay, were the Indians materially and spiritually contented. The reason is obvious. Those "missions" faithfully reproduced the benevolent communism of the Inca Empire, automatically imposed by religious sanctions, which had worked so satisfactorily in pre-Columbian Peru.

Now thus far we have considered solely the economic, social, and cultural impacts of two wholly distinct racial types. The fact of race-mixture has been purposely left out of the equation; because all those mutual injuries would have been done, all those economic and social problems would have arisen even if the two races had kept physically distinct—even though not one mestizo had ever been born.

But we know that the two races did mix wholesale and that a large intermediate caste of mixed-bloods came into being. This, however, further complicated (and, in the main, worsened) an already unfortunate situation. For surely the interbreeding of such different human types could not fail to pass on incompatibilities to the common offspring who thereby acquired a discordant heredity.

Of course we are here dealing with broad averages. Among a class numbering millions there must naturally occur a considerable number of desirable variations. It is therefore possible to compile quite a list of mestizo individuals who rank high in ability and character. Yet the weight of evidence proves pretty conclusively that, throughout Latin America, the mestizos lack both the white man's initiative and the Indian's solid poise, thus constituting an essentially unstable element.[7]

This is notably true of the "cholos" of Bolivia, Ecuador, and Peru. Says Doctor Harris: "One who observes the Cholos and Cholas,

7 For more detailed discussion on this matter, see the following easily accessible works: Garcia-Calderon and Harris, already cited; Lord Bryce, *South America* (London, 1912); E. A. Ross, *South of Panama* (New York, 1866); G. W. Critchfield, *American Supremacy* (2 volumes, New York, 1908).

mestizo men and women, gathered at the market-place of La Paz on Sunday morning, and realizes that in them he sees the results of two or three centuries of interbreeding, must despair of any great future for a people who will be endowed with the inheritance which the Cholos have to transmit."[8]

Even the mestizos of Chile, the product of two unusually sound stocks, do not average well. Significantly termed *rotos*,[9] the Chilean mixed-bloods "ordinarily exhibit the pride of their Spanish ancestors and the dullness of the Araucanians."[10]

The mestizo's shortcomings are perhaps best shown by his failure to grasp the one big opportunity which was logically open to him. This was the formation of a stable, efficient middle-class—a crying social lack throughout Latin-American history. If the white-Indian cross had been a good one, the mestizos would inevitably have gravitated that way. But the logically obvious has not happened. The brighter mestizos ape the whites and try to get into politics or the professions; they share to the full their Spanish forebears' disdain for trade as well as for manual labor.

As for the less able mestizo majority, it remains at an economic level barely above that of the Indian—yet not borne with the Indian's stoical resignation. The result is that the mestizo has never made a definite place for himself in the social structure, and remains an ill-adjusted, chronically dissatisfied element of the population.

The relations of the white and Indian stocks thus give rise to a very difficult situation. But this is further complicated by the presence of a third racial factor differing radically from them both. The Negro multiplies Latin America's difficulties in literally geometrical ratio; it renders the complexities, not three-fold, but manifold.

Detailed consideration of the Negro will be deferred until we come to survey his African homeland and its problems. Yet it is obvious that the black race constitutes the least advanced branch of mankind.

"No matter how much one may admire some of the Negro's individual traits, one must admit that his development of group

---

8 Harris, *op. cit.*

9 Spanish word *rota* means: "broken; disrupted; lewd."

10 Harris, *op. cit.*

traits is primitive and suggests a mental development which is also primitive."[11]

This essentially primitive being entered the New World as a slave, torn violently from his own surroundings and thrust in contact with conditions and races quite foreign to him. The Negro had obviously little or nothing positive to contribute; in fact, the Negro, unlike the Indian, proved to be an eager imitator. Yet this imitation remained superficial. Broadly speaking, it is fair to say that the transplanted Negroes of the New World have shown scant ability genuinely to assimilate white civilization. Whenever they have been left to their own devices, as in Haiti or the jungle-bush of the Guianas, they have quickly reverted to conditions reminiscent of their ancestral homes in West Africa or on the Congo. The chief difference is that these reversions lack much of the original. They are imperfect attempts to reconstruct broken and half-forgotten social patterns.

As Reinsch well says: "In countries like Haiti and our own South, the vices of the Negro populations assume more repulsive aspects than they bear in the African home. This is due, no doubt, to the fact that the original social unity has in these cases been destroyed. An African society, although it may have barbarous customs, still has a certain character which preserves individual morality and dignity of life."[12]

The mere presence of this backward stock would tend to exert a negative, depressing effect upon Latin-American social and cultural life, especially when we remember the extent to which the stock was introduced. From the earliest days Negro slaves were imported wholesale until the entire Caribbean basin and Portuguese Brazil became predominantly black in population. Negroes were, in fact, scattered broadcast over Latin America, though they are today mainly concentrated in the West Indian islands and the tropical coastlands of Central and South America.

Nevertheless, the racial effects of this African dispersion have been profound. The persistence of Negro blood and the tenacity of its emotional qualities are well known. Negro blood, percolating

11 Popenoe and Johnson, *Applied Eugenics,* p. 284 (New York, 1920).

12 S. Reinsch, "The Negro Race and European Civilization," *American Journal of Sociology,* September, 1905.

widely even in unsuspected quarters, accounts in large part for the notoriously unstable characteristics displayed by the truly mongrelized populations of tropical Latin America. Garcia-Calderon aptly analyses their chaotic psychology when he writes: "The mixture of Iberians, Indians, and Negroes has generally had disastrous consequences. None of the conditions established by the French psychologists are realized by the Latin-American democracies, and their populations are therefore degenerate. The lower castes struggle successfully against the traditional rules; the order which formerly existed is followed by moral anarchy . . . These tropical republics display a tendency towards atomic disintegration Given to dreaming, they are led by presidents suffering from neurosis."[13]

This racial medley attains its climax in the Caribbean—the American Mediterranean. Hither have flocked numerous representatives of every race on earth, including various Asiatic breeds to add their special savor to what has been humorously termed "The West Indian Pepper-Pot."

An American writer thus vividly portrays the resultant ethnic situation: "Islands and mainland swarm with races of every hue, living in every epoch of society from that of the primitive African jungle to the effete degeneracy of Havana creole aristocracy Habitats originally thousands of miles apart have been lifted and set down side by side. The Caribbean is a vast ethnological laboratory. Spaniards and Portuguese meet French and Dutch, English and Americans. Jews fled thither from the Spanish Inquisition. Full-blooded Negroes practice the fearsome Obeah. East Indian coolies and Hindus tread new tropics. Chinese have flowed in by tens of thousands. The descendants of native Indians who greeted Columbus still lounge under the royal palms. Interbreeding has created many mixed types all along the chromatic scale from black to white—ash-grey, yellow, red, golden brown, bronze."[14]

What will ultimately emerge from this welter of castes and colors, no one can say. Yet certain facts are reasonably clear. First and foremost, the Caribbean is racially ceasing to be part of the white

13 Garcia-Calcleron, *op. cit.*, pp. 361–62.

14 Carleton Beals, "The Black Belt of the Caribbean," *American Mercury*, October, 1931.

man's world. Throughout the West Indies the native white minority is dwindling, and in some islands it has almost disappeared. White political control will perhaps long continue to be maintained from without. Royal Governors may uphold standards of law and order in the British West Indies. United States proconsuls, more or less discreetly backed by United States marines, may elsewhere prevent ticklish situations from getting out of hand. Nevertheless, this vast Caribbean area, the world's supreme melting-pot, will simmer and boil with the ferment of forces, primeval and incalculable.

Because of this elemental instability, the Caribbean must be a region of chronic unrest. To think that these polychrome, caste-riven lands can within any imaginable future evolve stable forms of democratic self-government is the vainest of illusions. The West Indies and Central America[15] must be governed by the strong hand, if order and social security are to be maintained. The sole choice is whether such governments shall be enlightened or corruptly despotic. There is no other real alternative.

Despite the Caribbean's many racial elements, one easily outweighs all the rest put together. Everywhere Negroes swarm—and breed. The Indian has well-nigh vanished; the white man dwindles; Asiatics are local incidents. But the Negro thrives and multiplies exceedingly. The tropic islands are prodigious incubators of black men who, having populated their sea-girt homes down to the starvation level, are literally thrust out to make a living elsewhere. The rapid agricultural development of many Caribbean regions during the past few decades has been largely due to this ever-flowing tide of cheap black labor. But this means that lands like Cuba, once predominantly white, rapidly darken;[16] that the Negro's racial conquest of the Caribbean is being accelerated.

The West Indies and adjacent continental coastlands are thus destined to be a chronically unstable region which, unless controlled by outside forces, is liable to engender grave political and social troubles. However, out of this endemic turmoil nothing coherent or

15 With the exception of Costa Rica, where a predominantly white population renders orderly self-government possible.

16 The process of Africanisation in Cuba and elsewhere through the wholesale influx of black plantation-labor is vividly described by Luis Araquistain in his book, *La Agonla Antillana* (Madrid, 1928).

positive is likely to develop; certainly, nothing of much more than local significance.

Very different is the situation in the great land-block stretching from the southern frontier of the United States, down through Central America, to the borders of Chile and the Argentine. Here, we encounter a deep-going trend with far-reaching possibilities for the whole Western Hemisphere; even for the world balance-of-power and the future of the white race. This trend, though still in its early stages, has already crystallized in Mexico (our next-door neighbor), into a militant, aggressive movement. And its name is *Indianism.*

Indianism, as the word implies, is the conscious resurgence of those native stocks overcome by the fiery onset of the Spanish conquest four centuries ago. We have already surveyed the heyday and subsequent decline of Spanish power over those regions of Latin America where the whites did not actually settle and populate the land. We likewise saw that where the whites were merely a ruling aristocracy, they tended to become less strong and capable. Finally, we noted the rise of a discontented mestizo element, most of whom gravitated toward the Indian masses rather than to their white superiors.

Such weakening of white control long ago encouraged the lighter mestizos to demand and to seize an ever-larger share of white prerogatives, so that in time the so-called white upper-class in certain Latin-American countries became mostly near-white mestizo. But that was not Indianism. It merely paved the way for Indianism by further undermining white prestige and diluting white blood. Those lighter mestizos, once become part of the ruling class, adopted the slogan of white supremacy and paid at least lip-service to the ideals of white culture and the standards of white civilization.

Indianism is something radically different from all that. *Indianism means a deliberate repudiation of everything white;* a revolt, not only against white political and economic control, but also against white civilization, culture, and ideals—Christianity included. In short, Indianism spells a sweeping rejection of the white man and all his ways.

The Spanish conquest is to be utterly undone and Red America is to revert to its primeval self. Such is Indianism's objective. And in Mexico, at least, the Indianising process, though as yet far from complete, seems to be well on its way.

Why Indianism should have come to a head first in Mexico instead of elsewhere becomes clear from a glance into the past. When "Stout Cortez" undertook the conquest of Mexico he tackled a vastly harder job than did Pizarro in Peru. The Aztecs were a very different breed from the docile Incas; they were born warriors delighting in blood and slaughter.

Furthermore, they had plenty of opportunities to indulge those pastimes, because their Indian neighbors were fighters, too. The Aztec "Empire" was, indeed, quite unlike that of the Incas. It was a sort of glorified Iroquois Confederacy; a league of kindred clans banded together chiefly in order to dominate and levy tribute upon all the surrounding tribes.

Cortez and his little army landed among some of those tributary folk who, besides reverencing the mail-clad white strangers as gods also saw in them possible saviors from Aztec domination. Even so, Cortez and his men saw plenty of stiff fighting, and in the final death-grapple with the Aztec hosts Cortez might not have triumphed without the aid of no less than 50,000 Indian allies. This is enough to show the warlike nature of the native Mexicans at the time of the conquest. And the past two decades of Mexican history abundantly prove that the ferocious fighting strain still survives.

The Conquistadores, however, were good tamers. After one or two bloody revolts the Indians resigned themselves to the inevitable. As usual, the Spaniards became a ruling caste and spread over the land a veneer of white civilization. But it never really touched the Indian masses, who withdrew into themselves, clinging obstinately to their old ways and secretly cherishing even their ancestral paganism under a thin veil of Christian practices.

The War of Independence against Spain was in Mexico just what it was elsewhere in Latin America—a revolt of the native-born whites against Spanish rule. The Indian continued to be effectively kept in his place. And all the subsequent revolutions of the last century were essentially squabbles between various white factions, including a growing number of lighter mestizos who were gradually admitted to the charmed circle of the dominant race.

These interminable broils not merely undermined white prestige; they likewise led to grave national misfortunes. A disastrous war with the United States was presently followed by a French conquest which might have been permanent if France's puppet "Emperor" Maximilian had not been forced out by American action under the Monroe Doctrine.

The meaningless revolutionary cycle was closed by the advent of a strong ruler—Porfirio Diaz. Though a mestizo, Diaz thought like a white man. He wanted to make Mexico a strong, progressive nation, able to hold its own in our strenuous modern world. To do this as quickly as possible, he started an intensive process of Westernization. Gathering about him a group of able administrators, mostly white aristocrats and known as *scientificos*,[17] Diaz welcomed foreigners and foreign capital, European and American. Railroads, mines, factories, large-scale commercialized agriculture, the whole material paraphernalia of modern civilization was brought in pell-mell.

There was just one thing wrong with the picture—the Indian masses did not get on well in most of what was happening. But that did not stop Diaz. If the Indians were too obstinate or stupid to adjust themselves willingly, they must be coerced. The transformation of backward, half-barbarous Mexico into an up-to-date Western nation was a paramount national necessity. Let the good work go on!

So Don Porfirio and his *scientificos* laid on the Western veneer while, underneath this splendid material showing, the Indians and the dark mestizos, reluctant or unable to fit themselves profitably into the new scheme of things, gloomed and glowered. Presently Don Porfirio grew old; his iron grip relaxed—and the Great Revolution began.

The upheaval which unseated Diaz in the year 1911 was something profoundly different from anything that had happened before. This was a *real* revolution—the overthrow of a ruling caste; the shattering of an economic and social order. Above all, it was a

17 Meaning "scientific-minded ones."

race-war, which accounts for the ruthlessness and fiendish cruelty with which it was waged.

To be sure, the revolution was precipitated under the leadership of Francisco Madero, a wealthy white idealist who put forward a program of liberal reforms to culminate in democratic, parliamentary government. Such Western notions, however, did not matter much to the guerrilla chieftains who marshaled the rebel hosts. "Pancho" Villa, the arch-bandit, represented the mestizos of northern Mexico, while Emiliano Zapata typified the full-blooded Indian masses of the center and south. Both, however, were fired with the same fierce hatred of the white man and his works

"Death to the Spaniards!" was a favorite insurgent war cry; and "Spaniards" meant primarily the white Mexicans—though foreigners were plundered and killed wholesale. So this elemental upheaval went on through its varied phases for nearly twenty years until the revolution-wrecked land attained its present condition of relative stability.

Mexico's present ruling group are mostly mestizos and represent that intermediate class rather than the full-blooded Indians, despite a certain number of full-bloods in important official posts. Nevertheless, a basic change has taken place. Not only has the former ascendancy of the whites been definitely broken; the Mexican national attitude has radically altered. Indianism is today the popular cult. No longer do most Mexicans regard their country as a daughter of Spain or their culture as an offshoot of Latin civilization.

Instead, they emphasize Mexico's Indian origins and hark back to the legendary glories of the Aztec and Mayan Empires. Leading Mexican artists like Diego Rivera exalt the Indian and flay the Spanish Conquistadores as alien oppressors An imposing memorial has been erected to the last Aztec monarch, while Cortez, his conqueror, is vowed to popular execration.

Some Mexican intellectuals have even dropped their Spanish names and taken others of Indian derivation. The prevailing idea is that Mexico will become increasingly Indian, not merely in blood but in culture and institutions as well. It is, indeed, highly probable that Indianisation will go rapidly on. Certainly, the whites have become not merely politically impotent, but numerically a hopeless minority. When the Great Revolution began twenty-odd years ago, the native whites numbered fully 10 per cent of the total population, to say nothing of a large foreign-white residential element. Today, the white Mexicans have shrunk to probably less than 5 per cent. Death and exile have done their work only too well.

With the whites definitely out of the picture, what will probably occur in the relatively near future is a new revolutionary struggle, this time between the dominant mestizos and the Indian full-bloods Despite present professions of Indianism, the lighter and more influential mestizos usually deem themselves vastly superior to the Indian masses below them in the political and social scale, and likewise tend to look down on the darker mestizos who approximate the Indian in temperament as well as blood. By its very makeup, the mestizo class is an inherently unstable element which cannot act as a unit in the long run. How, then, can the present mestizo rulers long maintain themselves against a movement so dynamically elemental in character? For, basically, "Mexico is an Indian land."[18]

But the definite triumph of Indianism would transform Mexican national life out of all semblance to its former state. As Doctor Gruening (a leading authority on things Mexican), justly remarks: "The implications of Mexico's Indianism are profound."[19] How profound, the researches of many skilled investigators abundantly show. It is their well-nigh unanimous verdict that a thoroughly Indianised Mexico would spell not merely a reversion to more primitive economic and social conditions, but likewise to startling changes in attitudes and ideals. Carleton Beals well says: "Today, Mexico is in the throes of a vast revolution that has scarcely begun; it is seething with the re-emergence of unknown, aboriginal Mexico."[20]

Indianism's deeper implications are perhaps best observable in the field of religion. The bitter disputes between Mexico's revolutionary governments and the Catholic Church, and the strongly anti-

18 Ernest Gruening, *Mexico and Its Heritage.* p. 69 (New York, 1928).

19 Gruening, *op. cit.*, p. 79.

20 Carleton Beals, "Carrying Civilization to Mexico," *American Mercury*, February, 1924.

clerical attitude prevailing among the present ruling group, are well known. So far as Mexico's mestizo rulers are concerned, this means little more than one phase of a readjustment in the relations of Church and State which is going on in all white countries once solidly Catholic where the extensive privileges of the Church are today deemed incompatible with a society tolerant of religious differences and lay-minded rather than ecclesiastical in tone.

The real significance of the chronically strained relations between Church and State in Mexico is the attitude of the Mexican people, which, though statistically rated as almost solidly Roman Catholic, has offered no effective opposition, or even objection, to the government's most anti-clerical policies. "This naturally raises the question why this overwhelming majority has permitted what the clergy decries as persecution and, unquestionably, at times is so. The answer to this apparent paradox is simple. The Mexican people are not Catholics. Of the 15,000,000 *nominal* Catholics who inhabit Mexico, at most 2,000,000 are Catholics in the sense accepted in the United States, an equal number are agnostic or indifferent, and the remainder, while observing in their worship some of the outward form of Roman Catholicism, are in reality pagans."[21]

We have already noted that the Spanish conquest affected the Mexican Indians as superficially in religion as in everything else; that beneath a thin camouflage of Christian rites the old idolatrous gods lived on. Christianity was instinctively regarded as something external, aloof, foreign. "In Mexico, through the centuries, white gods have been associated in the Indian mind with the alien blood of the *blancos,* the whites. Whatever their surface acceptance of them, the difference in color between the white and the Indian has been a barrier which has resisted any acceptance of Christianity in the more valid sense.[22]

The close student of Mexican folkways just quoted goes on to show that the famous Virgin of Guadalupe, popularly rated as Mexico's patron saint, is not only a "red" Madonna, but is identified by the Indians with an Aztec female deity whose shrine occupied

21 Gruening, op. *cit.,* p. 229. On the religious question, as on other Mexican problems, Doctor Gruening's book is a mine of information.

22 Frederick H. Martens, "The Race Factor in Mexican Anti-Clericalism," *Current History,* November, 1927.

the very spot where his *Guadalupana* is now adored by hosts of pilgrims from far and wide. Indeed, the same attitude crops out in the Pueblo Indians of our own Southwest. "To this day, despite missionary effort, the Savior of the Hopi Indians of Arizona is a red Christ, Poseyemo, born of an Indian virgin beneath a pinion tree, and not the white Christ of Judea."[23]

The basic and apparently ineradicable idolatry of the Mexican Indian is strikingly revealed by an amusing yet deeply significant episode cited by Gruening, who writes: "Mr. Carleton Beals, who has wandered far and wide in Mexico, recounted to me that when crossing the lonely sierra of Durango on foot he passed an Indian kneeling before a wayside crucifix. Presently the native overtook the traveler and related that he had come from his village five miles away to pray.

"'Have you then no *Cristos* in your pueblo?' asked Mr. Beals.

"'We have several,' replied the Indian. 'But as there are many people there, those *Cristos* are kept very busy, and I felt my chances of being attended to out here were much better, for this Christ has almost nothing to do.'"[24]

Surely, we have here a stock inherently incompatible with, and refractory to, almost every phase of Western civilization. But, in so far as this stock molds Mexico to itself, the United States (indeed, the white race generally) will confront a very serious situation. An Indianised Mexico will mean that the white world definitely stops at the Rio Grande; that below an often invisible frontier-line arises something essentially antagonistic and profoundly alien. Not a pleasant next-door neighbor!

Mexico's Indianisation is not an isolated phenomenon. It is merely the most advanced phase of a trend which reaches far down into South America. What is happening in Mexico cannot fail to influence the adjacent Central American states, which are largely Indian in blood. In fact, this influence is already apparent. But even that is a minor matter compared to the great block of Indian population in the Andean plateau regions of Bolivia, Ecuador, and Peru—the former seat of the Inca Empire.

---

23 *Ibid.*

24 Gruening, *op. cit.*, pp. 238–39.

Despite their dejected abasement, the Andean Indians have long displayed symptoms of increasing unrest. The lessening prestige and ability of the ruling white or near-white minorities in all three republics has presumably stirred vague hopes of liberation among the Indian masses; or, perhaps, their dull minds were first quickened by suggestions from discontented mestizos. Whatever the initial impulse, this inchoate Indianism is an undoubted fact. Nearly half a century ago that far-sighted student of racial problems, Charles H. Pearson, predicted that the inefficiency of white rule in these Latin-American lands would ultimately engender Indian resurgence.[25]

Shortly before the Great War, Lord Bryce, in his South American travels, noted the growing intensity of the racial situation,[26] while Ross, the American sociologist, returned from a tour of investigation convinced that serious trouble lay ahead, especially in Bolivia, where the whites were living "in the crater of a slumbering volcano."[27]

Sporadic disturbances had already occurred, but genuine uprisings did not break out until after the Great War. During the past decade several have taken place. The worst was in Bolivia. In 1927, 80,000 Indians took the field and despite an almost total lack of modern weapons, they were put down only after hard fighting by an entire division of the Bolivian army. Three years later another large-scale rising was just nipped in the bud through the uncovering of an elaborate conspiracy which involved La Paz, the capital. Since then, Bolivian national sentiment has been solidified by the Chaco War against a foreign foe. Still, the conscription drain is resented by the Indians of the remoter regions, who probably have only a vague idea of what it is all about.

Not long ago, the Indians of a certain village killed and ceremonially ate white army officers who had come thither to levy recruits—certainly a quaint and emphatic method of registering discontent! The close of the Chaco War may usher in grave domestic troubles in Bolivia, for the long struggle with Paraguay must inevitably leave Bolivia so exhausted that the government will be proportionately weakened.

---

25 Pearson, *op. cit.*, p. 60.

26 James Bryce, *South America*, p. 181 (London, 1912).

27 Edward Alsworth Ross, *South of Panama*, p. 89 (New York, 1914).

The gravest aspect of recent Indian revolts and conspiracies in South and Central America[28] is the fact that they have all had Russian Communist backing. In every case the leaders included either Russian agents or Latin-American professional agitators, many of whom had been to Moscow and had there been trained in Communist revolutionary tactics by the Third International. This is highly significant, because it denotes a linking-up of two distinct types of Communism the primitive agrarian Communism of the American Indian, and the highly elaborated Communism of Marx and Lenin.

The possible effects of this synthetic propaganda upon the Indians are thus indicated by a former Ecuadorian Minister of Foreign Relations:[29] "In the South American republics which have a large Indian population the Soviet agents have found a most effective aid in the sentiment of the aboriginal Indians; a sentiment transmitted from generation to generation. Under the Incas, the ownership of land was communal, regulated by the individual needs of the people. Labor was obligatory for all . . . This memory of common land-ownership is the sentiment which the intelligent and active agents of Russian Communism are exploiting. And the subtle and tenacious Soviet propaganda is accomplishing its end slowly, and the multitudes of Indians are beginning to awaken from centuries of submissive lethargy. How far will they go when this awakening is complete?"

Although the Indianism of South America lags far behind that of Mexico, its goal is equally uncompromising and far-reaching. Garcia-Calderon, probably the most competent Latin-American student of racial problems, states that "Indianism believes itself appointed to create an entirely new and unique civilization, now that European culture, as it asserts, is destined to decay and die." And he goes on to quote a leading *Indianista* of Peru as saying: "Conquered and destroyed, we do not forget, and we will never forget. Our hope and our patience are as strong as our mountains. We will have nothing to do with the white man, who is our enemy

28 A serious Indian uprising took place in the Republic of El Salvador, early in 1932. It was suppressed only at the cost of several thousand lives.

29 Homero V. Lafronte. Reported in special correspondence of *The New York Times* from Quito, Ecuador, June 2, 1932.

today as he was yesterday. Someday the red race will again be what it was in its customs and its soil. The civilization of the Incas will be reborn for us, and for us only."[30]

The future of the vast land-block stretching from Mexico to Bolivia and Peru is thus far from bright. Throughout this area[31] white blood and white civilization are alike on the decline, while a regenerative large-scale white immigration is unlikely because it is economically inhibited by the presence of abundant low-standard Indian labor. The revolutionary cycle of Mexico will therefore presumably extend southward down the Andes. This means first the breaking of white and near-white supremacy, followed by an unstable period of mestizo rule merging into a new revolutionary phase as the Indian full-bloods seek to realize their desires and gain control.

Assuming that Indianism triumphs, what will be the logical consequences? Economically, it will spell agricultural communism, essentially primitive in type though perhaps modified by Russian influences. Politically, it will mean loose federations of more or less self-contained local units lacking a strong national consciousness. The Indian is still in the clan or tribal stage. He loves his *tierra*—his little corner of the land. But the *patria*—the larger concept of nationhood, is for him either a vague abstraction or quite beyond his mental horizon. Content to live an intensive group-life on a rather low level of economic well-being, and instinctively averse to change, the Indian may qualify as the world's arch-conservative. He shows less aptitude for, and far less interest in Western civilization than either Asiatics or Africans, and is therefore more resistant to its impacts—material, cultural, or spiritual.

Now it is arguable that we should view Indianism with a serene or benevolent detachment. That, of course, is the "liberal" attitude.

30 Francisco Garcia-Calderon, "Blood in Latin America," *Current History*, November, 1926.

31 The geographical continuity of this Indian-inhabited block is broken in two places: Costa Rica and Colombia. The little republic of Costa Rica is a white enclave in the otherwise Indian or mongrelized Central America. In Colombia, the high plateau country and mountain valleys are mainly white, while the lower valleys and hot coastlands are either mongrel or Negro, thus pertaining racially and socially to the Caribbean area. Colombia has no solidly Indian districts of large extent. Therefore the racial basis for Indianism is absent in the republic.

Your typical liberal promptly rises to remark: "If the Indian wants to be that way, let him. It's none of our business."

But is this true? It is one thing to make due allowance for the Indian's peculiar traits such as lack of individual initiative; to shield him from the harsher impacts of our civilization by measures like land-tenures on a group basis. It is quite another matter to envisage the Indian dominating whole countries intimately connected with our world, and remolding those lands to suit his special mentality.

However, leaving aside for the moment the question whether we should view with equanimity the rooting-out of our race and culture over vast regions adjacent to us, suppose we look at certain larger implications.

This planet is not the home of benevolent supermen. It is a world of close-packed races and peoples competing strenuously for survival. No large area richly endowed with natural resources and thinly inhabited by a backward, unprogressive population is going to be long left alone. More ambitious, aggressive stocks are bound to penetrate, seeking to grasp neglected opportunities. An Indianised block from Mexico to Peru would be an area not merely of scant achievement, but also a weak resisting power. And if the white man stands aside, this extensive low-pressure area will be filled by a vigorous indraft from Yellow Asia.

The Far East teems with virile and laborious life. It thrills to novel ambitions and desires. Avid with the urge of swarming myriads, it hungrily seeks outlets for its superabundant vitality. What other field would offer such tempting possibilities for Mongolian race-expansion as those mid-Americas in process of Indianisation? Vast areas of unexploited wealth sparsely inhabited by stagnant populations, revolution-ridden and reverting to more primitive economic and social levels—how could such lands resist the onslaught of tenacious and indomitable millions? The answer is self-evident. They could not resist; and such an invasion, once it got well under way, would be consummated with a celerity and thoroughness perhaps unexampled in human history.

This is no mere theorizing. Yellow Asia is well aware of the momentous possibility. In fact, Mongolian penetration of the non-white regions of Latin America has already begun. Japan, especially, has glimpsed in Latin America golden opportunities for that racial expansion which is the keynote of her foreign policy. For nearly thirty years Japanese statesmen have busied themselves with the problem and have elaborated a technique of penetration which is being methodically worked out.

Even before the Japanese, the Chinaman had pointed the way. Over half a century ago Chinese were numerous along the west coast of Latin America from Mexico to Peru, and even in the islands of the Caribbean where they have long formed a prosperous and influential element. The largest Chinese influx was into Peru, where they came so fast that the government grew alarmed and stopped the inflow by an exclusion law. The reason for this drastic action was that the Peruvians seemed unable to stand up against Chinese competition. The Indian or mestizo laborer was hopelessly undercut by the Chinese coolie, while the white or near-white merchants and shopkeepers were equally outdistanced by Chinese business methods. Given a free hand, these indefatigable Celestials might soon own the country!

The striking successes of these Chinese pioneers, won entirely on their own initiative, fired the Japanese imagination. What might not be accomplished by careful planning and skillful co-ordination with strong official backing! That was the line of reasoning behind a policy which started to function as soon as her epoch-making victory over Russia gave Japan the proper degree of self-assurance, enhanced her prestige, and freed her hands for wider aims.

The first overt moves occurred in 1906. Hitherto there had been almost no direct contacts between Japan and Latin America. When Japan started, however, things began to happen. That very first year several official missions toured Latin America, investigating trade prospects and studying immigration possibilities. Indeed, before the year was out, a Japanese steamship line had been established and Japanese immigrants were landing on Latin-American soil.

That from the very start Japan's aims were far-reaching is shown by utterances of her officials and merchant-princes made at the time. As early as 1907, for instance, Marquis Okuma, one of the best-known "Elder Statesmen," expressed a strong preference for Latin-American countries as fields for Japanese immigration, because most of them were "much easier to include within Japan's future sphere of influence."

White Chile, which had always excluded Asiatics, duly noted these Japanese activities and utterances and instantly took alarm. Using Marquis Okuma's remarks as a text, Senor Augustin Edwards, one of Chile's most prominent citizens and the owner of its leading newspaper,[32] called for a Pan-American rampart against Asia from Behring Strait to Cape Horn—"an invincible weapon against the plans and intentions of that Empire of the Orient which has so lately risen up to new life and already manifests so dire a greed of conquest."

The non-white republics, however, evinced no such fear of Japanese intentions. Indeed, Japan has tended to concentrate her Latin-American activities, especially her immigration projects, in two fields: the Andean republics of Peru and Bolivia on the west coast, and Brazil on South America's eastern side. In these countries Japanese immigration was at first welcomed, though of late years this attitude has changed.

The European War gave a great impetus to Japanese trade throughout Latin America, and immediately after the war Japan began a campaign to acquire important concessions and other opportunities for large investments of capital. These activities aroused widespread comment. Early In 1920, *La Razon* of Buenos Aires, a leading Argentine newspaper, published a detailed survey, concluding:

"There is no doubt that there already exists a vast plan of Japanese colonization in Peru and Bolivia; a plan which, considering the very dispersed native population and their relative incapacity for certain kinds of work, is susceptible of extremely rapid development. . . . Japan, according to one of its most authorized newspapers, is thinking out a very ample commercial program, and nobody ought to be surprised if within the next ten or twenty years its South American trade were far ahead of most other nations, as she is working for this unceasingly. These initiatives and tendencies are worthy of our earnest consideration."

---

32 *El Mercurlo,* one of the most famous and most influential newspapers in Latin America.

This was a true forecast. Japan's trade with Latin America has grown by leaps and bounds, especially during the past few years. In no phase of her current world-wide export campaign has Japan achieved more striking success than in Latin America. With some of the South American countries Japanese trade has increased 200 per cent or 300 per cent at the very time when the trade of Europe and the United States with those same countries was either stationary or retrograde.

Turning to Japan's immigration achievements, we find that there are today some 250,000 Japanese settled in Latin America. More than half of them are in Brazil, Peru and Bolivia ranking next as centers of Japanese colonization—for that is what it has consistently been.

The story of Japanese immigration to Brazil is an interesting one. The Brazilian Federal Government[33] has long favored the amalgamation of all racial elements within its borders. It therefore had no objection to Japanese immigrants. On the contrary, it welcomed them, provided they were healthy and good workers.

The Japanese were enchanted. Immigration societies were promptly formed in Japan to organize this opportunity. Prospective immigrants were carefully selected and trained. They were then shipped in large groups to Brazil and settled mostly in agricultural colonies where everything was prepared for them. These colonies have been materially successful. Visitors testify to their neatness and efficiency. The Japanese have adapted themselves to climatic and other conditions.

But there is one thing these immigrants have not done. They have politely declined to fuse into the great Brazilian melting-pot. With rare exceptions, the second generation is just as Japanese as their immigrant parents. So these settlements are "Little Japans," which tend to expand and flourish at the expense of their less efficient and more easygoing neighbors. This has aroused a growing uneasiness in Brazilian public opinion. In consequence, the Federal Government has recently restricted Japanese immigration.

---

33 To be carefully distinguished from the state governments. Brazil is a "United States" of a type much looser than ours. The states have powers which, in many respects, make them almost sovereign.

Whether this represents a permanent change in Brazilian policy remains to be seen. It certainly displeases Japan, which may find ways of bringing pressure upon Brazil to relax or rescind the restrictive regulations.

Brazil presents a spectacle in many ways unique. Here, not only are all the main racial branches of mankind in contact, but their amalgamation is favored by the national government backed by the prevailing trend of public opinion. The vastness of this melting-pot enhances its significance. Brazil is a great sprawling giant stretching over nearly one-half the entire South American continent and with a population of 40,000,000. Its area is, indeed, practically the same in size as that of the continental United States.

Brazil's history has been very different from that of its Spanish-speaking neighbors. The separation from Portugal was almost bloodless and resulted, not in a republic, but in a limited monarchy under a cadet branch of the Portuguese Royal House. The present republic is less than fifty years old.

The Portuguese are less race-conscious than any other European people. Already in colonial times the early settlers mixed rather freely with the nomadic Indians, and this mestizo populace took up some Negro blood. Negroes were numerous, for African slaves were imported as heavily as into the West Indies until Brazil's tropical provinces had a preponderating black population.

Intermarriage between blacks and lower-class whites or mestizos was checked not so much by race-feeling as by slavery, which was not abolished until 1888. Almost simultaneously the monarchy gave place to a republic.

Thenceforth race-mixture became more rapid. Under the monarchy, the ruling aristocracy and the upper classes generally had maintained a fairly definite color-line. The republic was, from the first, led by politicians dependent upon the votes of the masses, including the recently freed Negroes. Consequently, throughout tropical Brazil, racial lines became less and less distinct.

Although a color-line in our sense of the word has practically vanished, social gradations still correspond roughly to the degree of white blood. "The desire to be white is no less marked in Brazil than elsewhere in Latin America."[34] And this is not mere snobbishness. Success in life tends to be correlated with a white skin. Despite almost complete equality of opportunity, neither the mixed-bloods nor the Negroes have averaged well in most lines of endeavor. The Brazilian mixed-bloods show the same temperamental instability as do those of Spanish America. One of Brazil's leading sociologists, though favoring amalgamation, has to admit that "The *metis*[35] have shown scarcely any capacity for commercial or industrial life. As a rule, they squander what they have, are irresistibly fond of ostentation, are unpractical in their affairs, versatile, and intemperate in their enterprises."[36] Only in the more emotional forms of culture such as lyric poetry and oratory, together with the arts of politics, do the mixed-bloods make a good showing.

As for the Negroes, after emancipation they generally quit work on the plantations, flocking wholesale to the cities and towns. Black labor in Brazil is deemed inefficient and unreliable. Alike in town and country, the mass of full-blooded Negroes lie at the bottom of the social scale, remaining poor and backward.

Despite the charm of Rio de Janeiro, the Brazilian capital, and the culture of its upper classes, competent observers are not enthusiastic over the conditions prevailing in tropical Brazil or the quality of its inhabitants. Some Brazilian scientists also have grave doubts as to the wisdom of general race-mixture. A prominent biologist of Rio goes so far as to say: "I am not in accord with the opinion of those who believe that the mixture of the white race, Negro, and Indian is a useful process of selection. In examining the mixed bloods of Brazil one can see their great inferiority. To sum up: the crossings between different races are a disturbing element of natural evolution and accordingly does not constitute a means of ethnic perfection."[37]

Thus far, we have been considering tropical Brazil. A strikingly different situation exists in the southern part of the republic.

34 L. L. and J. S. Bernard, "The Negro in Relation to other Races in Latin America," *Annuals of the American Association of Political and Social Science,* November, 1928.

35 That is, the mixed-bloods.

36 Doctor de Lacerda, in *Inter-Racial Problems,* p. 381 (London, 1911). This volume is a collection of scientific papers, edited by G. Spiller.

37 Renato Kehi, "Ethnic Elements in the Population of Brazil," *Publication of the Eugenics Research Association,* October, 1929.

This extensive region, with a climate almost as temperate as that of neighboring Uruguay and adjacent districts of Argentina, has been similarly transformed by a tide of European immigration, including a great influx of Northern Italians and nearly half a million Germans. The result is that racially as well as climatically, Southern Brazil is "white man's country." It is certainly far and away the most prosperous and progressive section of the republic. This is notably true of the great State of São Paulo whose capital city is Brazil's southern metropolis.

These sharp differences have already had important political consequences, which will probably become more decisive as time goes on. The antagonism between tropic North and antipodean South cuts deep. It has already engendered several civil wars which, in the last analysis, are based on distinctions of blood and temperament. In this connection, it must not be forgotten that Brazil is a loose federation in which the States have such wide powers as to be quasi-sovereign. State and regional sentiment is very strong. There is a distinct likelihood that Brazil will ultimately split in twain. Anyhow, the republic is today far from being a well-knit, strongly unified nation.

Our survey of racial trends in Latin America reveals the following picture: a thoroughly white antipodean South, contrasted on the one hand with a retrogressive Indianised region stretching from Mexico to Peru, and also with two chronically unstable, mongrelized regions in the Caribbean and in Brazil.

It is against this background that we should evaluate political and social unrest culminating in Communism, and likewise the process of Asiatic penetration. Japan is today the spearhead of this Oriental invasion and we have seen how methodically successful are her tactics of business and colonization. But behind Japan stands an entire Orient, the homeland of more than a billion human beings astir with new wants and aspirations. The basic weakness of the whole middle zone of the Western Hemisphere offers tempting opportunities for Asiatic expansion which, unless checked by more than local forces, will almost inevitably be grasped and attained.

Momentous, indeed, would be the consequences. They would spell nothing short of an upset in the world balance-of-power.

Sensing the potential magnitude of the Asiatic menace, Garcia-Calderon thus reproves Latin Americans whose antagonism to the primacy of the United States in the Western Hemisphere blinds them to an even more disagreeable alternative: "The Japanese would invade western America and convert the Pacific into a vast closed sea, closed to foreign ambitions, *mare nostrum*, peopled with Japanese colonies. Japanese hegemony would not be a mere change of tutelage for the nations of America. Despite essential differences, the Latins oversea have certain common ties with the people of the United States: a long-established religion, Christianity, and a coherent, European, Occidental civilization. Perhaps there is some obscure fraternity between the Japanese and the American Indians; between the yellow men of Nippon and the copper-colored Quechuas. But the ruling race, the dominant type of Spanish origin, which imposes the civilization of the white man upon America, is hostile to the entire invading East."[38]

Furthermore, Asiatic penetration would not only imperil the white race and culture, it would likewise doom the Indian and mestizo elements. For, as Ross points out: "The Indian could make no effective economic stand against the wide-awake, resourceful, and aggressive Japanese or Chinese. The Oriental immigrants could beat the Indians at every point, block every pathway upward, and even turn them out of most of their present employments. In great part the Indians would become a cringing *sudra* caste, tilling the poorer lands and confined to menial or repulsive occupations. Filled with despair, and abandoning themselves even more than they do now to pisco and coca, they would shrivel into a numerically negligible element in the population."[39]

It is true that a certain school of thought advocates the forging of all Latin America into a great confederation able to withstand both the rising peril from the East and the traditional bugbear of the Yankee "Colossus of the North." We hear eloquent appeals for a "Continental Nationalism" or for *La Patria Grande*—the Super-Fatherland.[40]

---

38 Garcia-Calderon, op. *cit.*, pp. 329–30.

39 Ross, *op. cit., pp.* 92–93.

40 These are the translated titles of two books by well-known South American writers. They are: Joachim E. Bello, *El Nacionalismo Continental* (Madrid, 1926);

Yet such suggestions, however impressive in theory, break down before the iron logic of realities. Facts abundantly prove that the superficial unity which existed during the colonial period is disrupted beyond recall. Despite surviving ties of language and culture, the brood of independent states hatched by the revolution against Spain have for more than a century been pursuing divergent paths until today the differences between them are amazing. A recognized authority on Latin-American affairs brings this out when he says that Argentina, for instance, is in all things save speech more unlike Peru or Nicaragua than Germany is from Spain; that white Chile is mentally and spiritually far closer to France or Italy than to mestizo-Indian Bolivia, its next-door neighbor.[41] In the light of all this, the idea that Latin America could be welded into an effective unit for any major policy is seen to be mere illusion.

The one center of effective power in all Latin America is the block of stable, progressive nations in the extreme south: Argentina, Chile, and Uruguay. They alone can be depended upon for constructive opposition to Asiaticism, Indianism, mongrelism, and Communism; against all those retrograde or destructive forces which threaten Latin America with further disruption and with possible dissolution. North of the antipodes there is nothing solid and enduring until we reach the frontier of the United States.

However, from this stern reality there emerges the ideal of a true Pan-Americanism; of a genuine understanding between the strong, constructive elements, North and South, through the assumption of a common task—the saving of the Western Hemisphere for the white race and white civilization.

---

and Manuel Ugarte, *La Pania Grande* (Buenos Aires, 1927).

41 Henry Kittredge Norton, *The Coming of South America* (New York, 1932).

PART I
CHAPTER V
FRANCE AND THE BLACK POWER

THE position of France in Europe and in the contemporary world is one of the great perplexities of our time. There can be no hope either of re-establishing the comity of Europe or of broadening it into a larger white-Western comity unless France has her proper place therein. Unfortunately, just what that place should be is something on which most Frenchmen differ markedly from most other people.

The traditional French attitude, like France itself, is in many ways unique. The French believe that their country is entitled to a certain peculiar status as a matter of right; almost as part of the order of nature. To the average Frenchman this is axiomatic—not to be disputed. To it, in French eyes, all else is subordinate. Since other nations are not disposed to accept this thesis, the French are ready to go to any lengths in order to maintain it. As a result, France is today embarked upon certain policies which, if pressed to their logical conclusion, must almost inevitably spell disaster for Europe, for the white race, and ultimately for France herself.

The most difficult aspect of the situation is that it far transcends questions of politics or armaments. These are merely the surface aspects of a problem which roots deep in the past and which is largely psychological. To get at its true inwardness we must understand the French attitude of mind. And that is not easy for those who have not lived in France, learned the language, and got to know the people. Still, a careful analysis should reveal the major difficulties involved. But it must include not only France's present status but her historic evolution.

More than any other people, the French have attained a mature, well-rounded nationhood. Manners, methods, ideals, cultural forms—all are nicely timed in a vital rhythm which, like a pendulum, perpetually traverses the same path. Restricted adjustment and absence of basic change are the salient features of French life, which reveals itself as an exquisite finished product.

This is naturally the outcome of a long evolutionary development. French nationalism is, in fact, the oldest as well as the most perfect of its kind. Germinating far back in the Middle Ages, it became dynamically articulate five hundred years ago in the mystic personality of Joan of Arc.

Thenceforth, almost down to our own days, France stood in a class by herself. Indeed, by the beginning of the seventeenth century, France was the leading state of Europe; the indubitable head of the European comity. This primacy was firmly based on the realities of the period. France then outweighed every other European people in political power, in cultural prestige, and even in population.

Take the population factor alone. Under Louis XIV, France had thrice the population of Britain, twice the population of what is now Germany, and almost twice the population of Russia.[1] Politically, also, France's primacy was unassailable. In those bygone times, insular England was, practically speaking, almost as remote from Continental Europe as America is now, while both Germany and Italy were mere geographical expressions. As for Russia, she was then beyond the pale of Western civilization.

Thus, century after century, France maintained her leadership of Europe. By the reign of Louis XIV, France had come to set the tone of everything, from literature and diplomacy to mistresses and perukes. Under Napoleon, French armies ranged from Portugal to Moscow and came within an ace of bringing all Europe under France's lasting sway.

The collapse of Napoleon's Empire did not outwardly jeopardize French primacy in the larger sense. Though shorn of her extreme pretensions, France, down to 1870, was still unquestionably the leading power of Europe. Nevertheless, her traditional ascendancy was being rapidly undermined. The spread of nationalism throughout the Continent, the coalescence of Germans and Italians

1 Contrast this with the situation today. Both Britain and Germany outweigh France in population, while Russians outnumber Frenchmen nearly five to one.

toward adult nationhood, and the slowing-down of France's population-growth implied that her politico-military primacy was no longer inevitable. It was France's rash efforts to block German unity which led her to disaster in the Franco-Prussian War. The War of 1870 (termed by Frenchmen "The Terrible Year") was the worst blow France had ever received. Not only was she defeated and bereft of Alsace-Lorraine; she was also demoted from her traditional headship of Europe.

This last it was which rankled most. Indeed, the French people refused to accept the demotion as a reality. They insisted that it was a mere abnormal episode which must, and should, presently pass. Bismarck did his best to reconcile France to the new situation. By mingled pressure and persuasion (quite similar to France's present policy toward Germany) the Iron Chancellor tried to make France acquiesce in a German hegemony of Europe. Once she did that, France could have ample "security" in the sense of a self-contained nation attending to its own affairs.

But that sort of security France indignantly refused—precisely as she refuses it today. To the vast majority of Frenchmen, German ascendancy in Europe was something unnatural, monstrous, almost immoral. The natural, the *right* status was the political and cultural primacy of France—traditionally known to her devoted sons as *La Grande Nation.*

Almost all of France's leading spirits after 1870—Clemenceau, Delcassé, Foch, Poincaré, and others, worked grimly, inflexibly toward one goal—the bringing of Germany's intolerable hegemony to an end. Of course, they did not openly avow this; they "rationalized" their larger hidden grievance around Alsace-Lorraine, and took to heart Gambetta's astute counsel: "Speak of it never; think of it ever!" So France bided her time.

She did more than bide her time. Besides an astute diplomacy working tirelessly to forge an invincible anti-German combination of European Powers, France proceeded feverishly to build up a great colonial empire. And that empire was amassed primarily not to obtain outlets for trade or excess population, but to acquire fresh man-power for *La Revanche*—the Day of Reckoning when France would cast down the Prussian upstart and regain usurped primacy, at one and the same stroke. That was the supreme objective; a task inspired not merely by patriotic duty, but also in the true interest of civilization! Believing this from the bottom of their hearts, Frenchmen could not be expected to weigh objectively the larger consequences of their colonial policy when they called in Africa, and especially Black Africa, to help attain what most Frenchmen deemed a profoundly righteous end.

The French attitude towards other peoples involves such far-reaching possibilities that we should do well to understand it. Most foreigners lack a clear comprehension, because Frenchmen rarely disclose it to outsiders and even strive to disguise it in various ways.

Convinced as they are of the supreme excellence of their civilization, the French, far more than most peoples, grade mankind into two categories: themselves and others. The typical French attitude is strikingly like that of the Ancient Greeks, who divided the world into Hellenes and Barbarians. In fact, among themselves, Frenchmen often refer to foreigners collectively as le*s barbares.* A foreigner in France is judged mainly by his ability to adopt French ways and his enthusiasm for French culture. A good French accent is a most effective passport to social favor. It is deemed fair evidence that a barbarian is getting civilized; that another cultural conquest is being achieved.

This desire to extend the realm of French civilization motivates France's policy toward its colonies and also toward questions of race. The widespread idea that the French have little or no race-consciousness is incorrect. The average Frenchman feels himself to be a white man and takes pride therein. Only *La France* and all that she implies takes precedence over race, as over everything else. The seeming shift in attitude toward racial matters since the Revolution has been due far more to the pressure of external forces than to altered ideals.

The basic French attitude toward race when uncomplicated by patriotic considerations is revealed by the colonial policy of the Old Régime, before the French Revolution of 1789. In France's former colonial empire in America, race-problems were handled quite differently from the methods employed by either the Spaniards and Portuguese on the one hand or by the English and Dutch on the other. We have already seen the Spanish and Portuguese way in our survey of Latin America. We should likewise recall that the British and Dutch colonists everywhere maintained a strict color-line in which the integrity of the white race was the paramount consideration.

The French stood midway between these two extremes. They never doubted the innate superiority of the white race and they intended to maintain white supremacy in their colonies. But they were willing to take unto themselves such exceptional individuals as had *demonstrably* assimilated French culture and acquired a French type of mind; thus connoting an assimilation, not of mere external superficialities, but of basic attitudes and ideals.

This policy is clearly expressed in the official instructions of Colbert, Louis XIV's great Colonial Minister, to the Governors of New France or Canada. Therein, Colbert says:

"Call the natives to a community of life with the French, but only after instructing them in the maxims of our religion, and even in our manners, so that they may ultimately make, with those of ours who migrate unto Canada, one and the same nation." In other words, there was to be no hasty or general intermixture of whites and Indians. Only the qualified Indian elite was to be progressively incorporated with the French stock. The results of this policy show today in the fact that, while the present French Canadians show occasional traces of Indian blood, they are essentially a white breed—and are proverbially ultra-French in culture and in feeling.

Utterly different was the racial policy of the Old Régime in its West Indian colonies, where the non-whites were almost entirely Africans. The Negro was regarded as congenitally incapable of truly assimilating the French culture and mental attitude. Furthermore, he was deemed racially so different that even a slight admixture of black blood would dangerously alter the white colonial stock. Therefore all thought of attempting to incorporate even an elite was eschewed and intermarriage between pure whites and persons in any degree African was prevented by a strict color-line.

This is abundantly shown by official documents. As early as 1681, the Intendant of French San Domingo[2] reported to the Home

2 The island of San Domingo was divided into a Spanish colony, of the same

Government: "I do not think that marriages of whites to mulattresses, or of mulattoes to white women, would be good for the colony . . . It is true that the debauchery of the Spaniards and Portuguese has brought them to alliances with such an impure stock; but I can also say that their colonies are abodes of abomination, vice, and filth, and that from these unions there has sprung a people so wretched and so weak that a hundred of our buccaneers can put to rout a thousand of that *canaille*."

The Church authorities were of the same mind, for in 1722, the Superior of Missions states in an official report that the increasing numbers of mulattoes is exposing the colonies "to the terrible punishment of those famous cities of abomination, which were destroyed by the fire of Heaven. The mingling of these races is a criminal coupling of men and women of different species, whence comes a fruit which is one of Nature's monsters."

The Home Government fully shared this attitude. A Ministerial letter of 1741 addressed to the Colonial authorities states that "His Majesty's pleasure is not to permit the mixing of the bloods." And a similar letter of 1771 asserts that nothing can destroy that difference "which Nature herself has created between white and black, and which policy has ever been careful to uphold as a barrier which the mulattoes and their posterity may never overcome."[3]

The French Revolution radically altered this policy and attitude. The revolutionary watchword was *Liberty! Equality! Fraternity!* The Jacobin rulers of France were apostles of complete racial equality. Indeed, they aimed at a world-revolution similar to that planned by Communists today.

However, these revolutionary internationalists were in power less than three years. Their successors, despite lip-service to revolutionary slogans, stressed French national interests above aught else. If the

---

name, in the eastern portion, and to the westward a French colony officially termed *La Partie Frangaige de Saint-Domingue.* This is today the Black Republic of Haiti. The name *Haiti* is an Indian word, revived by the revolted Negroes when they gained their independence, in order to mark the break with the French colonial past.

3 The documents just cited are quoted from my book, *The French Revolution in San Domingo,* pp. 41–43 (Boston and London, 1914). The book is based mainly on personal research in the French Archives.

color-line thenceforth became fainter, it was largely because French thought even after the Revolution continued to be influenced by Rousseau and the Encyclopédistes, who asserted that men of all races could be formed in the same mold by training and education. Hence the idea that not merely exceptional individuals but whole populations might be transformed into genuine Frenchmen in every respect save the color of the skin. The extension of French power and culture, however, was still the primary consideration. The scope and technique had altered, but the objective remained the same.

These ideas were at first little more than academic speculation, because during the Napoleonic wars, France lost all her colonies. At the peace-settlement of 1815, England handed back some shreds and patches, chiefly as a salve for French pride. Some small bits in the Caribbean; a few trading-posts on the West Coast of Africa—these were about all that was left of France's former colonial empire. Chiefly through sentiment, those exotic remnants were declared part-and-parcel of the Mother Country and were given the right to send representatives to the French Parliament. In time, colored Senators and Deputies appeared from the "assimilated" colonies, and since they spoke measurably good French they were benevolently received as extensions of French culture. Anyhow, the colonies did not then matter much, one way or the other.

Presently France began to acquire new colonial possessions, first in North Africa, and later in Indo-China and the Pacific. The motives were those prompting other nations to colonial expansion—new outlets for trade or population. France was still the leading Power of Europe. Her traditional primacy had not yet been assailed.

The disaster of 1870 transformed French colonial policy. In the hour of defeat and humiliation there came the idea of building up a great overseas empire which should furnish the reservoir of man-power needed to accomplish France's European aims. Then began that intensive drive for African territory which brought almost the entire northwestern quarter of the Dark Continent under the Tricolor. This, added to her previous acquisitions, gave France a colonial empire second only to Britain's in size, and with a population exceeding 60,000,000 souls.

The basic purpose of this hectic expansion was naturally not publicly avowed and for a long time was not generally recognized abroad. Why France should spend so much blood and treasure conquering the barren wastes of the Sahara and the economically less desirable parts of West Africa mystified most foreign observers, who usually laid it to a mere desire for prestige. Lord Salisbury typified British opinion of the time when he is said to have jocularly remarked: "They tell me that the soil there is rather on the light side. Surely we can let the Gallic cock scratch in it."

A few keen-sighted foreign observers seem to have glimpsed what was in the wind. Henry M. Stanley, the famous African explorer, judged that France was acquiring the best part of Africa because she had got "the lands of soldiers." French officials occasionally dropped a hint, as when General Faidherbe urged the speedy conquest of Senegal because "other colonies give us products; this colony will give us men." Gabriel Hanotaux, French Colonial Minister during the closing decade of the nineteenth century, always kept man-power to the fore in his aggressive colonial policies. Indeed, he himself avows what was in his mind, for he writes: "In 1885, I was at Constantinople. I watched the Sultan's Black Guard march past. They were Sudanese soldiers sent by the Khedive. As they passed, marching to the fifes and clashing cymbals, I said to myself: 'Here are the great, the invincible armies of the future! These men know how to die.'"[4]

In the opening years of the present century France was assured uncontested possession of West Africa and the Sahara by the general settlement of colonial disputes with England which was then negotiated. Under this same agreement France likewise got a free hand to conquer Morocco, the home of the best Arabo-Berber fighters in North Africa. These North African peoples, however, had to be judiciously handled. They probably would not endure general conscription, and thus could not be depended upon to supply soldiers in the same ratio to population as the black tribes south of the Sahara. These black millions, especially the "fighting Senegalese," were the ultimate reservoir of man-power which the French General Staff had so long been seeking. Experimental battalions had proved the Senegalese's fighting quality. Quantity

4 Quoted from General Mangin's book, *La Force Noire*, p. 261 (Paris, 1910).

alone was lacking. And since reticence was no longer needed, the French public was duly informed, and enthused over the idea.

In 1910, General (then Lieutenant-Colonel) Mangin published his celebrated book aptly entitled, *La Force Noire*—"The Black Power." The book made a great sensation, not only in France but throughout Europe. It begins with an historical survey of the Negro's excellence as a soldier when competently trained and led by higher races.

The book then goes on to analyze the high fighting qualities of the Senegalese in particular, the author having had long experience as a commander of Senegalese troops Mangin concludes "Tenacity in long struggles is one of the most necessary qualities in modern war, where battles may last many days The black man's lack of nerves renders him precious in such fighting . . . The *insouciance* of the black and his fatalism are thus invaluable qualities. His confidence in his leader is unshakable . . . Especially in the final shock, the black excels, pouring forth his pent-up rage unimpaired by any nervous depression. In future battles, these primitive beings, for whom life counts so little and whose youthful blood boils with such ardor, as though eager to shed itself, will surely attain the old *June française*.[5]5

While General Mangin was advocating a great Black army, other French officers sought to develop Indo-China's man-power into a great Yellow army. The leading spirit of this group was General Pennequin. But the idea never amounted to much. Besides the low average fighting quality of the Indo-Chinese, the civilian officials, and white colonists of France's Far Eastern empire took alarm. Already a nationalistic ferment was visible throughout the colony. Sporadic revolts and conspiracies had already taken place. To arm and train large numbers of these discontented yellow men might be highly dangerous. So the plan was quietly dropped.

However, the mobilization of the Black Power went rapidly forward. When the Great War broke out, West Africa was able to furnish large numbers of trained black troops. By the close of the war France's colonial empire had furnished nearly 1,000,000 soldiers and laborers, most of whom saw European service. Fully

5 Mangin, *op. cit.*, p. 257.

200,000 fell on the battlefield, and an equal number died of wounds or disease. The Senegalese made a notable showing except under prolonged artillery fire Their bayonet charges were famous A German officer gives us the following vivid description of the fury of their onset:

"They came. First singly, at wide intervals. Feeling their way, like the arms of a horrible cuttlefish. Eager, grasping, like the claws of a mighty monster. Thus they rushed closer, flickering and sometimes disappearing in the cloud. Entire bodies and single limbs, now showing in the harsh glare, now sinking in the shadows, came nearer and nearer. Strong, wild fellows; their log-like, fat, black skulls wrapped in pieces of dirty rags. Showing their grinning teeth like panthers, with their bellies drawn in and their necks stretched forward. Some with bayonets on their rifles. Many armed only with knives. Monsters all, in their confused hatred. Horrible their unnaturally wide-opened, burning, bloodshot eyes. Eyes that seem like terrible beings themselves. Like unearthly, hell-born beings. Eyes that seemed to run ahead of their owners, lashed, unchained, no longer to be restrained. On they came like dogs gone mad and cats spitting and yowling, with a burning lust for human blood, with a cruel dissemblance of their beastly malice. Behind them came the first wave of the attackers, in close order, a solid, rolling black wall, rising and falling, swaying and heaving; impenetrable; endless."[6]

The Great War, which more than once brought France to the verge of destruction, ended with the glorious attainment of that which she had dreamed for nearly fifty years. Not only were the "Lost Provinces" restored; France was once more the leading Power of Europe.

The Teutonic giant was prostrate, disarmed, bankrupt; and French diplomacy quickly forged a network of alliances to guard against a revival of German strength.

An extraordinarily favorable status won by France on the battlefield was codified in treaties which formed the charter of a League whose membership was world-wide and which was ostensibly the basis of a new world-order. The French army and

6 Captain Rheinhold Eichacker, "The Blacks Attack!" *Current History,* April, 1917.

the French air-fleet were unrivaled. The vaults of the Bank of France bulged with gold, while French thrift piled up fresh capital. Apparently, an unbeatable combination.

Yet France becomes increasingly ill at ease. Feverishly she girds her frontiers with the most stupendous bulwarks erected since the Great Wall of China. Plans for disarmament, for treaty revision, for any real change in the *status quo* leave her cold. Deaf alike to argument and entreaty, she monotonously iterates one *word—security.*

Security for and from what?—from unprovoked attack? Naturally. But also security for those traditional values so enshrined in French idealism; so deep-rooted in the French soul.

Thus only can we fully comprehend France's inflexible determination to maintain at all costs her revived hegemony over Continental Europe; because France sincerely believes it to be best, both for herself and for the other European peoples, that the Continent evolve under her beneficent sway. We are likewise in a position to understand France's conception of her hegemony. The French are no crude militarists. Wisely they realize that wholesale European conquests and annexations would fatally dilute their culture and dissolve their nationhood. What they visualize is political and cultural *primacy:* the France of olden time, crowned with prestige and authority, setting the tone to her neighbors, and by them acknowledged as *La Grande Nation.*

Unfortunately for this beatific vision, the material and even the psychological bases which once automatically gave France leadership no longer exist. Other European peoples have attained adult nationhood and rebel at the prospect of even the mildest tutelage. Both Germany and Italy have long since ceased to be geographical expressions. Russia looms ever more insistently in the background. And, upon the far horizon, rise America and the Orient—factors which, in the days of France's pristine glory, had not effectively come into being. Europe is no longer the focal point of human affairs. The past does not return.

Yet there stands France: wedded to the past; staunch in her nationhood and her specialized culture; strong in herself, her traditions, her faith.

This is the great impasse underlying all the current perturbations of European politics. Until the dilemma is solved there can be no genuine assurance of European stability; no hope of a revived European comity. And of such a solution there today appears no sign. Whatever the temporary diplomatic shifts, the moral deadlock remains unbroken.

France is not averse to a restored comity of Europe. On the contrary, she deplores its loss and desires its revival—in what she deems the only legitimate way.

But the French mind is lucid; it sees clearly the obstacles to such an outcome. The French mind is skeptical; it doubts whether those obstacles can be surmounted. The French mind is proverbially logical. Therefore it has envisaged an alternative. If a European comity be impossible, there must be a Gallic comity. And its name is *Greater France.*

At the height of the international crisis of 1923, when French armies had poured into the Ruhr and Europe seemed on the verge of a general explosion, Premier Poincaré uttered his memorable phrase: "France is not a country of forty millions, she is a country of one hundred millions!" Almost simultaneously, General Mangin, the indefatigable advocate of the Black Power, echoed Poincaré almost word for word, and went on to assert that this Power was the best instrument by which France's expansion in the world might be furthered. These are merely two outstanding instances of what seems to be the prevailing attitude in France today.

Just what does this mean? Such statements imply, not simply an effective political structure composed of diverse elements but a real union bound together by common sentiments and ideas. Does such a union today exist between France and its far-flung colonial empire? Or, if not yet actually realized, is it definitely in the making?

Let us analyze this French colonial empire a bit in detail. Surely M. Poincaré could not seriously have included Indo-China in his prospective synthesis. Even the most ardent "assimilationists" know in their heart of hearts that this big Far Eastern dependency will never become truly "French." Its remoteness from France; its tenacious native culture, its exposure to the strong winds of nationalistic and racial self-consciousness now sweeping the entire

Orient make Indo-China's Gallicization a vain dream. Indeed, Frenchmen who really know Indo-China have long admitted that the duration of French rule is uncertain. A French publicist put the matter in a nutshell with his celebrated verdict: *Lachons l'Asie, prenons l'Afrique*—which, freely translated, means: "Let's discount Asia and concentrate on Africa." Practically speaking, therefore, Indo-China with its 20,000,000 inhabitants is out of the picture, and "Greater France" boils down mostly to French Africa.

What does that amount to? French Africa divides naturally into four significant regions. First comes North Africa, the belt of territory stretching between the Mediterranean and the Sahara Desert, from Tunis to Morocco. Its total population is about 12,000,000.[7] Of this, a trifle over 1,000,000 are Europeans, mostly concentrated in Algeria; and of this European population three-fourths are French citizens.[8] The 11,000,000 natives are basically Berbers—a Mediterranean "dark-white" stock, considerably mixed with Semitic Arabs, and in the towns at least slightly tinged with Negro blood.

Racially, therefore, Frenchmen and Berbers do not stand very far apart. The great barrier to fusion is religion. These North Africans are Moslems, and Islam is not merely a faith but also a culture and way of life profoundly different from that of the Western world. It is a noteworthy fact that whereas in Asia, Islam is being disrupted by Western ideas, in Africa Islam seems to be the nucleus around which is growing a nationalistic movement embracing all these North African peoples. At any rate, despite their best efforts, the French have thus far had scant success in Gallicizing the North Africans. Only a small minority can be considered as in any real sense French.

Despite the Sahara Desert's vast area, its nomadic population is so small and so scattered that it can be left out of consideration. The Sahara's significance is that of a connecting-link between North Africa and the French possessions to the southward. Once across the desert we come to French West Africa, an extensive region

---

7 Excluding the Spanish Zone of Morocco and the internationalized district of Tangier.

8 Not all of French blood, however. A considerable proportion are naturalized Spaniards and Italians, or their offspring.

with a population of some 14,000,000. They are Negroes, of various types. It should be noted that Senegal, the chief power-station of *La Force Noire,* has less than 1,500,000 inhabitants. Conquered by France within the last fifty years, these West African peoples are only one step removed from savagery. France's best efforts have thus far produced, at best, a superficial veneer of Western ways. Only in the old trading settlements of the coast, long in French hands, do we find a black or mulatto life which has imbibed some measure of French culture and declares itself to be French.

The southernmost extension of French Africa is the Congo area.[9] As yet, it is of scant importance. Largely tropical rain-forest, its relatively small population of 3,000,000 is of a decidedly low or even degenerate Negro type. Some tribes are rapidly dying out, chiefly because of new diseases, alcoholism, and other imported vices.

Such are the bases upon which the grandiose structure of "Greater France" is to be reared. The goal is clear enough—a modernized version 'of the Roman Empire, wherein all creeds and colors will be spontaneously united by the bonds of a common language, culture, and mental attitude. Paris is to be the New Rome of this unique creation.

How is this goal to be attained? Basically, by the method which Colbert prescribed to the Governors of New France; by "calling the natives to a community of life with the French" and incorporating among the French as rapidly as possible elites which genuinely respond to French civilization. Those elites, and they alone, are deemed worthy of special interest and favor. As always, he advancement of French power and culture transcends every other consideration.

We now understand the true French attitude toward racial equality. 'Whatever their theoretical professions, in practice the French mean *equality for Frenchmen and those in process of becoming French.* All outside that category are simply beyond the pale. To paraphrase a French witticism, equality is not an "article of exportation."

Herein lies the peculiar character of French imperialism, which differs markedly from that of any other Western nation. The French

9 Of course, to be distinguished from the adjacent Belgian Congo.

imperialist ideal is unalterably opposed to all indigenous cultural developments; it definitely vetoes aspirations not only towards independence but even towards local autonomy. *La France* comes first, last, and all the time. As a competent English writer well says: "The basic policy, both in theory and practice, is the propagation of French civilization and the French language on as wide a scale as possible. The touchstone of every administrative proposal is, how far it will advance or retard assimilation to France. The question of the ethnic type of the future French subject is subordinated to the desire for numerical strength, the suitability of the kind of education prescribed for Africans to the question whether it will assist the economical and rapid development of this Greater France. The benefits of French medicine are, in a word, conferred on both Berber and Negro, not only or even primarily for the sake of their health, but for political reasons. The same motive underlies the equipment and selection of officials . . . *La France* is, in fact, to be the goddess to whom the Franco-African of the future is to devote his life."[10]

Although Frenchmen dislike having this discussed by foreigners, they avow it frankly enough among themselves. A well-known French publicist, Augustin Bernard, puts the matter clearly when he writes: "We do not want to coerce the North Africans, but we want it clearly understood that we are just as much at home there as they are. France has fastened herself with all the fibers of her soul to these countries, and looks upon them less as colonies than as parts of the Mother Country. France has taken over the work that Rome used to perform when she incorporated provinces into her empire. We want to make all our African subjects, regardless of their racial origins, into a single people who will accept our speech as their common language. This common relationship will gradually produce a unified will." And such views are not confined to "imperialistic" groups in France; they permeate all shades of political opinion.

A radical "left-wing" newspaper, for instance, states: "Eighty million French-speaking people in a firmly knit stretch of territory—France, northern and central Africa—form an army that enables us

10 "Great Britain and France in Africa," *The Round Table* (London), September, 1929.

to march forward with the sure knowledge that the future of our race is secure."[11]

Out of more or less thoroughly Gallicized elites, white colonists, and their progeny, it is hoped fairly soon to develop a new ruling caste which will zealously further the development of Greater France, and which in return will naturally enjoy high favor and special privileges. The new caste will, of course, be racially very mixed, for French imperialism envisages "miscegenation on a vast scale . . . in French Africa miscegenation is frankly welcomed, especially if the male is French."[12]

Some "assimilationists" view the process of race-mixture in the colonies with an enthusiasm well-nigh apostolic. A good example of this attitude is the following account of a trip through the island of Martinique, written by the Director of the French Colonial Institute of Paris.

The trip was taken in company with a colored colleague, former Deputy for Martinique in the French Chamber of Deputies and just appointed Under-Secretary for the Colonies. This appointment aroused great enthusiasm among the population of this French West Indian island, where the former colonial whites have almost entirely disappeared. Having enjoyed much festive hospitality during his tour, the Director benignantly concludes:

"Martinique constitutes the first phase in that interpenetration of fraternal races in our overseas regions, and will prepare that fusion of which the Martiniquais prove so magnificently the happiness and success. A policy of 'association' is, at best, only temporary; whereas a policy of true assimilation—the marriage not merely of interests but of bloods—has produced in this fortunate isle both the idea and the living flesh of the French soul; it will be reproduced everywhere, if we practice this policy patiently and constantly.

"May you always keep alight these magnificent sparks of desire, courage, and high hope, Dear Little France of the farthest Atlantic! Martinique is a prodigious foreshadowing of our perpetual renovation. It is the basis of our great departure towards the Greater France; towards the French Universe—la *Patrie neuve, aux mille*

---

11 *L'Euvre* (Paris), March 1, 1930.

12 *The Round Table*, op. *cit.*

mamelles, l'avenir clair, les beaux enfants, la force, l'argent facile, l'espoir!"[13]

The concluding lines just quoted have been purposely left in the original French, so that their almost untranslatable lyric fervor may be duly appreciated, together with the writer's mental attitude.

Greater France cannot be divided into watertight (or, rather, blood-tight) compartments. A new Roman Empire welded by systematic miscegenation in the provinces cannot fail to have profound repercussions upon the imperial nucleus itself. As time passes, there must be racial give-and-take. The Gallicization of Africa necessarily implies a correlative Africanisation of France.

The Africanizing process has, in fact, already begun. To supplement French man-power, the General staff insists that between 65,000 and 100,000 colonial troops must be garrisoned at all times in France. And a large proportion of these colonials are Senegalese or other Negroes. Furthermore, since the war, many discharged colonial soldiers (including some Indo-Chinese) have remained in France. There is also a certain amount of immigration into France from the colonies. This miscellaneous collection of Berbers, Arabs, Negroes, Malagasy, and Orientals tends to settle in the port-towns, the large cities, and the big industrial centers. There it falls naturally into ranks of low-paid marginal or casual labor—a situation not displeasing to employers. Mingling with the lowest elements of the French population, this colonial riff-raff constitutes the beginnings of a mongrel urban proletariat. The story of Imperial Rome thus tends to repeat itself. Did not the cosmopolitanised Roman plebs cause Latin moralists to dub the Mistress of the Ancient World *Cloaca Gentium*—"the Sewer of Peoples"?

These ominous portents make some Frenchmen increasingly uneasy. A reflective minority, including biologists such as Count de Lapouge and the eminent psycho-sociologist Gustave Le Bon, have condemned the policy of "assimilation" from the start and predict dire consequences to France herself.[14] However, the idea of Greater

13 J. L. Gheerbrandt, "La Martinique–Jeune France des Tropiques," *Revue Bleue*, March 7, 1931.

14 The author has discussed these problems at some length with both those eminent scientists. They expressed themselves even more strongly in private conversation than they have in their writings.

France continues to captivate the popular imagination, while the insistence of the General Staff upon the Black Power's vital role in French security reconciles moderate-minded men to whom the imperialist dream does not, of itself, greatly appeal.

So France is today dotted with brown, black, and yellow garrisons; and these colonials have the same privileges as other French soldiers, including access to white women as a matter of course. Norman Angell strikingly depicts this phase of the situation. "Recently," he writes, "I had occasion to visit Strasbourg, to the liberation of which so many myriads of the youth of France gave their lives. On a sunny Sunday morning . . . an attempted short-cut back to my hotel landed me within a hundred yards of a street in which this scene was being enacted: under the summer sun long queues of Negroes, hundreds of them, were lining up in orderly fashion outside the doors of certain houses. From time to time a few Negroes emerged from those houses, a few were admitted, and the doors were closed—those outside patiently waiting their turn. Through this street wandered Alsatian children, girls and boys, watching a spectacle which, after all, must be an inevitable incident of the age in which the new Africa comes to the aid of old France. For those houses outside the doors of which the Negroes were waiting, were brothels, and inside were white girls, the Liberated Daughters of France."[15]

Possible effects of such occurrences upon the maintenance of white prestige and authority in the colonies seem to be ignored by French public opinion, in face of the military efficiency of *La Force Noire.* And this force is effectively employed. Senegalese, like North Africans, were quartered in great numbers upon the Rhineland during the long period of French occupation. Indeed, some Frenchmen seem to have gotten an almost sadistic pleasure out of thus affronting the Nordicism of the *Boche.* One French publicist certainly suggests this state of mind when he wrote: "Already our black soldiers are put to good use, and there will be plenty more use for them. On the Left Bank of the Rhine—perhaps beyond, tomorrow, there are vast territorial or economic pledges which are, and long must be, kept in our hands. Let black battalions

15 Norman Angell, "France and the Black Power," *Contemporary Review,* February, 1922.

mount guard there!"[16] Such sentiments were, however, by no means universal. Many Frenchmen disapproved the large-scale use of colored troops in occupied Germany. One well-known writer on colonial problems voiced this feeling by stating: "We fancied that we could thus humiliate 'the barbarians,' forgetting that at the same time we were humiliating the entire white race."[17]

That was, in truth, something which the French would have done well to remember; because not only their military methods in the Rhineland but the whole idea of *La Force Noire* was arousing apprehension and resentment throughout the white world. France's use of the Black Power was clearly laying up trouble for herself in the field of foreign affairs.

To begin with, the use of African troops in the occupied territories quite needlessly envenomed Franco-German relations. The Germans have not forgotten what they term "The Black Horror on the Rhine"; nor will Germans forget so long as the generation lives which had to endure it. This further complicates a problem already serious enough, by unnecessarily injecting into it ulcerated emotions.

Besides exacerbating German hatred, this policy certainly did France no good with its Western allies. The Belgians by no means gave it their unqualified approval. As for the British, they were frankly shocked.[18] And this augmented the chorus of protest against France's whole Black Power policy which was rising from the English press and from many sections of British public opinion.

The pronouncements of Premier Poincaré and other prominent Frenchmen evoked British replies of a most uncomplimentary character. General Mangin's remarks, already cited, served as a

16 Alfred Guignard, "Lea Troupes Noires," *Revue der Deux Mondes,* June 15, 1919.

17 Pierre Khorat, "Soldats de Couleur," *Le Correspondent,* July to, 1922.

18 The author spent some time in the Rhineland and the Ruhr during the height of the great crisis known as the "Ruhr War." He found the French Rhineland Zone filled with colonial troops, and the inhabitants extremely fearful. The difference in psychological atmosphere between the French and British Zones was amazing. At British headquarters, at Cologne, the English officers made no attempt in private conversation to conceal their wrathful disgust at certain things that went on in the French-occupied territory. In justice to the French, the author will add that, in the Ruhr, all the occupying troops were apparently white first-line units.

text for the following editorial in the outstanding organ of British Liberalism:

"General Mangin made a speech at Strasbourg on Sunday which is grim reading for Europe . . . It does not need much imagination to understand the horrors that would be brought upon Europe if European nations came to rely on the weapon which General Mangin brandishes before the world. A Europe with black garrisons would symbolize a civilization even more desperately retrograde than a Europe armed to the teeth. White conscription would mean a Europe without hope, but black conscription would mean a Europe without self-respect. France is proud, and justly proud, of her superb services to mankind as a civilizing force. She has often led the mind and the imagination of the world. If she listened to this temptation she would lead the world once again, but she would lead it back to such degradation and misery as that into which mankind was plunged by the introduction of the slave-trade in the sixteenth century. Her allies are ready to pay a price in order to make the world safe for France, but no country in the world is worth such a price as that."[19]

Criticisms like this were not confined to Britain; they reverberated over the Continent. Italian public opinion, especially, voiced mingled fear and anger at this method of upholding France's war-born European hegemony.

The larger aspects of the Black Power are thus trenchantly set forth in a prominent American periodical:

"Monsieur Poincaré and General Mangin bid us contemplate a war in which the manhood of 60,000,000 natives, mostly blacks, will fight in Europe against the white peoples. They do not concern themselves—as we do—with speculations about the effect which the training in arms of large numbers of West Africans may have on the relations of white man and black in Africa itself. But the phrase that they have used will go echoing down the years, and its effects will be incalculable.

"The West Africans are savages. They can kill and get themselves killed with great efficiency and courage. In a mutual slaughtering-down, such as war between nations has now become, they will

19 *The Manchester Guardian* (editorial), August 31, 1923.

be admirable material for the French General Staff . . . They are thus a really economical form of gun-fodder, turned out by mass-production methods and the nearest approach to the Robots of Czapek's play that the world has yet seen. Only, they are worse than the Robots in that they do possess a mentality and culture of a definitely low type . . .

"It is not unlikely that this question will in a few years become one of the most disturbing elements in European politics. France's neighbors will not contentedly contemplate the use against them of hordes of Africans. They will disapprove a method which they believe is degrading to the self-respect of Europe and of the white man.

"These blacks, since they are in no sense equal to the white man in intelligence or culture, will assimilate only his vices. They will mate with the lowest of his type, and such ideas as they carry back home will be demoralizing to their own countrymen and subversive of the position which the white man holds in Africa . . .

"These black soldiers are conscripts and mercenaries, upholding for their French masters the dominion which those masters are too few, too weak, or too decadent themselves to maintain. That is the news which they will carry back to the millions of Africa with an arrogance born of the 'equality' with the white race which they have learned in the wine shop and the brothel. Alike' in Europe and in Africa, the white man will pay dearly, one day, for *La Force Noire*."[20]

One thing is clear: the grandiose imperialist concept of a Greater France is an experiment fraught with such difficulties and dangers that it can be justified only by a reasonable prospect of success. We have already analyzed its material bases and have heard the pleas of its advocates who today have caught the popular ear.

Yet there is an opposition within France itself; an opposition, not very numerous, but intellectually formidable because possessed of knowledge and practical experience in colonial problems.

Their criticisms are unsparing. They condemn both "assimilationism" and the Black Power military system as alike dangerous and unsound.

---

20 W. P. Crozier, "France and Her 'Black Empire,'" *New Republic*, January 23, 1924.

To begin with, these opposition voices deplore from every angle the increasing influx of colonial elements into France. One objector remarks: "During their long absence from home on European service, many colored soldiers forget their native village and stay in France, 'to live like Europeans.' They find employment among us as common laborers and longshoremen, having learned no trades to qualify them for better occupations."[21]

Another critic points out: "Some of our industrialists are trying to bring native labor into France. They say there are tasks which white men don't want to do; so let Negroes do them. That was just the way men reasoned in the eighteenth century to justify slavery . . . Not to mention the fact that tropical Negroes brought to France mostly get tuberculosis in short order, such a policy is absurd when we realize that Equatorial Africa is today under-populated. So the same economic and political objections arise with reference to Negro labor as to Negro troops brought to France. The State ought to stop this immigration."[22]

Here is a forecast of highly unpleasant political and social results of wholesale cantoning of colored troops on French soil: "We already have mixed garrisons in some of our towns. We shall have more of them; and sometimes the troops will be exclusively black . . . What is likely to happen if serious strikes or political disorders occur in our large cities? The troops will be called out; and should these soldiers be yellow, black, or brown, shall we dare to use them against the rioters? Shall we not have a bigger task than we can handle, when race-hatred springs to the side of class-hatred? And will it be a pleasant thing to see men of our own blood cut down by those whom we believe destined by nature to obey? I blush with shame when I contemplate the prospect that our civilization is to be defended by people whom we snatched but yesterday from anarchy and barbarism. No man with a vestige of racial self-respect can contemplate without apprehension the role which these colored troops may play in France, should they ever be made the tools of the social policy which so many ambitious innovators now desire."[23]

---

21 Khorat, *op. cit.*

22 Jean Bourdon, "Colonies Françaises et Population," *Mercure de France*, September 15, 1931.

23 Khorat, *op. cit.*

Considerations such as those just quoted naturally involve the whole Black Power policy, which its critics do not view with the enthusiasm of General Mangin and his colleagues. The same writer above cited points out that before the Great War "these colored troops did not leave Africa. Military service was usually welcome and imposed no heavy sacrifices. Nor did it leave bitter memories behind. Now, however, the colored race is swept up in a cyclone of militarism of which we are the center. They sent 80,000 of their most vigorous young men to fight militarism in Europe, and the survivors brought back the infection to their native land. Before the war, our colonial soldiers lived with their families, except when actually upon military expeditions. Today these men languish for years in great barracks and cantonments far away in France."[24]

Even more sweeping is the following condemnation of the Black Power idea: "A huge native army is one of our favorite utopias. It is especially absurd when we persist in believing that we can have both it and a rapid economic development of our colonies. True, during the War we raised large colonial armies, and this has become our permanent military policy. But this big native army of ours has a very mediocre military value. Algeria does furnish good soldiers in proportion to her limited population. The pre-war corps of Senegalese was excellent, because they were recruited solely among a few notably warlike tribes. Since then, we have recruited also among peaceable tribes long subjected to warlike neighbors and harried by slave-raiders. The results have been deplorable—you can't make hunters out of game! Both during the Great War and even more in the Riff in 1925, many Senegalese units were little better than hungry mouths to feed. In short: with the Senegalese we can get quantity only at the expense of quality. As for the Annamites, they are practically worthless as soldiers. Hence, from our colonies we can draw many men, but few soldiers; and also, in order to train these soldiers, we need a strong contingent of long-term native under-officers.

"Furthermore, the very idea of a vast colonial army is against the modern evolution of war. Owing to growing mechanization, the *levée en masse*, the Nation in Arms, was outgrown even before the end of the Great War. Today, it is so much foolishness. Therefore, to

24 *Ibid.*

recruit native soldiers wholesale when we cannot afford the complex equipment to arm even the bulk of our own reservists would be not only useless, but harmful to the national defense. It would also be very dangerous to the Colonies.

"Here is the economic danger: With blacks as with whites, the man taken away from the land does not return to it. They drift to the cities. The more native soldiers called to the colors, the fewer laborers left in the fields.

"Here is the military danger: Native soldiers who have served in Europe and been treated as equals, on their return home have lost that spirit of submission which alone can assure the dominion of a handful of whites over the native masses. Every black or yellow man thus returned from Europe tends to be an agent of revolt. To recruit a great native army is therefore to prepare the revolt of our colonies.

"We can, and should, maintain a small, high-grade colonial army, destined primarily for colonial service; and which, in time of war, could be drawn upon for European service. But to seek, as we now do, to make it a major factor in our military scheme of things is merely to increase our army's essential defect, besides hindering the economic development of our colonies and there fomenting revolution."[25]

Leaving these military matters, what about French colonial policy, in itself? Here, likewise, we discover trenchant criticisms of present policies and methods. The dean of this dissident school of thought is Louis Vignon, long one of the most eminent professors at the *Ēcole Coloniale* of Paris, where future colonial functionaries receive their training. In his celebrated book on colonial policy,[26] Professor Vignon does not mince words. He dubs the whole "assimilationist" theory *La Sottise française;* which, freely translated, means "French Damfoolishness."

Frenchmen, argues Professor Vignon, have always tended to be lured by the hope of absorbing alien peoples into French life and French civilization. Even the great Colbert was led astray by this

---

25 Bourdon, *op. cit.*

26 Vignon, *Un Programme de Politique Coloisiak; Lee Questions indigenes.* (First published in 1919, the book has gone through several editions and is a standard work on the subject.)

chimera; though if he had ever visited Canada and actually studied Redskins, he might have come to realize that Indians were too alien in blood and temperament to be transformed into Frenchmen, save perhaps for a few individuals so unusual in mind and character that they constituted those exceptions which prove the rule.

However, continues Vignon, the colonial administrators of the Old Régime were wiser than their successors. Those old-time officials, at least, realized that the Negro could never be assimilated. Today, however, the average French functionary or politician, wedded to the sentimental abstractions of Rousseau and the Encyclopédistes, ignore those factors of race and culture which are the eternal, unchangeable bases of the entire problem.

"The assimilationists of today never doubt that society is a manufactured product, whereas we know that it is the slow development of a certain mental bent, whence flow all our social institutions."[27] He thus replies to assimilationist arguments: "Yes, yes; I know that man evolves; but slowly and within the bounds of his special mentality—not of ours.

"Yes, of course we ought to aid this evolution; but wisely, after special investigations and long experience—and above all, with due regard for the time-factor. Furthermore, should we not think of the future; even the distant future? Races and peoples preserve their personalities through the ages; and those personalities are irreducible . . . Do you mean to tell me that these African and Asiatic peoples; fetishists, Moslems, Confucianists, Buddhists, with social forms so different from those of Europeans, will not surely endure? . . . Wherefore, since peoples are irreducible, and since such peoples are beyond all hope of even partial assimilation, what is our best policy: that which stands self-condemned or that indicated by the law of nature?"[28]

Vignon's alternative is the policy termed "association." That is the policy today generally practiced by every other important colonial Power, and notably by England. This policy consists in regarding alien peoples objectively, analyzing their peculiar temperaments and ways of life, and seeking to develop them along

27 Vignon, *op. cit., p.* 193.
28 *Ibid.*, pp. 216–18.

their normal line of evolution. Above all, this policy neither seeks to stifle their individuality and culture, nor does it veto a growth of self-government which may ultimately ripen into complete independence. A few portions of France's colonial empire are actually administered along "associational" lines. This is especially true of Morocco, which is a French Protectorate. And that type of government has, in Morocco, produced excellent results. Unless the principle of association comes to prevail, concludes Vignon, France's colonial future is dubious.

Criticisms such as those of Vignon and others above-quoted are supported by the judgment of most foreign students of French colonial problems. Regarding French plans for wholesale miscegenation, previously described, a British authority writes: "Nothing is more remarkable than the rapidity with which in Africa, at all events in tropical Africa, the white strain grows weaker and the black stronger after racial intermixture. Even if the French scheme succeeds at the outset, can the high degree of centralization and the constant replenishment of French blood, upon which permanent success depends, be kept up indefinitely? Yet, without these artificial aids, the Negro strain would surely reassert itself, and a reversion to type and to the old outlook would follow. Africa herself seems to engender an aversion to assimilation with Europe, and the neighboring territories in which development is on African lines will be more likely to react in this sense upon a Gallicized French territory than it is to affect them. If, then, the only outcome of the French policy is likely to be the reassertion of the African type and the African will, British policy would seem to be based on sound sense; for it recognizes the inevitable, and going as it does with the trend of African aspiration it is more likely to place our relations with the African peoples on a permanently better footing."[29]

Another qualified analyst points out not only political and racial difficulties, but likewise economic shortcomings, all of which tend to make France's colonial empire a constant drain upon her resources and indicate ultimate failure. Says Professor Charles Sarolea:

"If colonization means the settlement of a country's surplus population and the exploitation of the colony's economic resources,

29 *Round Table, op cit.*

then French colonization has been an almost absolute failure, and milliards have been vainly sunk in the sands of the Sahara. The French population constitutes only one-half of 1 per cent, or 300,000 in a total of more than 50.000.000. No large fortunes are being made in French Africa. No large estates are being managed by Frenchmen. The French colonies, instead of being an asset, are a heavy fiscal and financial liability—they do not pay and cannot be made to pay. The results bear no proportion to the enormous expenditure, to the magnificent effort exerted, and to the tragic political sacrifices. The results do not justify the controlling influence of the colonies in French foreign policy . . . The third French colonial empire seems destined eventually to follow the vicissitudes of the first two, and will have been only an interesting political and military experiment. It will have been infinitely costly in blood and treasure. It will have deflected the whole course of French foreign policy. And yet it will not be a permanent achievement."[30]

We have analyzed the prevailing French attitude toward their position in Europe and in the world. We have likewise surveyed plans and methods for a Greater France intended both to buttress a present European hegemony and to constitute a vast yet tight-welded empire on the Roman imperial model.

Detailed examination and discussion of conditions in French Africa must naturally be deferred until the chapter devoted to the Dark Continent. Yet they will, in the main, confirm the general considerations which we have just elaborated. Thus far, France's momentous African venture does not look like a good gamble. Persistence in present policies may well lead to failure involving consequences both disastrous and far-reaching.

What tragic irony if "Greater France" should recall the melancholy tale of Roman decadence without even the transitory splendors of Rome's imperial glory!

---

30 Charles Sarolea, "The French African Empire a Heavy Burden," *Current History*. July, 1925.

PART I
CHAPTER VI
FASCIST HYPER-NATIONALISMS

ONE of the ills to which flesh is heir is that known as *hypertrophy.* This abnormal state consists in an overgrowth of some part or organ of the body. The abnormality is not basic, as in a malignant growth like cancer; it is rather an *excessive* development of something which, in itself, is quite natural. Hypertrophy usually arises from an unbalanced condition of the entire body and is thus an effect of some profound constitutional disharmony.

Though the parallel between society and a living organism is not perfect, our simile illustrates the character of certain political and social trends that have developed rapidly during the past two decades; trends which have crystallized in Communism on the one hand and in the various Fascist movements on the other. All these movements are, in the last analysis, due to the unbalanced state of our times. They are essentially abnormal symptoms of a disharmonic transition-period. Their excesses and exaggerations, alike in spirit and in method, thus reflect the temper of our age.

In our discussion of Red Russia we purposely avoided attributing to Communism in general all that applied to its particular Muscovite manifestation. We did this, first, because of the possibility that the Russian character might render workable there what would be clearly unworkable among peoples of different blood and temperament. Our second reason was that, under Stalin, Russia seems to be moving away from Simon-pure Communism toward State Socialism or even toward State Capitalism of a peculiar kind. Trotsky has undoubtedly remained much closer to Communist theory and tradition. He has logic on his side when he argues that the present Moscow bureaucrats are turning into "social fascists." Indeed, it is by no means impossible that Red Russia may evolve along lines quite similar to those on which Fascist states are now going.

Orthodox Communism is a one-sided attempt to solve our economic and social problems. Although its goal is a classless society enjoying economic equality, Communism proposes to attain this end by a Dictatorship of the Proletariat, thus exalting the interests of one class and summarily eliminating all other classes, however numerous, by a ruthless process of proscription amounting to physical extermination. Everything is subordinated to the proletarian ideal. Art, literature, knowledge, even science, are "proletarianized." Immemorial institutions like private property and the family are incontinently scrapped. Lastly, religion in the traditional sense is to be extirpated and replaced by a new social gospel whereby man worships his collective self.

Now, obviously all this implies a drastic transformation, not only of institutions and ideals, but of human nature as well. A new type of man is to be evolved. Communism thus flies in the face of both past human experience and modern scientific discoveries concerning our emotional and spiritual qualities.

The reason why Communists, nevertheless, believe that they can succeed in their unique experiment is because they are utter materialists. Zealously convinced by the doctrine of economic determinism, they assign material causes for all human activity. They likewise believe that racial and temperamental differences have no basic significance. They hold with Rousseau that heredity is nothing or next to nothing, while environment and training are everything; that the individual is, at birth, a blank sheet on which one can write virtually at will. Hence it follows that this plastic human creature can be molded radically and rapidly to almost any degree by sufficiently intensive and drastic methods. This is materialism pushed to its logical conclusion. And this hard, dogmatic materialism accounts for Communist ruthlessness, fanaticism, and uncritical enthusiasm for the machine.

Whether one regards Communism's ultimate aspirations with sympathy or aversion, no objective analyst can deny that orthodox Communists have single-track minds which view the world in an excessively over-simplified and one-sided way. Communism is perhaps the most striking example of the trend towards hypertrophy which is so obvious today.

It is unfortunate that no word has yet been coined describing collectively a series of "Fascist" movements which differ considerably amongst themselves. The so-called Fascist trends in Britain, France, Portugal, et cetera, are not mere copies of the Italian original. Germany's National-Socialism typifies quite a different model which has likewise been widely adapted abroad. Indeed, in Austria, the two types compete fiercely with one another. However, we must needs follow common usage, except where distinctions between the Italian and German brands of Fascism are in question.

Fascism differs from Communism in several vital respects. In the first place, Fascism involves no thoroughgoing breach with man's historic past, nor does it flout so flagrantly his spiritual side. Religion, marriage, and the family are not merely preserved but fostered.

National and racial distinctions are not condemned in favor of cosmopolitan uniformity; they are emphasized and exalted. Private property and individual initiative are encouraged by Fascism in so far as they do not conflict with the interests of a glorified Nation-State. And that political concept, the Nation-State, is itself a combination of two long-established ideals, one of which (State Sovereignty) goes back at least to the Renaissance, whilst Nationalism germinated in the Middle Ages.

Perhaps the sharpest contrast between Communism and Fascism is in their respective philosophical attitudes. Communism, as already remarked, is rigidly dogmatic. No medieval school men were more bound by Scriptural texts and pronouncements of the Church Fathers than strict Communists are by the gospel of Marx, the glosses of Lenin, and the doctrine of economic determinism.

Fascism, on the other hand, tends philosophically towards realistic experimentation. In Italy, especially, Fascism proclaimed an uncompromising revolt against sentimentality and phrase-worship of every kind. Mussolini and his colleagues so prided themselves on their realism that they denied having any doctrinal philosophy—save, perchance, that of William James, the celebrated American philosopher, who once pithily defined his "pragmatism" as: *Does it work?* Opposed to dogmatic theorizing on principle, Fascists strive consistently to keep their minds from crystallizing around formulas of any kind, except as working hypotheses which they may scrap tomorrow. Of course, tradition and emotion are recognized as useful tools; but these are to be valued in a relative, not an absolute, sense.

This truly formidable intellectual challenge to the contemporary world was at first ignored and is even yet ill-understood. That is why, for instance, most Americans long regarded the Italian Fascisti as nothing but a bunch of political rough-necks, violently assaulting the Goddess of Liberty, and then adding insult to injury by giving her a dose of castor oil.

Few outsiders realized that this assault was due, not to low-brow lack of thought, but to a deal of highbrow thinking, that Liberty was roughly cast down from her pedestal because, in Fascist eyes, she and certain other popular deities had not "delivered the goods."

Let us see how Fascist thinkers view our times. In their opinion, the world has long been going on the wrong track—especially since the days of Rousseau and his fellows. For the past century and more, say Fascists, we moderns have become increasingly obsessed by theoretical abstractions condensed into phrases or single words which we have set up like idols and to which we have superstitiously bowed down.

Consider some of our present-day idols. Their names are Democracy, Liberty, Equality, Inalienable Rights, Parliamentary Government, and more besides. Look at them closely. What do they really mean? In themselves, say Fascists, they mean nothing. Theoretical abstractions that they are, they have no concrete significance. Yet there they sit, like Gods in a heathen temple, paralyzing the creative thought and energy of mankind! Before them we meekly lay our problems.

Is this not so? Look you! A situation confronts us. What do we do? Do we study the special facts of the case and then act according to those facts in the light of our common sense? We may do this in our private lives, but we rarely act thus in public matters. Instead, we seek the will of our idols! In other words, we strive to find a solution which shall be "democratic" or which will not offend such "sacred principles" as liberty and equality. "What arrant nonsense!" cries Fascism. "And—what dangerous nonsense, too! Such idolatrous blindness gets us nowhere; or, rather, lands us in a bog of troubles. Wherefore: Down with our idols! Down with Democracy! Down with Equality! Trample the somewhat decomposed body of Liberty! Out with the word 'Rights'—save, perchance, when coupled with the word 'Duties'! Sweep these false gods into the dust-bin along with the other fallen idols of the past! Thus, and thus only, may we clear our vision, free our common sense, and regain the path of true progress."

Such is the uncompromising "pragmatism" of Fascism—a fierce revolt against precedent, formal logic, doctrinal authority, and phrase-worship of every kind. To be sure, the Fascists do not hesitate to use such things for propagandist purposes; to arouse popular enthusiasm and subdue the fickle passions of the crowd. But they do it with the tongue in the cheek, and this cynical disregard of consistency is, after all, another proof of their thoroughgoing realism.

By understanding the Fascist attitude of mind, we can better comprehend the inwardness of Fascist policies. Fascist programs, whether in Italy, Germany, or elsewhere, have often been criticized for their vagueness, and even more for the apparent contradictions between some of their proposals. The inference is, of course, that the movements themselves stand thereby self-condemned as unworkable and "utopian." Such criticisms, however, overlook the fact that Fascist leaders, from Mussolini down to Hitler and Sir Oswald Mosely, formulate such programs purposely, as part of their experimental realism. Whatever their public professions, they do not intend to be bound by hard-and-fast principles or even policies, but prefer to evolve them as they go along by dealing factually with particular situations as they arise.

The vital factor in Fascism is, therefore, something essentially subjective—a driving-force which may not know precisely whither it is headed, yet which, wherever it goes, is always sure of itself. The goal of Fascist policy is thus, not a fixed objective, but rather a *working-ideal,* itself evolving with the course of time. This concept of policy, always held by Mussolini, appealed strongly to Hitler and his colleagues. The German National Socialists argue that, if it has worked out successfully in Italy, it ought to have an even better chance in Germany; because the working-ideal is more congenial to the German temperament and attitude toward life. The Germans are a notoriously mystical, subjective folk; they are more interested in *becoming* than they are in *being;* more intrigued by the verb *werden* than the verb *sein.* A working-ideal, argue the Nazis, ought therefore to suit Germans very well, even though its realization may be remote.

We have seen that Fascism is a revolt against a prevalent worship of phrases. We also saw that its philosophy is one of pragmatic realism. Viewed from a purely intellectual angle, this represents a healthy, virile reaction against a cult of shams and unrealities. Again, Fascism's experimental attitude is akin to that scientific spirit which is the saving grace of our time. Had Fascism not attained unfettered political power; had it remained rather a movement of protest, it would probably have done far more good than harm. The galvanic shocks which it has administered to muddled or routine thinking are certainly all on the good side.

Yet this is by no means the whole story. Fascism is not simply a protest; it is an *exaggerated* protest. Fascism is not only realistically experimental, it is cynically opportunist. Furthermore, its realism knows no logical bounds, which implies the absence of a moderating sense of values. Lastly, in condemning the worships of phrases it tends to disparage those moral and spiritual ideas which stand behind the phrases; to flout the wisdom garnered by ages of human experience. These unfortunate tendencies have been intensified by the attainment of power and authority. The upshot is that Fascism's attempts to solve our political, economic, and social problems have been marred by much the same partisan fanaticism, callous cruelty, and narrow-mindedness that have characterized Communist methods and policies.

Take the Fascist attitude towards the political idea known as democratic self-government. In so far as Democracy and Parliamentarism are deemed political panaceas applicable at all times and in all places, the Fascist critique is undoubtedly sound. Sensible men are coming to realize that some peoples are not, and perhaps never will be, suited to democratic self-government. They also realize that even in lands where self-government normally works well, abnormal conditions may require a temporary modification of democratic institutions by more authoritarian methods.

The typical Fascist, however, surveys the world in no such open-minded way. Mussolini proclaims the advent of a Fascist Era, and Hitler says much the same thing. Fascist spokesmen everywhere laud the principle of the Dictator heading a virtually deified Nation-State as the true political world-ideal, while conversely they ridicule democratic self-government as everywhere outworn and doomed. But this is merely setting up a new panacea in place of the one contemptuously discarded. It is just as irrational and opposed to observable facts. Your Fascist has thus rejected not merely the phrase, but all that caused the coining of the phrase. To use a homely simile, he has thrown out the baby with the bath!

He has been led to do this because his reason and common-sense have become subordinated to his beliefs and prejudices. Fascism's sound intellectual core has been warped and largely perverted by its violent emotional bent. That is why Fascism and Communism display the same unlovely traits of fanatical unreason, cynical ruthlessness, lack of moderation, and inability to appreciate the importance of the time-element in the framing or carrying out of policies.

The Spanish thinker, Ortega y Gasset, clearly analyses this spirit, shared by Fascists and Communists. "Any one," he writes, "can observe that in Europe, for some years past, 'strange things' have begun to happen. . . . Under both Syndicalism[1] and Fascism there appears for the first time in Europe a type of man who does not want to give reasons or to be right, but who simply shows himself resolved to impose his opinions. This is the new thing: the right not to be reasonable; the 'reason of unreason' . . . The 'new thing' in Europe is 'to have done with discussions,' and detestation is expressed for all forms of intercommunion which imply the acceptance of objective standards, ranging from conversation to Parliament, and taking in science. This means that there is a renunciation of the common life based on culture, which is subject to standards, and a return to the

1 By "Syndicalism," Ortega y Gasset means what we usually term Communism.

common life of barbarism. All the normal processes are suppressed in order to arrive at the imposition of what is desired, by 'direct action.'"[2]

The essentially primitive emotional nature of both Fascism and Communism is shown by the types of persons to whom each makes its strongest appeal. Communism is a distinctly proletarian gospel, so its followers are mostly urban workingmen, though its officers' corps contains individuals from all social strata.

Fascism, on the other hand, has solidified the hitherto unorganized middle classes, including peasant farmers as well as the town "bourgeoisie"—shopkeepers, handicraftsmen, and miscellaneous "white-collar" workers. Crushed as they have been between the upper and nether millstones of Capital and Labor, the middle classes, for the first time, sense their latent strength, and thrill to Fascist promises of security and power.

Yet, in Continental Europe especially, "the bulk of these people are hampered by no appreciation of the complexity of the economic and political tasks which their movement sets out to accomplish; by no tradition of liberal culture; by no philosophical prejudices in favor of individualism; by no conception of the role played in history by the principle of political liberty and freedom of thought; by no notion of what a nation loses by strangling freedom and driving scholars into exile.

The cultural heritage of their country or of Europe means little, if anything, to them; for they have not shared in it and would hardly miss it if it disappeared."[3]

Fascism and Communism have been equally successful in winning the allegiance of the rising generation. One of the most extraordinary developments of post-war Europe is the way its "Youth Movement," which began as an ultra-pacifist reaction against war and "militarism," has been almost wholly enlisted in the ranks of either Fascism or Communism. And in either case, high-spirited, idealistic youth has been carefully taught a creed infused with violence and hate.

---

2 Ortega y Gasset, *op. cit.*, pp. 80–86.

3 Harold Callender, "Fascism's Tide Sweeps Onward," *New York Times Magazine*, November 26, 1933.

An American student of European affairs thus vividly depicts the results: "When we talked of 'cannon-fodder' in the old days, we had visions of sullen conscripts . . . But now, thanks to the complete perversion of the Youth Movement, Europe prepares armies of conscripted men, to be sure, but armies trained from childhood in the use of daggers, rifles, and machine guns, and imbued with such super-patriotism and hatred of one's neighbor that it is possible to envisage battles in which there would be real joy in the killing . . . The *Balilla* and *Avanguardia* in Italy, and the League of Communist Youth in Russia, which are the brightest achievements upon which the others model themselves, begin military training at the age of eight; they are taught the use of arms at about fourteen, and before they are called to the colors they are masters of all the means of death and destruction. In addition, their minds are completely fashioned in the ideology of the masters; they are fanatics for their class or their party; they hate what they have been taught is their enemy; they are inspired for the coming war.

"Like the Church, the dictators offer youth a religion. If not of love, then one of hatred. Hate your neighbor. He is your enemy; he plots against you; he prepares war against you. Arm; make ready; the day is coming; we will conquer in the name of Saint Benito or Saint Lenin!

"Religion of hatred and militarization are welded in Russia and in Italy . . . In Italy, the young become braggarts and bullies; they are actually taught the nobility of violence, while the Church strives to continue its preaching of humility. But Mussolini prepares an army equal to that of France and (rare in history) one composed of class-conscious and intelligent soldiers; in other words, an army just like the Soviet's.

"For in Russia also, millions of youth are trained in arms from childhood; they are urged to destroy other people's goods as well as their fathers'; they are taught to hate other people whose philosophy of life is not that of the orthodox Communist party-member. They hate not only the aristocracy, the old monarchy, and the world's middle classes, but even the radicals who do not conform to the narrow version of Marxian Socialism . . . This new Russian youth is a generation of militant, idealistic, passionate Communists, ready to fight the world for the Leninist religion. Since the Children's Crusade, such a thing has not happened in world-affairs."[4]

This systematic fanaticizing of youth; this methodical inoculation with the virus of intolerant hatred for everybody and everything not precisely in accord with a particular point of view, startlingly discloses the spirit which animates both Fascism and Communism. It likewise explains what might otherwise be interpreted as evidence of sadistic mania. We refer to measures such as mass-imprisonment, mass-starvation, and mass-executions, whereby dissident minorities (even very large minorities), are summarily "liquidated." That is the sinister word employed alike by Communists and Fascists to describe a technique inspired by what we may truly term *the philosophy of liquidation.*

Take, for instance, Hitler's recent "purge by blood" that has aroused such widespread reprobation outside Germany, especially in Britain and America. Summary shootings of suspected persons without even the semblance of a trial go against the Anglo-Saxon grain. We are accustomed to the idea that everyone has certain legal rights which the state is bound to respect; that a man should be considered primarily as an individual, and only secondarily as a member of a class or group.

That is not the ideal in Hitler's Third Reich. Neither is it the ideal of Fascist Italy or Red Russia. In all three countries the state comes first, and if any individual or category of individuals does not fit harmoniously into the designated state scheme, he or they, no matter how numerous, may be made to disappear from the scene. In short, they are liquidated.

This was the word used by an official spokesman of the Nazi régime to explain why traitors to the party and the Reich were so informally disposed of; though, as already remarked, the term originated in Soviet Russia and has long been the stock phrase used there to denote a similar method of state action.

Communists certainly do not object on principle to Hitler's blood-purge. Neither does Fascist Italy; which, indeed, gave Hitler's action its prompt endorsement The very day after the Nazi *coup, a* leading

4 George Seldes, "Is the Cannon-Fodder Ripe?" *Scribner's Magazine,* February, 1931.

editorial appeared in Mussolini's organ, the *Popolo d'Italia,* to that effect. The editorial, to be sure, regretted the need for such ruthless action, but it went on to say that summary executions were within the Nazi Government's "revolutionary rights," and it commented approvingly that "the ability to put an end to such a situation is an excellent example of power." The editorial concluded with the statement that while executions should usually be carried out only on the authority of courts, there are "exceptional occasions when the individual servant of revolution has the right to administer justice with his trigger-finger."

We are thus confronted with a political philosophy which is officially upheld by three European Great Powers, and which is sympathetically regarded by large numbers of persons in other lands, including our own. Communists everywhere are definitely in favor of such methods wherever their party gets in control; all brands of Fascists have substantially the same attitude, while many persons of radical leanings are apt to consider the individual citizen as a pawn to be moved about and experimented on as part of some social scheme or policy, with scant regard for his own wishes or for the effects of state action upon his particular well-being.

Now there is no use going up in the air and getting hysterical over all this. We are faced with a widespread political and social trend which has triumphed in three great nations and which may spread to other lands. Furthermore, there is very little we can do about it outside our own borders. But certainly we should carefully scrutinize these doctrines and see what, in actual practice, they lead to. We will then be in much better position to make up our minds whether we want similar things to happen here; whether, in short, we are willing to pay the price for such economic and social benefits as a Communist or Fascist state may conceivably bring.

The effects of this philosophy of liquidation in Nazi Germany are well known. So are its effects in Fascist Italy, from castor-oiling up or down. However, both those countries are rank amateurs compared to Communist Russia, where the method was first put on an efficiency basis.

Russia's Communist rulers first liquidated several millions of the old upper, middle, and professional classes. They later liquidated some millions of individualistic peasant-farmers, termed *Kulaks,* who objected to the Soviet Government's collectivizing of agriculture. But the liquidating process is by no means ended. It is now functioning busily among the collectivized peasants themselves.

For the last two years, rumors have been current of acute famine conditions in certain Russian areas. These rumors were always officially denied or minimized. A well-known American press correspondent has now lifted a corner of the veil. William Henry Chamberlin, having been transferred to another field after ten years of news-gathering in Russia, has recently written a series of special articles, significantly entitled: "Russia,—Without Benefit of Censor."[5] Herein he speaks his mind freely, since he is no longer on Russian soil.

In the autumn of 1933, he managed to visit some of the reputed famine districts, from which foreign correspondents had been rigidly excluded. He relates, in detail, his truly harrowing experiences, and comes to the horrifying conclusion that famines had occurred which cost between 4,000,000 and 5,000,000 lives. Furthermore, he concludes that this was mainly an artificial famine, due less to natural causes than to excessive grain-requisitions by the Soviet Government and to its deliberate withholding of food in short-crop districts.

According to Chamberlin, the government's idea was apparently to "teach the peasants a lesson." In these districts not only were there still many obdurate Kulaks, but even the collectivized peasants were half-hearted and did not function as they should. So no food at all was given the starving Kulaks, while backsliding collective farms were granted relief on a scale so inadequate as to cause the loss of countless lives.

This deliberate starvation policy was pithily summarized by President Kalinin, the official head of Soviet Russia, when he stated in a party address: "The collective farmers this year have passed through a good school. For some, this school was quite ruthless."

5 This series of articles was published in *The Christian Science Monitor* during the spring and early summer of 1934. The article here summarized appeared in *The Monitor* of May 29, 1934.

There, in a nutshell, you have the philosophy of liquidation. It is an attitude, not of cruelty or brutality in the ordinary sense, but rather one of more or less serene and quite detached objectivity. This attitude regards individuals, not as human beings, but much as the experimental scientist views his fruit flies and guinea pigs.

The political and social experimenter makes up his mind that certain people block his projects or mar the symmetry of a plan he has formulated. That settles the matter in principle. Logically, they should be eliminated from the picture—"liquidated." And this, be it noted, whether it involves hundreds, thousands, or millions of persons. The only factor thenceforth to be considered is whether or not the job can actually be done.

The philosophy of liquidation is the logical outcome of a mental attitude which concentrates so fiercely upon one objective that it loses sight of everything else. The consequence is a decidedly abnormal condition in which a single factor is magnified to gross excess whilst other factors are unduly minimized or distorted out of all relation to their true significance The final result is a radically unbalanced situation wherein a sense of values, proportion, and appreciation of the time-element have been virtually lost.

What better proof do we need that Fascism and Communism are alike afflicted with that essentially abnormal trend toward *hypertrophy* which is perhaps the most disquieting phenomenon of our day?

For, surely, hypertrophy is the only valid term to describe the overgrowth of a single factor so excessive that it dwarfs everything else, and perverts ideals and policies, in themselves sound and natural.

Under these circumstances, whatever is touched by this abnormality runs to excess. We therefore observe a whole series of these overgrowths: hyper-dictatorships, hyper-regulation, hyper-planning, hyper-solidarity, hyper-racialism; and, above all, hyper-nationalism.

Nowhere is the hypertrophic trend so striking as in the field of nationalism. Here it has exacerbated an already unhealthy situation, the result being a condition profoundly pathological. Although, theoretically, Communism is anti-national, the rapid growth of a nationalistic spirit in Red Russia may soon bring it emotionally into line with Fascism in this, as in other, respects.

We have seen that there is nothing inherently wrong with nationalism, *per se;* that besides being deep-rooted in human nature, patriotic sentiment engenders values which would be sorely missed in a cosmopolitanized world. We likewise saw that Fascism, by stimulating patriotism, discovered an effective antidote to the spread of Communism, thus preventing what might have been a widespread epidemic of class-wars, proscriptions, and massacres. This important service rendered by Fascism should not be forgotten in drawing up its balance-sheet. The trouble is, however, that Fascism has let loose an evil spirit quite as formidable as the one which it exorcised.

Especially is this true of Continental Europe. Our survey of Europe's historical background revealed the growth of a disruptive trend that was the root-cause of the Great War by which Europe's traditional comity was shattered. Long before 1914, Europe's many peoples were stressing their respective differences to a degree so unwarranted by basic likenesses in blood, ideals, and culture that the disruptive factor could even then be justly termed hyper-nationalism.

The Great War and its aftermath immeasurably worsened an already bad situation. But Fascism has still further inflamed nationalistic passions until they have attained a fanatical intensity which virtually knows no bounds.

The way in which Fascist hyper-nationalism has complicated and aggravated all Europe's problems is truly deplorable. "Nationalism was virile and disquieting enough before it was systematically cultivated and excited by marching columns of black shirts, brown shirts, and blue shirts. The problem of excess population was serious enough before Fascist governments began urging their people to multiply at a greater rate. Territorial difficulties were sufficiently acute even before Fascist leaders proclaimed their countries' need and longing to expand. Fascism cannot, of course, be held entirely responsible for either sentimental nationalism or that economic form of it which sharpened the antagonisms of European nations in the latter half of the nineteenth century and helped pave the way for the World War. But it seized upon both forms of nationalism (which had been intensified by the Versailles Treaty and the economic crisis), and used them, as it used so many other instinctive impulses, for its own ends."[6]

The sound and unsound aspects of the Fascist mental attitude are clearly contrasted by Christopher Dawson. "Hitherto," he writes, "we have had nationalism and internationalism, but no third alternative. Socialism bases its appeal on international class-consciousness—on the common interests which unite the proletariat of every land against their exploiters.

The nationalist, on the contrary, feels, as Wyndham Lewis puts it in his recent book on Hitler: "The fact that a man is a sorter at the post-office or a metal-worker is not of such importance as that he is English, German, French, or Chinese. Take a Chinese metalworker and a German metal-worker, for instance. The fact that both were metal-workers would not be so important as that the essential nature of one came out of all the past of China, and the essential nature of the other came out of all the past of the white Northern race.

"This is true enough. Unfortunately, the pure nationalist (Nazi or Fascist) fails to recognize what is implied in the second part of the above passage. He concentrates on the national consciousness and ignores the existence of all that common culture which has made us what we are.

He is prepared to let Europe go to hell, in the interests of his own particular unit. And Europe is not a mere abstraction or a geographical expression, it is a true society; and it is only through their communion with it that the nationalities of Europe are what they are. Germany or France, apart from Europe, is nothing. They draw their life from their membership in the European society. Thus every great European war is of the nature either of a civil war or a revolution."[7]

The English thinker above-quoted specifically raises the issue underlying our own survey. Only, instead of confining it to the

---

6 Callender, *op. cit.*

7 Christopher Dawson, "The New Decline and Fall," *The Commonweal,* January 20, 1932.

European homeland, we have regarded the problem from its larger aspect by including the outlying portions of the far-flung white race.

Is it possible to reforge the broken links, first in distracted Europe, and then to extend the regenerative process so as to bind all organic units into an effective White-Western Comity?

That is a question whose pros and cons we will analyze in succeeding pages.

PART I
CHAPTER VII
CAN A TRUE COMITY OF THE WEST BE ATTAINED?

SHORTLY after the Versailles Conference a German thinker, convinced that this maladjustment of the Great War inevitably entailed catastrophic misfortunes on a planetary scale, dedicated the rest of his life to travel and study throughout the globe, in order to try to grasp the meaning of current events from a truly world point of view. After ten years of constant wandering, the expected crisis did arrive in the shape of the Great Depression. When, by the close of 1930, the Depression was visibly attaining the intensity of an economic blizzard, he thus summarized his observations and reflections on the post-war decade:

"The world-crisis is here. That is the one great conclusion that I reach. I am convinced that it is really a world-crisis; not a stock-market depression, nor one of those regular dips in the business cycle. Rather is it a convulsion of all the intellectual and spiritual foundations that underlie our culture. Indeed, the crisis even represents a gradual crumbling of these foundations themselves.

"Those parts of the great spiritual revolution through which the world is passing that take the forms of Communism, Fascism, and Nationalism are not, in my opinion, the real focal points of power. They are merely conglomerate lumps of will-power, born of the dull, fermenting consciousness of the masses . . . Above all, this is by no means a purely economic question, and all this talk about the sovereign importance of economics must eventually cease, because the economists have been as mistaken as the politicians.

"I do not believe there is any set formula or any one text that will bring salvation. I believe that one must learn the whole vast parallelogram of forces which determines our line of development. Therefore my new wanderings will be more difficult, more wearying, because their end is shrouded in mist."[1]

No profounder judgment on our strange transition epoch has anywhere been penned. This wise observer portrays the complexity of the problem, stresses the presence of spiritual as well as material factors, and emphasizes the need of including all factors as the prelude to correct evaluation and genuine understanding.

The necessity of making due allowance for non-material elements cannot be exaggerated, because it is just these which modern man is prone to ignore. Yet he does so at his peril, for he thereby remains unaware of the deeper realities of our time.

Beyond the well-mapped region of concrete facts and figures lies the nebulous realm of the Imponderables. There we encounter a maze of psychological factors bewildering in their complexity and generally ill-understood. The materialistic pseudo-realist either glosses over such factors or blandly disregards them. The true realist, however, appreciates their significance. Bismarck, most realistic of statesmen, warned that the Imponderables should never be forgotten.

Beliefs, emotions, attitudes of mind, can be neither weighed nor statistically tabulated. Collective passions and delusions are often inexplicable. Yet the most absurd aberration, if sufficiently widespread, is a *fact* of great importance. Regardless of its inherent falsity, it may determine the fate of nations and profoundly alter the course of human affairs.

It is characteristic of our machine age that proposed solutions of its problems usually imply an essentially materialistic end attained by mechanistic means. We have seen that nearly all internationalist thinking today envisages as its ultimate goal a cosmopolitan World-State run on an efficiency basis and subordinating everything to economic considerations. This is true both of "liberal" internationalists like H. G. Wells and of Communist internationalism, which is the most materialistic form of all. We should keep this intellectual trend in mind when considering

1 Cohn Ross, "A Wanderer's Testament," *Vossische Zeitung* (Berlin; translated and republished in *The Living Age,* January, 1931).

attempts to remedy current ills, either internationally by the League of Nations, or regionally by a European Federation.

As originally conceived, the League of Nations was to be endowed with powers so extensive that it would have been something very like a Super-State. The League actually embodied in the Covenant was in no sense that; yet it provided effective international controls—if its members had chosen to work them. However, the members did not thus choose, especially the big signatories who inevitably controlled League policies. That is why the League has so bitterly disappointed the hopes of its internationally minded supporters. As Frank Simonds well says: "The present failure of the League arises uniquely from the fact that it is an international institution in the hands of peoples who can only think and act nationally. As a consequence, each country seeks to employ the machinery of the League to its own ends . . . Thus, in the present attitude of peoples, the true explanation of the failure of the League is discoverable."[2]

Frank Simonds is, of course, no League enthusiast. But its staunch friends say substantially the same thing. Raymond Leslie Buell points out that "the success of the League depended upon the development in each country of strong political movements which would support the ideals of international co-operation; such movements had not come into existence by the fall of 1933 . . . The real trouble thus lay, not in the League itself, but in the spirit which animated its leading members, and in the character of world society."[3]

Furthermore, this nationalistic spirit was no post-war development; it permeated the League from its very inception, presided over its birth, and shaped its growth. The Covenant was tied to and predicated upon the Versailles Treaties which became the law of Europe—a law which League members automatically endorsed and, in a sense, pledged themselves to uphold.

That is just why the United States refused to join. When the victorious European Allies dropped the mask of propaganda and revealed their true war-aims, the eyes of the American people were opened—and they acted accordingly. Pro-Leaguers err when

2 H. Simonds, *Can Europe Keep the Peace? p.* 274 (New York, 1931).

3 Leslie Buell, *The World Adrift*, p. 7 (New York, 1933).

they see in America's popular rejection of what President Wilson strove to accomplish merely the triumph of a selfish, parochial nationalism; a blind and stupid reaction against the inevitable trend towards a new age which had already dawned.

Many who opposed America's entry into the League did so, not because they were hostile to the League on principle, but because they thought that the attendant conditions were too unfavorable or that the attempt itself was premature. Such critics contended that, though the Wilsonian ideal might someday be attainable, that day was so distant that it could not now be made the workable basis of world-politics. Where, they asked, was the proof that mankind as a whole, or any notable fraction thereof, was as yet willing to make the mutual concessions and sacrifices needed to establish a new world-order based upon the principle of international co-operation? How could a League of Nations (at least, the sort of League envisaged by Woodrow Wilson and the other framers of the Covenant) be made an authoritative reality? These questions require answers, for nothing is more dangerous than illusions—especially in crucial times like ours. And thus far the answers put forth have not been convincing except to those predisposed to be convinced.

The important point to remember regarding the epic contest in America over the League issue is that the nationalist reaction against Wilsonian ideals was due not so much to selfish parochialism as to the fact that the American people was not ready to assume the herculean task of imposing an internationalist order upon a blatantly nationalistic world. That was certainly the way it looked at the time. Does it look any different today? But if ours is still a nationalistic world, where is the people ready, virtually single-handed, to tackle the job of making it otherwise? The deeper reason for America's attitude is, therefore, not a blind and ignorant nationalism, but a growing realization by the American people that the psychological basis required for the carrying out of this bold experiment does not yet exist.

That does not mean that the League should be branded with utter failure, especially as it has evolved away from its Wilsonian origins into technical and consultative channels. Within limits the League has proved to be a useful institution. Yet those limits are today rather narrowly drawn and apparently cannot be notably extended, now or in the immediate future. By frankly recognizing those limitations and keeping within them, the League can work most effectively, whilst its existence will not be jeopardized. Above all, we should realize that the League is a piece of political machinery which functions, not of itself, but by virtue of the power generated by its members and by the spirit of the age.

Much the same is true of other international mechanisms such as the Kellogg Peace Pact and the World Court. International arbitration is an excellent instance of the way in which loose thinking may give rise to deplorable (and perilous) illusions. In certain respects, tribunals like the World Court can and do render much useful service. They are well fitted to handle that extensive category of cases where the interests of private individuals or groups are concerned, together with conflicts of domestic law or practice in matters like citizenship, marriage, and divorce, or commercial and financial regulations. Such things, though separately unimportant, collectively cause chronic friction which sometimes seriously affects international amity. Within this entire field, therefore, international tribunals can unquestionably be granted extensive jurisdiction.

Jurisdiction of a more limited sort not only can be, but already is, in effect for minor disputes between nations. But those burning questions from which modern wars usually arise are not *and cannot* today be unreservedly submitted to any tribunal, for the simple reason that, in a world organized upon a nationalistic basis, *they are neither arbitrable nor justiciable.* A court or board of arbitration, national or international, must function either upon agreed premises or upon the existing status. Issues of vital national interest are, however, precisely those which involve the *status quo* itself. One nation feels that the existing set-up is intolerable and is determined to obtain a revision more favorable to its aspirations. Another nation is equally resolved to oppose any such change, because the proposed new status would be equally intolerable in its eyes. What existing method of judicial procedure could be applied to such cases? How, for instance, "arbitrate" the problem of Oriental immigration? Or how adjudicate "a place in the sun"?[4]

4 The above passages regarding arbitration and America's reaction to the League have been taken, substantially unaltered, from the author's book, *Lonely America*

All these institutions arc thus mechanisms which may minimize friction and smooth contacts between nations but which cannot, of themselves, transform the general world-situation. They certainly offer no short-cuts to the settlement of major international issues dependent upon a worldwide process of evolution. When, for example, the economic and social changes wrought by the spread of our civilization shall have raised the standards of backward peoples and hence created a closer approximation of attitudes and aspirations, the basis for a real world-opinion will have been laid, and upon that foundation a structure of international government can possibly be reared. That, however, will be the task of future generations. Those who strive to usurp the future will be as disappointed as they are deceived.

Horrified by the shattering effects of the Great War and terrified by ominous portents of further catastrophes to come, certain Europeans have sought to salvage their distracted continent through some form of federation, either connected with or distinct from the League of Nations. Several such plans have been broached since the war, but they are typified by the two best-known projects: *Pan-Europa* and *The United States of Europe.*

Both movements originated from a growing realization that post-war Europe had lost its former world-primacy; that it was being rapidly outclassed (relatively, at any rate) by other great human aggregations. Two of these aggregates, immensely powerful and effectively federated, flanked disorganized, war-harried Europe to east and west. These portentous neighbors were the *U.S.S.R.* and the *U.S.A.*

To Europeans, this was a situation as disquieting as it was novel. For four centuries Europe had expanded at will. Now she was faced with the possibility of being squeezed on two sides by formidable entities which, though not wholly alien, were certainly more dissimilar from Europeans than Europeans were from one another. The shock of this discovery began to stir in many minds memories of that traditional comity of Europe which had been well-nigh forgotten in the tumult of internecine rivalries and broils. Like an electric shock, indeed, it bids fair to galvanize into new life

(New York, 1932).

an almost moribund *Europeanism*, thereby reversing the disruptive trend toward hyper-nationalism by reminding Europeans that they are joint heirs of a common culture and of kindred ideals. In short, the law of group-solidarity begins to operate—at least, in embryonic fashion.

Group solidarity is caused primarily by external pressure. Men normally combine *against* something or somebody else. This is the tendency universally shown in the forging of clans, tribes, and nations. That Europe, of all places, should experience such a unifying trend may appear absurd. Europe has been the classic example of dis-union. Every attempt to unite its diverse peoples from Czar to Kaiser has failed. But all those were conscious efforts arising from *within*. Europe's stubborn particularism is now exposed to automatic pressure from *without*.

The new unifying factor is, of course, in its tender infancy. Beside Europe's robust nationalisms it is a weak and fragile thing. Yet the new trend is there and it *may* develop with surprising rapidity under the pressure of events. Another big war might force the European peoples to come together quickly under the insistent urge of self-preservation from impending ruin On the other hand, such a war might leave Europe so devastated and chaotic that it would fall a helpless prey to a foreign conqueror, much as the city-states of Ancient Greece succumbed first to Macedon and then to Rome. Certainly the prospects of a federated Europe (indeed, of any effective European association) look none too bright, judging by the failure of attempts hitherto made.

Pan-Europa was first in the field. Its pioneer advocate was a talented young Austrian nobleman, Count Coudenhove-Kalergi. In the black year 1923, he launched the movement with a ringing manifesto whose tenor may be gauged from the following passages:

"Many men are dreaming of a united Europe, but few are determined to create one. As an object of longing, it is a sterile idea; as an object of will, it is fruitful. The only power that can make Pan-Europa a reality is the will of the people of Europe; the only power that can maintain Pan-Europa is that same will.

"Consequently, a part of the destiny of his world lies in the hands of every European . . .

"The European question is: 'Can Europe, subdivided as it is today both politically and economically, preserve peace and independence in face of the growing power of non-European nations; or will it be forced to federate in order to survive?'

"To ask this question is to answer it. Therefore it is not asked—it is suppressed. We do, of course, hear much of European questions, but not of *the European question* in which they all have their root. .

"Time presses. Tomorrow it may be too late to solve this problem; therefore we should begin today.

"Europe has lost self-confidence. It hopes for help from without. Some seek this from Russia; others from America. Both hopes are perilous for Europe. Neither the West nor the East wishes to save Europe. Russia would conquer it; America would buy it.

"Between the Scylla of Russian military dictatorship and the Charybdis of American financial dictatorship lies but a narrow path to a better future. This path is Pan-Europa, and means self-help through the welding of Europe into a politico-economic unit....

"Whether an ideal remains an Utopia or becomes a reality usually depends upon the number and the vigor of its adherents. So long as thousands believe in Pan-Europa, it is an Utopia; when millions believe in it, it will be a political program; when a hundred millions believe in it, it will be an accomplishment.

"I appeal to the youth of Europe to achieve this."[5]

Pan-Europa got off to a good start. Its noble sponsor's eloquent appeal evoked enthusiastic replies. In 1926, the first Pan-European Congress convened at Vienna, attended by many eminent personages. Famous literary lights delivered moving addresses. Emil Ludwig, for instance, chose as his text Goethe's memorable words on the battle of Valmy, a turning-point of the French Revolution: "This place and this day marked the beginning of a new epoch of world-history, and you can say that you were a witness thereof." Count Coudenhove-Kalergi repeated the phrase in his concluding speech, asserting that the corner-stone of Pan-Europe had now been laid.

5 First published in *Die Neue Rundschau* (Berlin), August, 1923; it subsequently formed the introduction to his well-known book, *Pan-Europa,* published late that same year.

The Pan-European Congress voted to convene next year at Brussels and appointed a committee to draw up the program for its proceedings. The Congress's opening session having laid the theoretical foundations, the next session would get down to business, especially on economic lines. The goal was a European *Zollverein* or customs-union, excluding Britain and Russia, but including the entire continent up to the Russian frontier.

The agenda committee duly met to itemize this project—and then the trouble began! So impossible did it prove to reconcile conflicting viewpoints among these "Pan-European" committeemen that all hands agreed that if their dissensions ever reached the convention floor, the Congress itself would fly to pieces. So the Brussels meeting was called off and that marked the end of Pan-Europa as an effective force, though it still lingers on as a mere shadow already forgotten save in certain restricted circles.

The reason why the economic obstacle proved insurmountable is set forth in a pamphlet published by a German critic at the time. A customs-union between politically independent states, asserts this critic, is utterly impracticable. "The analogy invoked by Coudenhove to prove the feasibility of his European customs-union—that of the German *Zollverein* before 1870—is a witness against him; for that union was concluded only between States which for a long period had represented a political unity, even though incomplete, in the Germanic Confederation and earlier in the Holy Roman Empire. To begin with a customs-union is, therefore, to set the cart before the horse."[6]

The kindred project known as *The United States of Europe* got its name and its first big publicity from a happy phrase uttered by the French statesman, Aristide Briand. Exalted with emotion as he formally welcomed Germany into the League of Nations, M. Briand exclaimed: "This is the beginning of the United States of Europe!"

These words seem to have been spoken extemporaneously. But the phrase stuck in Briand's mind and he soon began to sponsor the idea. Another French statesman, Edouard Herriot, likewise took it

6 The pamphlet was written by Doctor Waither Borgius and was published in Berlin, in 1927. The above quotation is taken from a review of the pamphlet by the Austrian publicist, Heinrich Kanner, printed in *Current History*, p. xxii, February, 1928.

up and elaborated his views on the subject in a book with the same title, published in 1929.

Like Coudenhove-Kalergi, Herriot paints a dark picture of Europe's present position in the world. "Already Europe has lost her position as the world's banker. The financial power of the United States is growing. Japan increases in strength." He does not blink the formidable stumbling-blocks of national sovereignty and nationalistic feeling. However, like most international planners, Herriot believes that economic factors today dominate political, intellectual, and moral considerations. Once Europeans become convinced that federation would spell heightened power and material prosperity, self-interest will bring and keep them together. He therefore exclaims: "First give Europe a body, then give it a soul!"[7]

It is noteworthy that this movement was, from first to last, chiefly French in guidance and popular backing. Hence it is not strange to find French interests well looked after. The mental attitude involved is amusingly revealed in a rather flamboyant book by the French *littérateur,* Gaston Riou, entitled: *Europe, Ma Patrie.* Offhand this sounds quite Pan-European. Yet on almost every page, that King Charles's head, French primacy, sticks prominently out.

To begin with, M. Riou feels that Europe has been on the downgrade ever since it ceased to be under France's benign tutelage, away back in the last century. And though he solemnly warns against the danger from certain alien, uncultured, yet highly organized blocs like Russia and the United States, which threaten to dominate Europe and thrust her down into some sort of dark age, "it is unnecessary to ask what this European civilization is which M. Riou finds so indispensable to the race . . . M. Riou would not contend that a French peasant or a Paris bricklayer could contribute some of his surplus culture to the enlightenment of an university-trained American. Nor does he imagine that London and New York, in their slow advance towards civilization, must draw spiritual sustenance for Albania or Latvia. Since he is remarkably broad-minded, he probably would concede that Germany, Italy, and Spain contained elements of civilization. But one does not have to live in

7 This summary of Herriot's book is drawn from a review of it by T. R. Ybarra in *The New York Times Book Review.* November 23, 1930.

France or read French books and periodicals very long to become aware that the real source of enlightenment is the Rue d'Ulm and is called the *Ecole Normale Supérieure*. It is well-known that its graduates, with the incidental aid of those of the universities, are all that keeps the world from slipping into barbarism."[8]

M. Riou's United States of Europe is a strictly Continental affair. Russia, of course, is in every way beyond the pale. But Britain is likewise hostile to European unity. England does not consider herself as a member of the "European fraternity," but as a colonial nation. Even Europe is, in British eyes, a sort of colony. Therefore, Britain cannot enter the charmed circle.

America, however, is the real villain of the piece; the arch-menace to Europe and consequently to civilization. American culture is, at best, embryonic. Furthermore, there is that matter of her part in the late war and those infernal debts. Nevertheless, despite all these shortcomings, "can it be denied that America feels herself the mistress of the white world? Americans come to Europe to play. For American millionaires we are a distinguished and grandiose extension of Long Island and Atlantic City. The Yankees, in relation to Europe, are somewhat like the Roman conquerors after Actium, the herdsmen of the Tiber in relation to the Graeculi."[9]

All things considered, it is not strange that the Gallic flavor of the federative project championed by Briand and Herriot (to say nothing of M. Riou), failed to evoke much enthusiasm elsewhere. In fact the idea was denounced by staunch nationalists in other lands as just one more French scheme for European hegemony. And internationalists were quite as unfavorable. Although the projected European federation was to be within the League framework, the idea did not sit well at Geneva. An eminent League spokesman, Salvador de Madariaga, asserted that it might "imperil the League's very foundations. The League must remain a universal institution."

Señor Madariaga need not have worried himself. This French-sponsored scheme soon fell flatter than *Pan Europa*. Barely had it been launched when the Great Depression excited nationalistic

---

8 These excerpts are taken from a review of Riou's book by Harold Callender in *The New York Times Book Review*, April 28, 1929.

9 Special article in *The Times* (London), September 12, 1929.

passions, political and economic, to a new pitch of intensity. The peoples of Europe became far too busy building tariff walls and furbishing up their armaments to toy with either international or regional ideas.

Why, despite the insistent pressure of a perilous present and a gloomy future, has each recent attempt to organize Europe so egregiously failed? The political and economic obstacles have already been indicated. We need not elaborate upon them because they are known to every one even moderately well informed. But are these the sole reasons for failure? May there not be others more basic in character?

As we analyze current pleas for European union we can hardly fail to be struck by a close similarity between them and those commonly advanced for international projects. Whether the goal be a continental or a world federation; whether the institution advocated be Pan-Europa or the League of Nations, the arguments are addressed mainly to sentiments of fear or material self-interest. Economics usually has the last word. At any rate we never find it subordinated to cultural or spiritual values. Herriot typifies this attitude when, as already noted, he asserts: "First give Europe a body, then give it a soul!"

However, do not his own words prove why Herriot and his ilk have not succeeded? How can they expect to create anything truly constructive and enduring unless it possesses from the very first that vital spark which kindles lofty enthusiasms and engenders a burning idealism evoking self-sacrifice? Unless the soul be ever-present, you have either a corpse or a robot—a lifeless automaton.

If this view be correct, any attempt to organize Europe must rest upon a cultural and spiritual basis. In short: a political and economic "Pan-Europe" can come into being only as the lost comity of Europe is regained. The new tendency toward group-solidarity produced by external pressure, being an essentially negative factor, will not, of itself, suffice to overcome the prevalent disruptive trend. Positive cultural and spiritual forces can alone turn the tide.

This is what certain European thinkers are today insistently proclaiming. Christopher Dawson writes that "apart from the external feuds which divide Western nations and the class conflict that destroys the inner unity of every European State, there is a still more profound disunity of spirit that divides the European mind against itself."[10] He therefore concludes that if a divided Europe is not to destroy itself by the friction of its parts, it must recover "a common European consciousness and a sense of its historic and organic unity." In similar vein Ortega y Gasset believes that this "would give new life to the pulses of Europe. She would start to believe in herself again, and automatically to make demands on, to discipline, herself."[11]

Count Hermann Keyserling gives us an impressive analysis of the deeper aspects of the European situation. He writes:

"We must learn to see historical reality as it truly is—something that no one attempted before 1914. If the whole edifice of pre-war Europe has crumbled to ruin within a half-dozen years, it is because its external reality no longer corresponded with an interior and essential reality. The ultimate forces that created and sustained the life of nations were not those which all the world believed them to be . . .

"It is Europe as a whole that is ruined today; and if she is ever to recover, she can do so only as a whole. Europe is a unit; upon that will depend her political influence hereafter . . . No merely external reform will reach the heart of the evil, until the spirit of man has been converted to the truth of our new condition.

"The World War, let me repeat, was but the physical symbol of a soul crisis . . . In the domain of politics, Germany and France no longer matter; it is only new Europe that we need consider. But, in a truer sense, we are not concerned with politics at all. The future of Europe is essentially a spiritual question."[12]

Keyserling not only stresses the spiritual basis needed for a regenerated comity of Europe, he likewise indicates the broader implications of that comity. We have already seen how projects for a European federation are restrictive in character. Britain as well as Russia is excluded in principle, while the Americas are entirely out

---

10 Dawson, *op. cit.*

11 Ortega y Gasset, *op. cit.*, p. 198.

12 Count Hermann Keyserling, "L'Avenir de l'Europe," *Revue de Genève*, October, 1922.

of the picture. Furthermore, all these excluded groups are regarded as more or less antagonistic and dangerous. That is the natural result of thinking solely in politico-economic terms and of considering only those factors.

If, however, we change our mental focus and seek primarily a Europe regenerated culturally and spiritually, our field of vision automatically widens until it includes all peoples, no matter how geographically remote, who truly share in Europe's idealistic and cultural heritage. In other words, we glimpse the ideal of a larger white-Western comity in which the peoples of Continental Europe, the British Commonwealth of Nations, the United States, and the genuinely Westernized portions of Latin-America will all partake in a true *symbiosis* or common life; will all gravitate about the sun of a common civilization.

This would repeat on an enlarged scale the process which we saw was normal to Europe before the trend toward disintegration and disruption set in. Only one former member of the European constellation would presumably be missing. This is Red Russia, which has seceded so absolutely from Western ideals and culture and is traveling in such an eccentric orbit that it would seem impossible to bring her into an organic relation with the system we have in mind.

It must be clearly understood that this Western comity would in no sense imply political or economic union. That would depend upon other factors, notably upon the degree of group-solidarity engendered by the pressure of alien groups like the Mongolian East upon the white-Western world.

The vital element in this, as in every other true comity of peoples, is a mental attitude which stresses likenesses rather than differences and which cherishes those basic matters that are in common. That was what kept Europe together for ages and that is the only cement which will mend its shattered self—to say nothing of binding the enlarged Western comity of the future.

To many persons the bare idea of such developments may appear visionary speculation. As matters now stand they could admittedly not occur. Yet certain portents indicate the coming of an epoch wherein material forces will no longer go so largely unfettered;

where the human mind and spirit will assume control over mere things.

We have already noted many complications due to our mechanistic civilization and we shall encounter many more when we survey its impacts upon Asia and Africa. Having reached the close of our survey of the Western world, this seems a fitting moment to seek the basic reason why our present epoch is so materialistic and also why we may hope that a more spiritual age is at hand.

The predominantly materialistic character of our times is due neither to human wickedness nor to some chance mental aberration. It is the logical outcome of an unprecedented situation brought about by the sudden advent of the machine.

Although power-driven machinery came in with the later decades of the eighteenth century, it became a major factor only toward the middle of the nineteenth century—when it swiftly and utterly transformed the face of things.

Here was something absolutely novel. Within a few decades Western man broke the immemorial tempo of material progress and leaped clear over into a new self-made world. Hitherto, man's material progress had been a gradual—a very gradual—evolution. His tools, though more numerous, were mainly elaborations of those invented by his remote ancestors. A few instruments like the printing press and the mariner's compass were about the only notable innovations.

Man's control over natural resources had likewise not greatly expanded. With the exception of gun powder, he had tapped no new sources of material energy since very ancient times. His chief source of power remained muscle, animal or human; for the rest he filled his sails with the breeze and turned clumsy water-wheels by using brooks and streams. But the ancients had done all these things. As for methods of communication they had, if anything, deteriorated. In the year 1800, there was no system of highways which equaled the Roman roads, no posting-service as quick as Caesar's, no method of signaling which could compare with the semaphore "telegraphy" of the Persians, and probably no ship which could not have been overhauled by a Phoenician galley in a moderate sea.

Suddenly, astoundingly, all was changed. The hidden forces of nature yielded themselves wholesale, as though at the wave of a magician's wand. Steam, electricity, petrol, and a whole series of mysterious "rays" and "waves" gave man powers of which he had not even dreamed. These powers were promptly harnessed to innumerable machines which soon revolutionized every phase of human existence. Production and transportation were alike stepped up to amazing velocities, distance was well-nigh abolished, and the very planet shrunk to the measure of human hands. In short man suddenly entered a new material world differing not merely in degree but in kind from that of his grandfathers.

What was Western man to do? Obviously he had to fit himself into this strange new world, just as any living organism has to adapt itself to changed surroundings. This had to be done because adaptation is an imperious law of nature. Also it had to be done quickly and continuously because man's new world was constantly and rapidly altering. Thus, re-adaptation has been the insistent problem with which Western man has been confronted during the past hundred years.

This adaptive process seemed, on the surface, to be concerned almost wholly with material aspects. Actually, the changed character of our civilization called for idealistic adaptations no less sweeping. These were neglected because their necessity was not so compellingly self-evident. Indeed, man was distinctly attached to his traditional idealistic outfit, which had fairly served the requirements of his simpler past. Therefore, modern man concentrated intensively, exclusively, upon materialistic problems, feeling that he could thus concentrate because he believed that he already possessed an idealistic equipment adequate to support the immense new material superstructure that he was raising.

Unfortunately, this was but partly true. Transformed material conditions required corresponding idealistic modifications. Unhappily, also, what had at first been merely a means to an end tended to become an end in itself. Losing sight of his ancestral idealisms, modern man evolved a thoroughly materialistic philosophy. The result was a warped, one-sided development which increasingly betrayed its lack of balance and proportion. The fact that man was much less culpable for his errors than many moralists aver is quite beside the point so far as consequences are concerned. Nature takes no excuses and inexorably inflicts her penalties. They have culminated in the Great War and in the chaotic state of our world.

Yet the very magnitude of his misfortunes appears to be arousing modern man to his perilous situation and spurs him on to seek a way out of his present ills. More and more, men of vision see the remedy in a better balance between the material and the spiritual—which can be best accomplished, not by scrapping material gains, but by harmonizing them to spiritual needs. This, in turn, implies the discrediting of purely materialistic attitudes and an increasing concentration upon spiritual problems. And that means the advent of an epoch devoted largely to the things of mind and soul—in short, to the coming of a characteristically spiritual and cultural age.

By "spirituality" we most emphatically do not mean anything like the fatalistic mysticism of the old Orient. Our dynamic civilization gives us scant time or inclination to sit down passively and await the happening of—what may happen. Nor do Occidentals normally seek to plunge themselves into mystic ecstasies through Yoga tricks like breathing exercises or prolonged contemplation of one's navel. The East itself is fast abandoning such practices. The West will hardly pick up what the Orient is discarding.

No. Mysticism is not the way to a better-balanced life. Modern Western man is the joint product of the Christian tradition and the new scientific spirit. And neither true Christianity nor true science offers any real obstacle to a harmonious blend of the spiritual and temporal that may best be described as *enlightened realism—a* broad appreciation of the varied elements in the problems that confront us and a mental attitude enabling us to deal with those problems in sane, constructive fashion.

Enlightened realism would avoid most of the pitfalls which beset our present-day thinking. Men would cease to pin their faith on formulas and phrases or upon the automatic action of laws and institutions. They would deal with problems, not by trying to frame a "solution," but by striving to formulate a *correct method* of action.

By thinking in terms not of a program but of a *process,* we would gain and retain the flexible attitude and the open mind needed to traverse the road leading out of our bog of troubles to the firm ground of better times.

Our world today looks dark. But there is light ahead. And modern man is on the march.

PART II: THE BALKANIZATION OF ASIA

CHAPTER I
ASIA'S FIVE-FOLD REVOLUTION

THE Orient today presents a stupendous crisis. An entire order of life seems to be passing away. No phase of Oriental existence is immune. Ancient political forms, ancestral economic and social patterns, venerable cultures, age-old religions are alike involved. All is in profound ferment.

This ferment arises not from within but from without. Its causes are external, foreign. The process is thus a dissolvent rather than an organic growth.

Herein lies the full gravity of the situation. Acute though our Western crisis may be, it is less serious than that of Asia. For our problems are fundamentally those of adaptation to changes engendered by ourselves and possessing a logical connection with our past.

The peoples of Asia, on the contrary, are suddenly compelled to rebuild from the ground up an edifice continuously shaken to its foundations by strange new forces.

How much of that crumbling edifice can be salvaged towards a new structure and how much must be scrapped is as yet uncertain, for the tearing-down phase is in full swing, whereas the building up has scarcely begun. Demolition today far surpasses construction and no one can estimate how far the destructive phase may go or how long it will endure. If the West is threatened with disintegration, the East is menaced with downright dissolution. One thing is certain: the old Orient, regarded as a whole, is clearly doomed.

The Unchanging East

The old Orient has often been represented as plunged in chronic lethargy; its peoples portrayed in the guise of Rip van Winkles drowsing time away.

This hackneyed picture of "The Unchanging East" is inexact. Asia's life was never lethargic; it was always active and colorful. Yet though the simile be at fault the underlying idea is substantially correct. In the traditional East despite much movement there was scant change. Political and social patterns remained unaltered. The "Cycle of Cathay" might whirl faster or slower; but, like any circle, it had neither genuine beginning nor end.

Of course a general survey of the old Orient must be sketched in broad strokes and many local differences will necessarily be ignored. Asia never was a unit. The distinctions between the Near East, the Far East, and India their common meeting-ground, are numerous and important. Nevertheless, the old Orient displayed certain basic features which clearly distinguished it from the West and it is these which we shall endeavor to portray.

The contrast between East and West appears most strikingly in the field of government. Our political institutions are founded upon the Roman ideal of law and embody notions of the worth and dignity of the individual which run back to Greece and to the forests of the North. The East knew little of all this. In the Orient the typical form of government has always been despotism—the arbitrary rule of an absolute monarch, whose subjects are slaves, holding their goods, their honors, their very lives, at his will and pleasure. The sole consistent check upon Oriental despotism has been religion. Some critics may add "custom"; but it amounts to the same thing, for in the East custom always acquires a religious sanction. The mantle of religion covers *its* ministers, the priests usually forming a privileged caste. But, with these exceptions, Oriental despotism has ordinarily known no bounds; and the despot, so long as he respected religion and the priesthood, has been able to act pretty much as he chose.

We Occidentals have never known despotism in its Simon-pure, Oriental sense; not even under the Roman Empire. In order to conceive what it means, let us cite an instance which has occurred in Asia many times. Some Sultan or King-of-Kings immures himself in his harem, casting the burdens of state upon the shoulders of a grand vizier. This official has thenceforth limitless power; the life of every subject is in his hands. Yet, any evening, at the pout of a dancing-girl, the monarch may send from his harem to the vizier's palace a Negro "mute," armed with the bowstring. And when that black mute arrives, the vizier, doffing his robe of office, and with neither question nor remonstrance, will bare his neck to be strangled. That is real despotism—the despotism that the East has known.

Now the annals of the East prove conclusively that despotism is a bad form of government in the long run. Of course there is the legendary "benevolent despot"—the "father of his people," surrounded by wise counselors and abolishing evils by a nod or a stroke of the pen. That is all very well in a fairy-tale. But in real life the "benevolent despot" rarely happens and still more rarely succeeds himself. The "father of his people" usually has a pompous son and a vicious grandson, who bring the people to ruin. That celebrated Biblical trio—David, Solomon, Rehoboam—has appeared with depressing regularity throughout Oriental history.

Furthermore, even the benevolent despot has his limitations. The trouble with even the best despot is that his rule is entirely *personal.* Everything, in the last analysis, depends on the despot's own will. Nothing is fixed or certain. Indeed, he may discard his benevolence overnight, and the fate of an empire can be jeopardized by the monarch's infatuation for a woman or by an upset in his digestion.

Eastern history is, in fact, largely a record of sudden flowerings and equally sudden declines. A strong, able man cuts his way to power in a period of confusion and decay. He must be strong and able, or he would not defeat capable rivals likewise seeking the coveted prize. Once on the throne, his energy and ability work wonders. He knows the rough-and-ready way of getting things done.

While the master lives, matters may go well. But the master dies and is succeeded by his harem-bred son, who is not apt to look after things as did his father. And as soon as the master's eye wavers, things begin to go to pieces. How can it be otherwise? His father built up no governmental machine, functioning almost automatically, as in the West. His officers worked from fear or personal loyalty; not out of a patriotic sense of duty or impersonal *esprit de corps.* Under the grandson matters get even worse, power slips from his incompetent hands and is parceled out among many local despots, of whom the strongest cuts his way to power, assuming that the decadent state is not overrun by some foreign conqueror. In either eventuality, the familiar cycle—David, Solomon, Rehoboam—is completed, and a new cycle begins—with the same predestined end.

Such, in a nutshell, is the political history of the old Orient. And it is surely obvious that under such a tradition neither ordered government nor consistent progress is possible. To be sure, this life, with its amazing vicissitudes, had its glamorous side which appealed to high and low alike. For the Prince, the pasha, the courtier, existence was truly an Oriental paradise. Of course, the prince might at any moment be defeated and slain by a rival monarch; the pasha strangled at his master's order; the courtier tortured through a superior's whim. But, meanwhile, it was "life," rich and full. "Each of these men enjoyed a position such as is now unattainable in Europe, in which he was released from laws, could indulge his own fancies, bad or good, and was fed every day and all day with the special flattery of Asia—that willing submissiveness to mere volition which is so like adoration, and which is to its recipients the most intoxicating of delights."[1]

But, it may be asked, what about the poor man, exploited by this hierarchy of capricious despots? What had he to gain from all this? Well, in most cases, he got nothing at all; but he *might* gain a great deal. Life in the old Orient was a gigantic lottery. Any one, however humble, who chanced to please a great man, might rise to fame and fortune at a bound. And this is just what pleases the Eastern temperament; for in the East, luck and caprice are more prized than the "security" cherished in the West. In the Orient the favorite stories are those narrating sudden and astounding shifts of fortune—beggars become viziers or viziers beggars, and all in a single night. Such happenings made the life of the Orient infinitely

1 Meredith Townsend, *Asia and Europe,* p. 104 (fourth edition, London and New York, 1911).

interesting to *all.* And it is precisely this gambler's interest which Westernization is eliminating.

Like the grand prizes in a lottery, a few dramatic strokes of fortune concealed a drab reality. Below the gorgeous luxury of the rich and powerful vegetated a great mass of people, not only poor but unable to better their condition by normal means. The lucky individual might rise suddenly to dizzy heights; the average man was bound fast in the meshes of economic and social patterns too tough and close-woven to be broken.

Oriental economics were as simple as they were primitive The East was virtually devoid of either industry or business, as we understand these terms today. Everywhere predominantly agricultural, the Orient's economic unit was the self-supporting, semi-isolated village. Oriental "industries" were handicrafts, carried on by relatively small numbers of artisans, usually working by and for themselves.

This primitive economy rested on the principle of status. The Western economic principles of contract and competition were virtually unknown. Agriculturists and artisans alike followed blindly in the footsteps of their fathers. There was no competition, no stimulus for improvement, no change in customary wages, no desire for a better or more comfortable living. Trades were stereotyped; the apprentice merely imitated his master and rarely thought of introducing new implements or methods. Instead of working for profit or advancement, men followed an hereditary "calling," usually hallowed by religious sanctions, handed down from father to son through many generations, each calling possessing its own unchanging ideals, its zealously guarded craft-secrets.

The few bolder, more enterprising spirits who might have ventured to break the iron bands of custom and tradition were stopped by lack of capital: Fluid "investment" capital, easily mobilized and ready to pour into a venture of demonstrable utility and profit, simply did not exist. To the Oriental, whether prince or peasant, money was regarded, not as a source of profit or a medium of exchange, but as a store of value, to be hoarded intact against a "rainy day." The East has been known for ages as a "sink of the precious metals." One form of financial activity did exist. This was usury, and therein practically all the scant fluid capital of the old Orient was employed. But such capital, lent not for productive enterprise but for luxury, profligacy, and incompetence, was a destructive rather than a creative force and merely intensified existing prejudices against capital of any kind.

The social pattern of the East was equally rigid and impersonal. Throughout the old Orient, the individual was strictly subordinated to the family, caste, or clan. China, for instance, should be regarded basically as a huge mosaic of compact family-units. And the Oriental "family" must not be taken in its ordinary Western sense—father, mother, and children.

In the East, the family means rather what we should call a clan, including all generations in the direct line together with collateral relations as well. To this narrow group the individual owes primary allegiance. A successful man must look after his relatives; indeed, kinsmen are the only persons he can really trust and with whom he can successfully co-operate. This is the main stumbling-block to the establishment of efficient governments on the Western model. Only in Japan has there always existed a sentiment similar to what we term patriotism.

The outstanding achievements of this essentially static Eastern world lie in the fields of religion and culture. Asia has produced much lofty spiritual meditation and profound philosophic thought, together with literatures of exquisite beauty and charm. Yet the relation of these achievements to the general scheme of things needs to be understood. Oriental saints and sages have usually dwelt in ivory towers far removed from the everyday world and oblivious of its affairs. The most brilliant cultural flowerings were confined to extremely small groups. The mass of the population, illiterate and devoid of understanding, remained unaffected by the most intense activity within those spiritually remote intellectual or artistic circles. And neither sage nor poet desired it otherwise. What the ignorant masses thought or felt did not concern him. The Chinese historians typify this attitude by recording the death of millions through famine, flood, or pestilence with the same serene detachment as when they note a plant blight or an epidemic among cattle.

Such education as existed in the old Orient was of an incredibly formal nature. The traditional system, from Morocco to China, was mainly a memorizing of classical or sacred texts combined with exercises of religious devotion.

The Mohammedan or Hindu student spent long years reciting to his master (a "holy man") interminable passages from books which, being written in classic Arabic or Sanskrit, were unintelligible to him, so that he usually did not understand a word of what he was saying.

No more deadening system for the intellect could possibly have been devised than this mind-petrifying nonsense. Every part of the brain except the memory atrophied, and the wonder is that any intellectual initiative or original thinking ever appeared.

We can now perceive the true significance of Eastern spirituality and culture. They did exist and were sometimes of high quality. Yet for the most part, they had slight concern with reality and they exerted an even slighter practical effect upon either the popular consciousness or the course of events.

On this matter the Chinese thinker, Hu Shih, remarks:

"The wheel-barrow civilization of the East is no less material than the motor-car civilization of the West. The term 'materialistic civilization,' which has often been applied to stigmatize the modern civilization of the West, seems to me to be a more appropriate word to characterize the backward civilizations of the East.

"For to me that civilization is materialistic which is limited by matter and incapable of transcending it; which feels itself powerless against its material environment and fails to make the full use of human intelligence for the conquest of nature and for the improvement of the conditions of men.

"Its sages and saints may do all they can to glorify contentment and hypnotize the people into a willingness to praise their gods and abide by their fate. But that very self-hypnotizing philosophy is more materialistic than the dirty houses they live in, the scanty food they eat, and the clay and wood with which they make the images of their gods."[2]

2 From the essay by Hu Shih in the collaborative volume entitled *Whither Mankind*, edited by Charles A. Beard, pp. 40–41 (New York, 1928).

Such was the static, impersonal, formalized East which, after ages of seclusion, was suddenly exposed to the impact of a supremely dynamic West.

The Impact of the West

The relations of East and West form one of the basic factors in history. For ages Europe and Asia have reacted upon each other. Yet these reactions have not consistently balanced. Down to our modern epoch, the impetus usually came from Asia. Only in recent centuries did the tide turn and a reverse current set in, growing ever stronger as time went on.

Asia presumably cradled the human species. Asia was certainly the birthplace of civilization and of the great religious movements. From time immemorial a stream of culture and ideas flowed out of the Orient toward the more backward West. And the East sent forth human streams as well. The steady drying-up of Central Asia caused vast migrations, many of which flooded westward, deluging Europe with conquering hordes. In all this, Asia was the positive, aggressive factor. Asia was the hammer and Europe the anvil on which our West was forged.

Now and then, to be sure, the roles changed and Europe took the lead. This happened in the palmy days of Greece and Rome, while medieval Europe followed suit during the Crusades. Seen in historical perspective, however, such happenings were little more than episodes. Even Alexander's conquests stopped at the borders of India, while neither Romans nor Crusaders got far from the shores of the Mediterranean. Furthermore, the cultural effects of these incursions were local and fleeting. The West then had little to offer which the East cared to accept. The Orient remained substantially unaltered.

A stupendous shift in the relations of East and West began with the voyages of Columbus and Da Gama four centuries ago. Those voyages of discovery, as already remarked, transformed Europe from a dead-end peninsula of Asia into the potential overlord of the planet. Yet this momentous change was not at first apparent. Though Europe had grasped the talisman of sea-power and was forging ahead in the art of war, Asia still bulked large in European eyes, with its façade of four extensive empires which, though inwardly declining, looked imposing from without. Three of these—Turkey, Persia, and India of the Grand Mogul, represented the Moslem civilization of Western and Middle Asia. In the Far East, China stood in solitary grandeur, heading an isolated world of its own.

Neither the Moslem nor the Mongolian East then saw in the expanding West anything more than an annoying interloper. They certainly had no desire to copy Western ways. Indeed, so far as possible, both maintained an attitude of haughty aloofness, keeping the despised Westerners strictly at arm's length.

Only one Oriental land was temporarily receptive to Western advances. This was Japan, which at first toyed with Westernism, displaying the eager curiosity characteristic of its people. But Japanese statesmen presently glimpsed disruptive effects of Western ideas upon their exquisitely wrought yet essentially fragile civilization. Determined to prevent this, they took the drastic step of excluding all things Western and immured their island homeland in a hermit isolation which lasted almost down to our own days.

For some three centuries the logical outcome of the new trend in world-affairs was undisclosed. All this time the West grew rapidly in power and efficiency while the East got steadily weaker. Europe nibbled at the outskirts of Asia, founding colonial empires and developing profitable lines of trade. But the sharply contrasted civilizations of East and West had not yet come decisively to grips. The two worlds were still essentially their separate selves.

The full impact of the West upon the East is surprisingly recent. The "big push" of our civilization into the Orient began only about a century ago, while the decisive breakthrough did not occur until very recent times.

Furthermore, the driving-force behind this shattering impact was not what is usually supposed. It was less a deliberate campaign of imperialistic aggression by arms and diplomacy than a semi-automatic process of economic penetration. Western political ascendancy in Asia was paralleled by an economic ascendancy more complete and destined to produce changes far more profound and enduring.

The root-cause of this decisive Western ascendancy was the Industrial Revolution. Just as the voyages of Columbus and Da Gama gave Europe the strategic mastery of the ocean and thereby the political mastery of the world, so the technical inventions of the later eighteenth century which heralded the Industrial Revolution gave Europe the economic mastery of the world. These inventions in fact began a new age of discovery, this time into the realms of science.

The results were, if possible, more momentous even than those of the age of geographical discovery three centuries before. They gave our race such increased control over natural forces that the ensuing transformation of economic life swiftly and utterly transformed the face of things, first in the West and later in the East as Well.

The two outstanding features of the new economic order were the rise of machine-industry with its limitless stepping-up of mass-production, and the accompanying development of cheap and rapid transportation.

Both these factors favored a prodigious increase in economic power and wealth in Europe, since Europe became the workshop of the world. In fact, during the nineteenth century, Europe was transformed from a semi-rural continent into a swarming hive of industry, gorged with goods, capital, and men, pouring forth its wares to the remotest corners of the earth, and drawing thence fresh stores of raw material for new fabrication and exchange.

Such was the industrially revolutionized West which confronted an East as backward and stagnant in economics as it was in politics and the art of war.

We have glimpsed the old Orient, with its rigid economic and social patterns centering about the self-sufficient village and supplemented by a few luxury goods made by craft-artisans working by such slow, antiquated methods that their products, though often exquisite in quality, were limited in quantity and relatively high in price.

Despite very low wages, therefore, Asiatic products could not hope to compete with Western machine-made, mass-produced articles even in their home-markets, once Western economic penetration got fairly under way.

Soon the flood of cheap Western goods was invading every Eastern land, driving the native wares before them. The way in which an ancient Oriental handicraft like the Indian textiles was literally annihilated by the destructive competition of Lancashire cottons is only one of many similar instances. The assertions of Indian nationalists that this was mainly due to British favoritism seem to be largely special pleading, because the textile crafts of independent Oriental countries like Turkey and Persia suffered the same fate. Indeed, there is no doubt that Oriental peoples, taken as a whole, have bought Western-manufactured products in preference to their own hand-made wares. To many Westerners this seems incredible.

Such persons cannot understand how Orientals could buy the cheap, shoddy products of the West, manufactured especially for the Eastern market, in preference to native wares of better quality and infinitely greater beauty. The answer is that the average Oriental is not an art connoisseur but a poor man living perilously close to the margin of starvation. He not only wants but must buy things cheap, and the wide price-margin is a deciding factor.

Yet in addition to price there is also the element of novelty. Besides goods which replace articles he has always used, the West has introduced many new articles whose utility and charm are irresistible. Novelties like the kerosene lamp and the sewing-machine have swept the Orient from end to end. They have become part and parcel of the daily life of the people. New economic wants have been created; standards of living have been raised; canons of taste have been altered.

The root-cause of this apparently insatiable demand for Western novelties is the lure of *comfort*. The idea of comfort, imported from the West, has disrupted the East more profoundly than all our guns and missionaries put together.

Let us see why this is so. Few contrasts could be sharper than the living conditions prevailing respectively in the traditional East and in the modern Western world. This basic difference lies, not in wealth (the East, like the West, knows great riches as well as great poverty), but rather in comfort—using the word in its broad sense. The social structure of the old Orient was extremely simple. It consisted of a few very rich, the masses very poor—and almost no comfort for anybody. Even the wealthiest Oriental of olden times spent most of his money on Oriental luxuries like fine raiment, jewels, women, horses, a palace, and a great retinue of servants. But it is safe to say that the mightiest Eastern potentate lived under domestic conditions which a self-respecting Detroit factory-worker would despise.

Today, however, the Oriental is discovering comfort, as we know it. And, high or low, he likes it very well. All the mechanical gadgets which make our lives easier and more agreeable, from wrist watches and safety razors to electric lights and sanitary plumbing—all those things which we take more or less as a matter of course—are to the Oriental so many delightful discoveries, of irresistible appeal. He wants them, gets them, in ever-increasing quantities. And in the process, not merely his material surroundings but also his whole attitude and outlook on life are subtly yet profoundly transformed.

The true conquest of the East by the West is thus not political but economic and social. Whatever else happens, *that* conquest will endure. We hear much talk about the current Asiatic reaction against the West. Now there is undoubtedly a great and growing determination throughout the East to get rid of every kind of Western political tutelage, every sort of commercial or financial exploitation.

There likewise exists in the East a widespread disillusionment regarding our political institutions, culture, and ideals. Superficially, this may seem like Oriental reactions in the past, as when the Hellenistic veneer imposed upon many parts of Asia by Alexander was stripped off and completely disappeared. The vital difference between past movements and that of today lies in the fact that nowhere in Asia, save possibly in India, is there any effective revolt against *Westernism, as a way of life.* Orientalism in its traditional sense cannot come back, because the old Orient has gone, never to return; because, for the first time in history, *the West has got under the Oriental's skin.* The white man may everywhere be thrown out bodily, but his ways will remain. Western ideas, methods, habits, tastes have struck roots in Asia too deep to be plucked up. "The unchanging East" has been changed at last—changed to its very depths. The Orient is today in full transition, flux, ferment, more sudden and profound than any it has hitherto known. Peoples contentedly stereotyped for ages are astir, on the march. Throughout its huge length and breadth, Asia writhes in *utter revolution.*

Asia's Five-Fold Revolution

The entire Orient is today undergoing a complete transformation. From fundamentals to trivialities, it is the same story. Asia is literally in the melting-pot. Nothing is immune from drastic change.

This prodigious transformation is more sudden, more intense, and above all more complex than anything the West has ever known. Our civilization is mainly self-evolved; a natural growth developing by normal, logical, and relatively gradual stages. The East, on the contrary, is in the throes of a concentrated process of adaptation which, with us, was spread over centuries. The result is not so much evolution as revolution—political, economic, social, cultural, religious—and all at the same time. The upshot is confusion, uncertainty, grotesque anachronism, and glaring contradictions. Single generations are sundered by unbridgeable mental and spiritual gulfs. Fathers do not understand sons; sons despise their fathers. Everywhere the old and the new struggle fiercely, often within the brain or spirit of the same individual.

A keen observer of Far Eastern affairs thus describes the process as seen in the chaotic China of today: "Every type of change in human activity and relations takes place simultaneously over wide areas. Stand at the corner of Nanking Road and the Bund in Shanghai. Here passes a laden wheelbarrow drawn by coolies, substitutes for horses because they are cheaper, sweating in the summer heat, straining at the loins; here passes a rickshaw coolie rapidly carrying a man from house to office; here rides a stockbroker in his cart drawn by an ex-racing pony; here goes by every form of motor vehicle; overhead flies an airplane carrying mail 600 miles up the Yangtze to Hankow. Hu Shili once called China a rickshaw civilization to contrast it with the airplane civilization of the West. That is much too simplified. China is all civilizations at once, all changes at once, all forms of human evolution and revolution at once."[3]

3 George E. Sokoisky, *The Tinder Box of deja*, p. 2 (New York, 1932).

Here is a description of the same process at work in India; a description, be it noted, penned nearly a quarter of a century ago. Yet even in those pre-war days, the revolutionary nature of India's Westernization was clear. Says this British economist:

"What could be more anachronistic than the contrast between rural and urban India? Rural India is primitive or medieval; city India is modern. In urban India you will find every symbol of Western life, from banks and factories down to the very sandwich men that you left in the London gutters. Yet all this coexists beside rural India. And it is surely a fact unique in economic history that they should exist side by side . . .

"The present condition of India does not correspond with any period of Europe's economic history. Imagine the effect in Europe of setting down modern and medieval men together, with utterly different ideas. That has not happened in Europe because European progress in the economic world has been evolutionary; a process developing through centuries.

In India, however, this process has been profoundly revolutionary in character . . .

"Rural India, though chiefly characterized by primitive usage, has been invaded by ideas that are intensely hostile to the old state of things. It is primitive, *but not consistently primitive.* Competitive wages are paid side by side with customary wages. Prices are sometimes fixed by usage, but sometimes, too, by free economic causes. From the midst of a population deeply rooted in the soil, men are being carried away by the desire for better wages. In short, economic motives have suddenly and partially intruded themselves into the realm of primitive morality. And, if we turn to city India, we see a similar, though inverted, state of things.

In neither case has the mixture been harmonious or the fusion complete. Indeed, the two orders are too unrelated, too far apart, to coalesce with ease.

"India, then, is in a state of economic revolution throughout all the classes of an enormous and complex society. The only period in which Europe offered even faint analogies to modern India was the Industrial Revolution, from which even now we have not settled down into comparative stability. We may reckon it as a fortunate circumstance for Europe that the intellectual movement which culminated in the French Revolution did not coincide with the Industrial Revolution. If it had, it is possible that European society might have been hopelessly wrecked. .

"But that revolution was not so sweeping as that which is now in operation in India . . . No, the Indian economic revolution is vastly greater and more fundamental than our Industrial Revolution, great as that was. Railways have been built through districts where travel was almost impossible, and even roads are unknown. Factories have been built and filled with men unused to industrial labor. Capital has been poured into the country, which was unprepared for any such development. And what are the consequences? India's social condition is being dissolved. The *Brahmins* are no longer priests. The *ryot* is no longer bound to the soil. The *banya* is no longer the sole purveyor of capital. The hand-weaver is threatened with extinction, and the brass-worker can no longer ply his craft. Think of the dislocation which this sudden change has brought about; of the many who can no longer follow their ancestral vocations; of the commotion which a less profound change produced in Europe, and you will understand what is the chief motive-power of political unrest. It is small wonder. The wonder is that unrest has been no greater than it is. Had India not been an Asiatic country, she would have been in fierce revolution long ago."[4]

Appalled at the chaotic turmoil of this transition stage and fearful of its ultimate outcome, a minority of staunch conservatives in every Oriental country assert that Asia is on the wrong road and must retrace her steps toward the traditional past. This essentially reactionary school of thought is strongest in India, where the mystical "other-worldliness" of Hinduism retains a strong hold on the popular imagination. Appealing to these sentiments, mystics like Gandhi and Rabindranath Tagore condemn the "accursed" spirit of the West, preach the ascetic gospel of renouncing all things Western, and urge India to go back to the spinning wheel.

Yet surely such counsels, however idealistic, are vain dreams. Whole peoples cannot arbitrarily cut themselves off from the modern world, like isolated individuals forswearing society and

4 D. H. Dodwell, "Economic Transition in India," *The Economic Journal*, December, 1910.

setting up as anchorites in the jungle. The time for "hermit nations" has passed, especially for a huge country like India, set at the crossroads of the East, open to the sea, and already profoundly penetrated by Western ideas. Ascetics like Gandhi and Tagore can no more wean their people from Western comforts than Mrs. Partington could sweep back the incoming ocean with her broom. Women who have once used the sewing-machine will not return to the bone needle; men accustomed to railway trains and motor buses will never revert to travel by bullock cart. As for the girls, they are coming out of the harem and seeing the world. Just try to shut them up again!

Convinced that the reactionary recipes of Asiatic "die hards" are impracticable yet fearing the consequences of thoroughgoing Westernization, other Oriental conservatives try to evolve a compromise policy through what may be called the "pick-and-choose" method. The aim is to keep whatever is most congenial in the old system, though making it more workable by grafting upon it a select set of Western improvements. In India, again, this middle-of-the-road conservatism has been intellectually most fully developed. Accordingly, we find in the writings of men like R. Mukerjee and Lajpat Rai elaborate programs for a "new order" based on a blend of Hindu mysticism, caste, Western industry, and socialism.

Now these schemes are highly ingenious. But they are not convincing. Their authors should recall the old adage that you cannot eat your cake and have it too. When we note the utter contrast between the economic systems of the old East and the modern West, any attempt to combine the best points of both while eschewing their defects seem like striving to reconcile irreconcilables and about as profitable as trying to square the circle. Lowes Dickinson wisely observes: "Civilization is a whole. Its art, its religion, its way of life, all hang together with its economic and technical development. I doubt whether a nation can pick and choose; whether, for instance, the East can say, 'We will take from the West its battleships, its factories, its medical science; we will not take its social confusion, its hurry and fatigue, its ugliness, its over-emphasis on activity' . . . So I expect the East to follow us, whether it like it or no, into all these excesses, and to go right through, not round, all that we have been through on its way to a higher phase of civilization."[5]

This seems to be substantially true. Judged by the overwhelming body of evidence, the East, in its present process of transformation, will follow the West—avoiding some of our more obvious mistakes, perhaps, but, in the main, proceeding along similar lines.

That, indeed, is what many Asiatics recognize. Going on the principle that it is foolish to try and put new wine into old bottles, these persons feel that compromise is impossible; that there must be a decisive break with the past and a frank acceptance not only of Western methods but of the Western spirit as well. From Turkey to China, such root-and-branch Westernizers are numerous and influential. Only in their emotional attitude towards Westernism do they differ amongst themselves. Some welcome the prospect, whilst others regard it as a disagreeable necessity.

This latter attitude seems to prevail in the Near East, especially in the Turkey of Mustapha Kemal. From his firsthand studies in those regions, Arnold J. Toynbee concludes:

"The several Islamic peoples that I have encountered are all trying to be Western—trying with all their might. But we must not flatter ourselves that they are adopting the ways of Western civilization because they are enamored of it. They do not really much like our ways; still less do they like ourselves. At the back of this astonishing metamorphosis there is, I fear, no love—nothing, for instance, that corresponds to the passion for Hellas and Hellenism that inspired and ennobled our Western Renaissance.

"The Muslims are Westernizing their life in a rather hard, matter-of-fact spirit and for rather prosaic reasons: because they have realized that they will go under if they do not do it, and because the thing is catching. You do not love chicken-pox, but you catch it all the same and you endure the incubation philosophically."[6]

The uncompromising spirit animating the rulers of present-day Turkey in their drastic Westernization of that hitherto backward land is almost brutally stated in a semiofficial volume

5 G. Lowes Dickinson, *An Essay on the Civilizations of India, China, and Japan*, pp. 84–85 (London, 1914).

6 Arnold J. Toynbee, "Islam and Ourselves," *Atlantic Monthly*, January, 1930.

called *The Book of Mustapha Kemal.* Its main thesis is that the old mentality of the Turkish people, shaped by the Koran and Arabic influences, should be summarily scrapped and replaced by the modern European mentality. "We have tried," says the author, "to compromise between the two, but this has proved impossible. That is why previous reform movements in Turkey failed; they tried to mix the old and the new, and the upshot was chaos . . . Asia has been dominated by a mystical mentality, and it has no capacity within itself to change this mentality. Salvation can only be gained by the vaccine of the European mentality . . . Some think that this superiority can be secured by the adoption of technical things alone. This is impossible. The Asiatic mentality must be rejected totally and the European mentality must be adopted totally; there is no alternative."[7]

The rather dour attitude of Turkish Westernizers may be contrasted with that of many Chinese who tend to show an almost apostolic zeal in demolishing their ancestral edifice as the prelude to new construction along Western lines. Nathaniel Peffer reports this striking conversation with a prominent Chinese administrator:

"We were walking on the shores of a lake which is hallowed in Chinese legendary. Here, in the golden splendors of the T'ang age, poets came to sing of its beauties, painters to set them down in swift strokes on silk. Here emperors came to take their ease in pavilions of red beams and green-and-golden tiled roofs built for their pleasure. On the hills which gently rise above it monasteries lie in cool, serene retreat half-hidden in groves of bamboo. About us lay the deposits of the greatness and glory of China's ancient days.

"He was telling me of his plans for the 'development' of the lake shore—he used just that word. There would be a public library, with classes for the illiterate; there would be a building for commercial exhibits, and so forth. What kind of buildings would they be? I asked. Would they follow the architectural lines of those around us, with dipping roofs and broad courtyards, and winding, shaded paths of old gardens? They would not, he answered vigorously; decidedly not. Would they be adaptations, then, from Western style to make them more comfortable and economical of space? No; that was

7 Cited from a summary of the book by Professor Albert H. Lybyer in *Current History,* January, 1927, pp. 583–84.

chop suey, neither one nor the other. They would be Western, pure Western—as complete a break with the past as possible. Yes, these that were here now were beautiful. They could never be surpassed. And they embodied the traditions of the race. That was just it—they tied the race to the past. Above all else, those ties had to be broken.

"Then he spoke with passionate intensity. 'If I thought it were necessary in order to make that break sure,' he said, 'I would tear all these down and put up New Jersey factory buildings in their place.'"[8]

Whether such absolute breaches with the past are feasible, or even possible, certain it is that the process will be difficult and painful, and that the goal cannot be quickly attained. The mental and spiritual transformations bound up with economic changes alone are very formidable. Why, even under the heaviest pressure of Western competition, has it proved so hard for Oriental artisans and shop-keepers to alter their traditional methods? Because not merely a change in technic but a basic difference in outlook on life is involved. The life of the old Orient, though there was much want and hardship, was an easy-going life, with virtually no thought of such matters as time, efficiency, output, and "turnover." The merchant sat cross-legged in his little booth amid his small stock of wares, passively waiting for trade, chaffering interminably with his customers, annoyed rather than pleased if brisk business came his way. The artisan usually worked by and for himself, keeping his own hours and knocking off whenever he chose. The peasant arose with the dawn, but around noon he and his animals lay down for a long nap and slept until, in the cool of the afternoon, they awoke, stretched themselves, and, comfortably and casually, went to work again.

To such people the speed, system, and discipline of our economic life are painfully repugnant, and adaptation can at best be effected only slowly and under the compulsion of the direst necessity. Meanwhile they suffer from the competition of those better equipped in the economic battle. Sir William Ramsay paints a striking picture of the way in which the Turkish population of Asia Minor, from landlords

8 Nathaniel Peffer, "The Death of Chinese Civilization," *Harpers Magazine*, March, 1930.

and merchants to simple peasants, were going downhill for a half-century before the war under the economic pressure not merely of Westerners but of the native Christian elements, Armenians and Greeks, who had partially assimilated Western business methods and ideas.[9]

One of the most difficult tasks of Mustapha Kemal and his colleagues has been to inculcate a Western attitude towards work and business among the Turkish people.

The social consequences of economic change are merely one aspect of a process which touches every phase of Oriental life. The undermining of the clan-family system in China and of the patriarchal Moslem family in the Near East breaks the hold of custom and authority, shatters traditional moral codes, and spawns bewildered individuals with no spiritual roots, no guide to personal conduct, no sense of duty.

This anarchic-minded younger generation is most prominent in China, where it goes in ostentatiously for cocktails, jazz, and any other Western frivolities it can pick up. But it exists in Japan and elsewhere. Even the social life of India, most conservative-minded of Oriental lands, is permeated with the same ferment. More than twenty years ago a well-known Indian student of social problems wrote:

"The clearest result of the breakdown of our old system of domestic life and social customs under the assault of European ideas is to be found in two directions—in our religious beliefs and in our social life. The old system, with all its faults, had many redeeming virtues. Today this old system, narrow-minded but God-fearing, has been replaced by a strange independence of thought and action. Reverence for age, deference to the opinions of others, are fast disappearing . . . Under the older system the head of the family was the sole guide and friend of its members. His word had the force of law. He was, so to speak, the custodian of the honor and prestige of the family. From this exalted position he is now dislodged, and the most junior member now claims equality with him."[10]

9 Sir William M. Ramsay, "The Turkish Peasantry of Anatolia," *Quarterly Review*, January, 1918.
10 S. Khuda Bukhsh, *Essays, Indian and Islamic, pp.* 221–26 (London, 1912).

From all this, he concludes: "We have commenced to despise our religion, our literature, our history, our traditions. We have unlearned the lessons of our civilization, and in their place we have secured nothing solid and substantial to hold society fast in the midst of endless changes Destruction has done its work, but the work of construction has not yet begun."[11]

Culturally and spiritually, the East is indeed passing through a peculiarly unhappy moulting period. Among Orientals the impact of the West has tended to discredit their native art and literature, besides weakening allegiance to their religious beliefs and practices. At first, this trend was accompanied by an uncritical admiration for Western culture and ideals. But the glaring contradictions between these Western values and the material aspects of our mechanistic civilization soon opened Oriental eyes to Westernism's seamy side. The Great War so speeded up the process of disillusionment that most Orientals today believe there is something very wrong with the ethical basis of Western life. How far, they ask themselves, does this affect the validity of Western culture and ideas? The first reaction of such disillusioned skeptics is a resolve to accept only our science and technology while rejecting everything else.

That, however, does not settle the difficulty which confronts them. How can Western technics be successfully grafted onto Eastern culture? How, indeed, under even partial Westernization can Oriental cultures be revivified? We saw that the art and literature of the old Orient were everywhere highly specialized, produced by and for a select few with no thought of a wider audience. How much of this old culture can be incorporated into a new culture which will be both popular and in harmony with imported Western elements? That is a problem which the East has as yet hardly begun to solve.

Equally difficult, and far more urgent from a practical standpoint, is the problem of government. We have seen that the political tradition of the East is the cycle of despotism—a cycle barren in itself and rendering sustained progress impossible. Few Westerners grasp the inwardness of this matter, because the Orient's political background is something quite foreign to Western experience. No European government, however autocratic, has been unrestrainedly

11 *Ibid* p. 240.

personal, arbitrary, and capricious up to the point where it transgressed some religious taboo. The most high-handed Western monarch ruled by means of an officialdom with established rules and standards; furthermore, his subjects all enjoyed, in varying degree, a definite legal status. In short, Western countries have been organized states run by governmental machinery of various kinds.

The East knew little of this until it began copying Western political models in relatively recent times. Therefore the root-problem for the Orient is, not so much acclimating advanced political institutions like parliaments or universal suffrage as making sure that it has established basic concepts of government which the West assumes as a matter of course but which, in the East, cannot be taken for granted.

There is thus little use in considering whether a particular Oriental country is fit for democratic government unless it already has a systematized government, no matter how undemocratic. To that extent, at least, the East must outgrow its political past before it can take further steps. This is what Lord Cromer had in mind when he wrote:

"From the dawn of history Eastern politics have been stricken with a fatal simplicity. Do not let us for one moment imagine that the fatally simple idea of despotic rule will readily give way to the far more complex conception of ordered liberty. The transformation, if it ever takes place at all, will probably be the work, not of generations, but of centuries . . . Good government, however, has the merit of presenting a more or less attainable ideal. Before Orientals can attain anything approaching the British ideal of self-government, they will have to undergo very numerous transmigrations of political thought."[12]

There are no short-cuts to the exalted heights of free institutions. Orderly self-government presupposes strong, stable government. Any attempt to dodge that issue invites disaster. That is why, during the past generation, most Oriental copying of Western political models have so lamentably failed.

Of this, China is the horrible example. More than twenty years ago a revolution against the Manchu dynasty changed China's form

12 The Earl of Cromer, *Political and Literary Essays, pp.* 25–28 (London, 1913).

of government over night from a slipshod, loose-jointed Oriental despotism into a republic with all the constitutional trappings of a Western state. Zealous young men educated in Europe and America descanted so eloquently upon the "New China" that for a while the world was inclined to believe them. However, these high hopes were grievously disappointed. Instead of reorganizing China on a sound basis, the Revolution of 1911 precipitated acute disorders which soon reduced the unhappy country to a condition bordering upon downright anarchy. Almost every province groaned under the despotism of some upstart "war lord" heading an army which was hardly more than enrolled banditry. Instead of evolving toward genuine nationhood, China seems to be degenerating into a political vacuum.

The Chinese Republic has thus merely made a bad matter worse. However, the cure for China's political ills is not the "strong-man" nostrum so frequently prescribed. That, of itself, might mean just a relapse to the old tradition of personal despotism. What China needs is, not a strong *man,* but a strong *government* in the Western sense. It does not matter much, in the long run, how far such a government might fail to qualify under the tests of liberty and democracy Indeed, an authoritarian government might be the only way in which the Chinese could learn their political ABC's and so ultimately be ready for something better.

Some such political apprenticeship is actually being served by another Asiatic people, the Turks, and the experiment is apparently going on well. Though Turkey is technically a republic, every well-informed person knows that effective power is lodged in the hands of a small group which, in turn, is dominated by the dynamic personality of Mustapha Kemal. Yet this perpetual President is not a despot in the traditional sense. His rule is orderly and he is building up a governmental mechanism on the Western model. Since the Turks are a notably well-disciplined people with a genuine national consciousness, we may expect that a real nation-state will presently become a stable fact.

The outstanding (and almost the only) example of political progress in the Orient is Japan. Here we find both a strong government and a political system which embodies Western parliamentary institutions. Yet it must be remembered that the Japanese are a singularly homogeneous people who, alone among Asiatics, have long possessed both deep patriotic feeling and iron self-control. Furthermore, their political tradition was not Oriental despotism but a feudalism much like that of Europe during our Middle Ages. Thus, when Japan began Westernizing herself in the middle of the last century, she could erect a political structure on foundations which, elsewhere in Asia, had not even been laid.

The gravest questions for the Orient's political future arise in connection with the immense regions under Western control. Many of these lands are today clamoring for either full autonomy or absolute independence. Few informed students believe that any of these lands would be capable of running an efficient, orderly government—let alone a government truly democratic in character. On the contrary, most qualified observers are convinced that, in almost every case, independence would spell misgovernment, acute civil strife, and perhaps chaos. A free Philippines would presumably soon turn into a bear-garden of warring factions, whilst it is well-nigh certain that India, left to its own devices, would quickly degenerate into the most frightful welter of racial and religious passions that the modern world has ever seen.

Nevertheless, the power and prestige of the West is waning so rapidly throughout the East that the emancipation of these Asiatic dependencies from Western control seems to be inevitable in the near future, regardless of consequences. To point out the disastrous results of immediate independence, not only to the West but perhaps even more to the Orientals themselves, is a mere waste of breath. The classes who really count in Asia; the men who mold public opinion and guide the ignorant masses, want the white rulers to *get out, no matter what happens afterward.* As one Filipino politician pungently expressed it: "We would rather be governed like hell by ourselves than like heaven by the Americans!"

That Manila *politico* cast a horoscope pretty accurately for an independent Philippines and for other emancipated Oriental lands as well. But political hades spreading through large parts of Asia would inevitably have far more than merely political effects. We have seen that Asia is undergoing a tremendous and essentially revolutionary transformation embracing virtually every phase of its existence. The maintenance of orderly government keeps this process from becoming uncontrolled. A widespread political breakdown, however, would unleash volcanic forces already simmering beneath the surface which might well produce eruptions of terrific intensity and hurl lava-floods of chaos far and wide. These portentous forces and their latent perils will be our next consideration.

The Rising Tide of Chaos

Many years ago, one of Britain's great proconsuls of her Oriental empire, wrote: "It is doubtful whether the price which is being paid for introducing civilization into these backward Eastern societies is always recognized as fully as it should be. The material benefits derived from European civilization are unquestionably great, but as regards the ultimate effect on public and private morality the future is altogether uncertain."[13]

Lord Cromer's warning words were little heeded at the time. To our self-confident pre-war world, the Westernization of the East appeared an eminently auspicious event. The price involved might be regrettably high, but the results would surely prove it to have been justified. Europeans and Americans descanted eloquently upon a "marvelous new synthesis" of Eastern and Western elements in the modernized Orient that was to be, and Orientals were inclined to agree with them. Japan's amazingly rapid and apparently successful assimilation of Westernism certainly seemed to point that way.

That facile optimism no longer prevails. Alike in the East and in the West, thoughtful minds ponder anxiously on what this fermenting Orient portends. Will the outcome be for good or for ill? Is the leaven of Westernism a vital tonic, or is it a baneful toxin infecting the East with death and decay? An old adage states that "one man's meat is another man's poison."

Now what we wish here to emphasize is, not the blackness, but the uncertainty of the outlook. Present conditions in the Orient are so extraordinary, so historically unique, that there are no precedents to guide us, no way of predicting the future. In the

13 Earl of Cromer, *Modern Egypt*, Vol. II, *p.* 231 (London, 1908).

course of our survey, we are about to consider the darkest aspects of a crucial situation. Yet, throughout, our mood should be one, not of pessimism, but of objectivity, always remembering that our discussion concerns, not what *will* happen, but what *may* happen. In this spirit, then, let us calmly confront what we may well term:

The Rising Tide of Chaos.

That the present-day East is not only revolutionary but increasingly chaotic there can be no reasonable doubt. The disruptive process is now most acute in China, where an entire order of life appears to be in the throes of dissolution. Those who best know the Orient realize that contemporary China is just a huge country adrift; an enormous human mass, writhing beneath the scourge of political and social anarchy, seeking blindly some new equilibrium which it seems unable to attain by its own exertions—at least, within any predictable period of time.

A close student of the Orient thus sets forth both the deeper aspects of the Chinese tragedy and its wider implications: "What is really happening in China, what is important as history and fundamental in influence, is that a *world is turning over.* This is happening everywhere in the East, but in China it is brought to the sharpest focus. A whole hemisphere seethes, and the revolutions, civil wars, disintegrated governments, nationalist insurgencies, and anti-foreign movements are but the froth at the top. They are interesting and dramatic; they are enlivening as feature articles, and grievous to foreign offices, and sometimes tragic to those immediately affected, but they are unimportant in themselves. They are symptoms. They are effects, not causes.

The truth about China, about the whole East, is much more serious than we think it is, than we are told it is in conventional channels of information. It goes deeper and, moreover, it is something we cannot 'do anything' about. There is chaos in the East now, not as the word is used in the professional slang of writers on foreign affairs, diplomatic observers, and outraged 'men on the spot,' but in its correct sense of *formlessness.*"[14]

Mr. Peffer is quite right in saying that there is nothing to be done about all this. He might have added that, for it all, no one

14 Peffer, *op. cit.*

is really responsible. In the larger sense, the impact of the West upon the East was inevitable. And its logical consequences were equally inescapable. Given the nature of the old Orient, Westernism was, from the very first, a disturbing element which was bound to produce increasingly disruptive effects. As Nicholas Roosevelt well says:

"When Western political and social ideals actually penetrate an Asiatic country they bring chaos in their wake. When the social order of the Orient, based on the family or clan and bound together by immutable traditions, meets the Western system, with its emphasis on individualism and personal liberty, it is obvious that the result can only be explosive. Disrespect for parental authority, insistence on the equality of the sexes, the flat disregard of age-old customs, and the introduction of the brusque manners of the West, are so subversive of the entire social structure of the East that social chaos is inevitable."[15]

Everywhere it is substantially the same story. Ramsay Macdonald sadly depicts the cultural chaos of a semi-Westernized India when he writes: "Beautiful Mogul palaces furnished with cracked furniture from Tottenham Court Road; that is what we have done to the Indian mind. We have not only made it despise its own culture and throw it out; we have asked it to fill up the vacant spaces with furniture which will not stand the climate. The mental Eurasianism of India is appalling. Such minds are nomad. They belong to no civilization, no country, no history. They create a craving that cannot be satisfied, and ideals that are unreal. They falsify life . . . We sought to give the Eastern mind a Western content and environment; we have succeeded only too well in establishing intellectual and moral anarchy in both."[16]

Even those Western gifts seemingly beneficial and which Orientals themselves certainly appreciate may entail highly disturbing results. We have seen how our numberless material conveniences are welcomed in the East; how the Western idea of comfort has captured the Oriental imagination. Yet this ever-growing and apparently insatiable demand for things Western produces grave

---

15 Nicholas Roosevelt, *The Restless Pacific, pp.* 231–32 (New York, 1928).

16 J Ramsay MacDonald, *The Government of India*, pp. 171–72 (London, 1920).

economic and social consequences. The Oriental's family budget is thereby thrown quite out of balance. This opening up of a whole vista of new wants means a drastic rise in his standard of living. And where is he going to find the money to pay for it? If he be poor, he has to skimp on bare necessities. If he be rich, he hates to forego his traditional luxuries.

The upshot is a universal growth of extravagance. And, in this connection, it is well to bear in mind that, taken as a 'whole, the peoples of the Orient have never been really thrifty. Poor the masses may have been, and thus obliged to live frugally, but they have always proved themselves to be "good spenders" when opportunity offers. The way a Turkish peasant or a Hindu *ryot* will squander his savings and run into debt over festivals, marriages, funerals, and other social occasions astounds Western observers. Now add to all this the fact that in the East, as in the rest of the world, the cost of life's basic necessaries—food, fuel, clothing, and shelter—has risen greatly for the past quarter-century, and we can realize the gravity of the problem which higher Oriental living-standards involve.

Certain it is that, throughout the East, the struggle for existence is growing keener and that the pressure of poverty becomes more severe. With the basic necessaries soaring in price, and with many things considered necessities which were deemed luxuries or were entirely unknown a generation ago, the average Oriental peasant or town worker is finding it harder and harder to make both ends meet. The cost of living has increased faster than the resources of the people.

One major factor in the Orient's present crisis is overpopulation. This is mainly due to Westernism. Of course, Orientals are proverbially quick breeders, and as a result Oriental peoples have always pressed close upon the limits of subsistence. In the past, however, this population-pressure was automatically lightened by war, pestilence, famine, and gross misgovernment, all of which combined to sweep off such multitudes that, despite high birth-rates, populations remained at substantially a fixed level. But here, as elsewhere, Western influences have radically altered the situation. They have largely abolished those "natural" checks on population-growth above mentioned, and in response to the life-saving measures of the West, the enormous death-rate of former days tends to compare with the low death-rate of Western nations. But to lower the Orient's tremendous birth-rate is quite another matter. The net result has been a prodigious increase of population wherever Western life-conserving methods have been adopted. Japan and India, both of whose peoples have tripled in a century, are merely typical examples.

Swarming populations and soaring living costs make a bad combination. We cannot be surprised to find all Eastern lands cursed with acute poverty and much social degradation. Throughout the Orient, the rural and urban masses alike live on the bare margin of subsistence. The filthy squalor of China's teeming millions is too well known to need description here, nor need we depict the pathetically neat yet equally stark poverty of overcrowded Japan. What we should realize is that conditions in the Near and Middle East are no better.

The English economist Brailsford thus portrays the condition of the Egyptian peasantry: "The villages are crowded slums of mud hovels, without a tree, a flower, or a garden. The huts, often without a window or a leveled floor, are minute dungeons of baked mud, usually of two small rooms neither whitewashed nor carpeted. Those which I entered were bare of any visible property, save a few cooking utensils, a mat to serve as a bed, and a jar which held the staple food of maize."[17]

As for the poorer Indian peasants, a British sanitary official thus depicts their mode of life: "One has actually to see the interior of the houses, in which each family is often compelled to live in a single small cell, made of mud walls and with a mud floor; containing small yards littered with rubbish, often crowded with cattle; possessing wells permeated by rain soaking through this filthy surface; and frequently jumbled together in inchoate masses called towns and cities."[18]

In the cities, indeed, conditions are even worse than in the country, the slums of the Orient surpassing the slums of the West. A well-known French publicist paints positively nauseating pictures

17 H. N. Brailsford, *The War of Steel and Gold,* p. 113 (London, 1913).

18 Doctor Ronald Ross, "Wretchedness a Cause of Political Unrest," *The Survey,* February 18, 1911.

of the poorer quarters in the great Levantine towns like Cairo, Constantinople, and Jerusalem.[19]

In India it is the same story. "Even before the growth of her industries had begun, the cities of India presented a baffling housing problem Into the welter of crooked streets and unsanitary habits of an Oriental city, great industrial plants are now wedging their thousands of employees Working from before dawn until after dark, men and women are too exhausted to go far from the plant to sleep, if they can help it. When near-by houses are jammed to suffocation, they live and sleep in the streets."[20]

An official report on conditions in Bombay tenements reads: "In such houses—the breeders of bacilli, the centers of disease and poverty, vice and crime—have people of all kinds, the diseased, the dissolute, the drunken, the improvident, been indiscriminately herded and tightly packed in vast hordes to dwell in close association with each other."[21]

The inevitable result of all this is a widespread and ever-growing social unrest. That unrest is of long standing. Even before the Great War had produced its shattering effects and aggressive social revolution had established itself in semi-Asiatic Russia, close students of the Orient were predicting social disturbances of increasing gravity.

A quarter of a century ago, the Hindu nationalist leader, Bipin Chandra Pal, stated: "This so-called unrest is not really political. It is essentially an intellectual and spiritual upheaval, the forerunner of a mighty social revolution, with a new organon and a new philosophy of life behind it."[22]

And a French observer wrote in similar vein: "There will be a series of economic revolutions in India, which must necessarily produce suffering and struggle."[23] Even thus early, increasingly hard living conditions, together with the adoption of Western ideas

---

19 Louis Bertrand, *Le Mirage Oriental,* pp. 111–12 (Paris, 1910).

20 Fred B. Fisher, *India's Silent Revolution,* p. 55 (New York, 1920).

21 Quoted by A. Yusuf Au, *Life and Labor in India,* p. 35 (London, 1907).

22 Bipin Chandra Pal, "The Forces Behind the Unrest in India," *Contemporary Review,* February, 1910.

23 J. Chailley, *Administrative Problems of British India, p.* 339 (London, 1910–English translation).

of comfort and kindred higher standards, were obviously causing friction between the different social classes. Some years before the war, a British health officer assigned "wretchedness" as the root-cause of India's political unrest. After describing the deplorable living conditions of the Indian masses, he wrote:

"It will of course be said at once that these conditions have existed in India from time immemorial, and are no more likely to cause unrest now than previously; but in my opinion unrest has always existed there in a subterranean form. Moreover, in the old days, the populace could make scarcely any comparison between their own condition and that of more fortunate people; now they can compare their own slums and terrible 'native quarters' with the much better ordered cantonments, stations, and houses of the British officials and even of their own wealthier brethren . . . Seditious meetings, political chatter, and 'aspirations' of babus and demagogues are only the superficial manifestations of this deeper disturbance."[24]

In Westernized Japan, social unrest has likewise been developing for decades. Soaring costs of living, affecting all classes but bearing especially hard upon the vast new factory proletariat, make many thoughtful observers fear for Japan's future stability. Revolutionary stirrings are not confined to the urban masses.

They also occur among the middle classes of the towns and the tenant farmers of the countryside. Both of these normally conservative elements have been so hard hit by heightened living costs and heavy taxation that they are shot through with discontent. Beneath the power and panoply of Imperial Japan lurk volcanic forces which may someday burst forth in violent eruption. Official Japan calls them "Dangerous Thoughts" and represses them with an iron hand. Yet, though suppressed, they remain.

Growing social friction in the East is intensified by the Oriental's lack of interest in the sufferings of all persons not bound to him by family, caste, or customary ties. Throughout the East, "social service," in the Western sense, is practically unknown.

This fact is noted by a few Orientals themselves. Says an Indian writer, speaking of Indian town life: "There is no common measure of social conduct. Hitherto, social reform in India has taken account

24 Doctor Ronald Ross, *op. cit.*

only of individual and family life. As applied to mankind in the mass, and especially to those soulless agglomerations of seething humanity which we call cities, it is a gospel yet to be preached."[25] As an American sociologist remarks of the glowing slum evil throughout the industrialized Orient:

"The greatest danger is due to the fact that Orientals do not have the high Western sense of the value of the life of the individual, and are, comparatively speaking, without any restraining influence similar to our own enlightened public opinion, which has been roused by the lessons of a century of industrial strife. Unless these elements can be supplied, there is danger of suffering and abuses in the East worse than any the West has known."[26]

All the diffused social unrest of the Orient tends to center around two recently emerged classes, both due to Westernization. These are the Western-educated *intelligentsia* and the industrial workers of the factory towns. Revolutionary tendencies of the Orient's "younger generation" are notorious.

This restless, spiritually uprooted class has taken the lead in every revolutionary disturbance of the modern Orient, from North Africa to China and Japan. As for the new industrial proletariat, it is as yet too unorganized, ignorant, and tradition-bound to have developed a radicalism corresponding to its increasing numbers. Nevertheless, Japan, China, and India today possess genuine labor movements on Western-lines, with the familiar accompaniments of strikes, picketing, and other forms of industrial struggle.

The Great War of course intensified every phase of Oriental unrest. Into this turmoil there now came the sinister influence of Russian Bolshevism, marshaling all this-diffused unrest by systematic methods for definite ends.

Russia's Communist leaders were frankly out for a world-revolution. To bring this about, they not only launched direct assaults on the West but planned flank attacks in the East as well. If Red Russia could set Asia on fire, it would kill two birds with one stone: The loss of great dependencies like India would shake

25 A. Yusuf Ali, *op. cit., pp.* 3, 32.

26 E. W. Capen, "A Sociological Appraisal of Western Influence in the Orient," *American Journal of Sociology,* May, 1911.

the colonial powers of Western Europe to their foundations, while the Bolshevizing of China, India, and other Eastern lands would further the World-Revolution.

Communist efforts have notably increased the difficulty of maintaining Western control over colonial dependencies in Asia and Africa. The gravest aspect of Red propaganda is its building-up of disciplined, strongly backed Communist groups to fight the well-trained colonial officials who have hitherto ruled Oriental lands more by skill and prestige than by armed force. In this way the "moral imponderables" of Western rule are being insidiously undermined. India, French Indo-China, the Dutch Indies, the Philippines—everywhere it is the same story.

A French writer explains very well what is going on. "The methodical organization of colonial revolts," he says, "is of recent origin. Before the war, it was non-existent; since the war, not a month has passed without some such revolt in some part of the globe. And not an hour passes, but what thousands of professional revolution-makers work toward the achievement of their larger ends . . . Everywhere the Third International has sown an infinite network of committees, associations, and emissaries of various kinds. These strive to bring about a condition of profound unrest—and then have chosen, disciplined groups on the spot, ready to take command when real trouble breaks out . . .

"Hitherto, we Europeans alone have had the advantage of an organization which permitted tiny minorities to govern immense peoples. In India, for instance, a single white resident, aided by a few ill-armed native policemen, has governed a great district with no thought of trouble. That was because, behind this frail visible authority, every native sensed the mighty power of England. But today the European minority is faced by another minority, equally well organized, conscious of whither it is going, and sustained by a distant power no less formidable."[27]

Red Russia's Oriental policy aims at something even more far-reaching than the shattering of Western colonial empires. In all the elaborate network of Communist intrigue which has enmeshed

---

27 "La Politique Coloniale et le Bolchévisme," *Revue des Deux Mondes*, May 15, 1930.

the East since 1917 we can glimpse the interplay of two distinct objectives: one immediate—the destruction of Western political and economic supremacy; the other ultimate—the Communizing of the Oriental masses with the consequent extirpation of the native upper and middle classes, precisely as has been done in Russia and has been planned in the countries of the West. In the first stage of its Eastern policy, Red Russia is quite ready to respect Oriental faiths and customs, and to back nationalist movements. In the second stage, however, religion and nationalism are to be branded as "bourgeois" and relentlessly destroyed.

As a matter of fact, this second stage has actually arrived throughout Russia's Asiatic dependencies. In Transcaucasia, Central Asia, and Outer Mongolia, Communism is today fully established—which means that all persons not rated as workers or peasants have been killed, imprisoned, or driven into exile.

Yet those "second-stage" proceedings, however successful in Russian territory, have seriously hindered Red efforts beyond Russia's borders. All Asia has been duly warned of what to expect, and strong reactions against Communism have set in. The upper and middle classes, even where bitterly antagonistic to Western control, tend to set bounds to their nationalistic agitation in view of a still more disagreeable alternative to Western rule. Indeed, nationalism itself, in the East as in the West, has proved to be the best antitoxin against Communist infection.

China's rapidly waxing nationalism is the chief reason why Red Russia's forward policy there, temporarily so successful, suddenly faltered and failed. In Japan, likewise, early Communist gains have been followed by a rapid decline, most Japanese radicals having recently abjured Communism for the ultra-nationalistic gospel of Japanese Fascism. As for the Moslem Near East, Communism has thus far failed to strike deep roots at any time. The strong nationalism of Kemalist Turkey seems to offer an especially staunch bulwark against Communist penetration.

Though Communism has not swept the Orient and has even suffered serious setbacks, the Communist threat remains. Oriental unrest is too widespread and deep-seated not to offer fertile ground for Communist propaganda. Though Asiatic conservatives may fear Bolshevism, they have no love for Western rule; so in all Asiatic lands under Western control, Communist support of nationalistic movements will hardly be rejected, even though accepted with due caution. Furthermore, the discontented *intelligentsia* are inclined to be extreme radicals, while the urban workers constitute an obvious source of Red recruits. Even the peasants, when impoverished and in hard circumstances, may lend a ready ear to Communist arguments. The persistence of Communist revolts in the agricultural hinterland of China shows how dangerous such risings can become.

Chinese Communism likewise reveals what we may expect from this and similar movements. It shows that the Communist threat in the Orient is not what we are apt to imagine. Those who fear the sudden emergence of Soviet republics on the Moscow model are mistaken; except Japan, no Asiatic country seems even remotely ripe for full-fledged Bolshevism.

Chinese examples are much more to the point. The Red regimes set up in Central China are decidedly primitive in character. Even though some of the Red leaders may understand Communist doctrines, their followers apparently know little about such matters and think almost wholly in terms of food and loot. Chinese Communism is thus an essentially destructive force similar to the great T'ai-ping Rebellion of the last century, which desolated the heart of China and swept away tens of millions of lives.

Should Asia go Red, therefore, the immediate result would presumably be, not organized Communism but chaotic barbarism. We should realize that throughout Asia (except in Japan) social discipline is maintained by relatively small upper classes. Beneath them lie swarming masses, miserably poor, densely ignorant, and with no traditions of self-government or self-control.

If, therefore, those native upper classes should be overwhelmed by a flood of social revolution, the upshot would be a descent to something like the level of savagery.

The sudden release of the ignorant, brutal Oriental masses from their traditional restraints of religion and custom would mean the wrecking of Oriental civilization and culture; a primitive reaction from which the East could begin to emerge only after the lapse of many years.

The effects of all this upon our Western world can easily be imagined. Billions of European and American capital invested in Eastern lands would, for the most part, be hopelessly lost. Our great foreign trade with the Orient would dwindle to relatively small and uncertain proportions. Sources of tropical products and other raw materials vital to our industrial life would be virtually closed to us. As for the political complications, who can estimate their magnitude? With one-half of the world and more than half of the human race weltering in chaotic turmoil, how could the rest of the world remain unscathed?

Now this is no alarmist picture, drawn to make one's flesh creep. It aims to be a sober analysis of what *may* happen, if Asia's five-fold revolution gets entirely beyond control.

Yet once more we wish to emphasize that this complex transformation may keep within evolutionary bounds; that it contains constructive as well as disruptive factors; lastly, that Asia should be regarded not merely as a whole but likewise as a broad diversity. And the prospects of the Orient's various parts can best be gauged by separate surveys of its outstanding regions.

PART II
CHAPTER II
CHINA: A COLOSSUS RUN WILD

PRESENT-DAY China presents a spectacle of stupendous tragedy. Before our very eyes an ancient civilization, a complex culture, a wisely ordered way of life is going to pieces. Thereby a great segment of humanity numbering at least four hundred millions has lost its bearings and drifts aimlessly towards an unknown fate. Nothing precisely like this has ever happened before. The break-up of Classic civilization at the downfall of the Roman Empire is the only event at all comparable.

Old China was the heart of an isolated world—the Mongolian East. Down almost to our own days, this group of kindred peoples lived virtually a life apart. Sundered from the rest of mankind by lofty mountains, burning deserts, and the illimitable ocean, the Far East formed a self-sufficing comity, whereof China was the enduring focus. About this "Middle Kingdom," as it aptly called itself, the other yellow folk were disposed—Japanese and Koreans to the east; Siamese, Annamites, and Cambodians to the south; and to the north the nomad Mongols and Manchus. To them all, China was the august teacher, sometimes rebuking their presumption, yet always instilling the principles of its ordered civilization.

China headed a Far East not only isolated from but strangely unlike the outer world—especially the West. The abysmal differences between Chinese and Western civilization made it certain that when they came in contact, neither would comprehend the other. The Chinese did not even try to understand the presumptuous "sea barbarians." And the men from the West, despite earnest efforts on their part, had scant success in grasping the inwardness of matters so foreign to their own experience. "Almost all Western studies of China are vitiated by the practice of applying to Chinese history and civilization, Chinese forms of dynastic structure, law, social order, war, nationalism, revolution, and so on, the concepts developed in the West out of Western history."[1]

To understand China we must forget all Western precedents and view it from quite a different angle. Old China was not a nation; not even a state, in our sense of the word. Its people were held together, not by public law or political institutions, but by customary codes applying primarily to social groups rather than to individuals. Even organized religion, as we know it, was lacking, its place being taken by a common-sense system of ethics elaborated by Confucius. In Western eyes, old China seems a mere geographical expression; a strange something little better than collective anarchy. But this "something" contained a social cement which, for thousands of years, kept together one-fourth of the human species, subdivided into an infinite number of tiny groups yet never losing social cohesion and always aware of belonging to a great community.

The clue to this seeming mystery is that, in China, the social unit is, not the individual, but the clan-family. Old China was, in fact, "a vast aggregation of community-families lying midway between the Western family and the primeval tribe which acknowledged no extra-family responsibilities . . . This social unit imposed on its members an unwritten code of immemorial custom more binding than law."[2]

Above this clan-family mosaic stood a personage whom we call an Emperor but who is much better described by his Chinese Title: "Son of Heaven." He was essentially the father of the great Chinese family-group in the sight of the gods, whose favor he was expected to retain. Though theoretically absolute, this patriarchal monarch usually went on the negative principle of letting well enough alone. The Chinese, as a people, were virtually free from governmental regulation because, through their family or guild codes, they effectively policed themselves. Such imperial officials as did exist were chosen, not by reason of administrative talents, but from a knowledge of the Chinese classics shown at competitive

1 Owen Lattimore's article on "China and the Barbarians" in the collaborative volume entitled *Empire in the East*, p.11; edited by Joseph Barnes (New York, 1934).

2 H. B. Elliston, "China in the World Family," *Foreign Affairs*, July, 1929.

examinations in which the test was ability to write an "eight-legged essay." The chief duty of these literary officials was the collection of a moderate imperial tribute. Otherwise, the central authority left them pretty much to their own devices. Thus an extreme localism in government prevailed and anything like a centralized machine was unknown. Indeed, the average Chinese could have no idea of what we mean by Government or the State—much less the Nation. He simply was not a political being, so, for him, words like patriotism or public duty had no meaning.

All this enables us to realize how hard it is for the Chinese even to think in Western terms; to say nothing of recasting their political, economic, and social life along Western lines.

Hiram Bingham points out some of the complications arising from the traditional Chinese ideal of the clan-family. "Family loyalty," he writes, "is so paramount in China that only an infinitesimal part of the Chinese people have the slightest conception what is meant by the term 'public welfare.' To them, whatever will benefit the family and its members is right. Whatever hurts the family is wrong. Consequently, the Chinese official who looks after his relatives at the expense of the state is right; while the Chinese official who permits them to suffer while he serves the state is wrong, wholly wrong, inconceivably wrong.

"The same ethical attitude makes it practically impossible for the Chinese joint-stock enterprises or business corporations to succeed. It is ethically the duty of the directors to look after their families. Similarly, it is the duty of the employees to look after their families. Neither directors nor employees have any conception of the Western attitude of loyalty to a corporation."[3]

An exceptionally close student of Chinese thought and ways goes so far as to doubt whether China can ever be transformed into a modern nation-state. Says Mrs. Buck:

"The Chinese have enjoyed such extreme individual freedom that one wonders if they will ever be able to endure the legal restrictions of even a liberal republic. The bond between ruler and subject has been of the slightest, many times going scarcely beyond the payment

---

3 Hiram Bingham, "Family Loyalty—the Chinese Problem," *Scribner's Magazine*, February, 1928.

of an annual tribute, and local autonomy has been carried very far. The first reaction of the average Chinese to any kind of control is to rise up against it in indignation."[4]

China's inadaptability to new ways is partly due to the sheer inertia of an immense human mass, but it is also due to the stubborn conservatism of a traditionally minded people. What is the reason for this outstanding Chinese trait? Basically it is inborn, no doubt. But this natural bent seems to have been intensified by the course of events. For ages, Chinese history is the story of an unwarlike agricultural people chronically harried by the exceedingly warlike Mongol nomads to the northward to guard against constant peril, the Chinese built their Great Wall—the mightiest engineering feat ever undertaken.

This defense blocked minor raids, but it did not prevent large-scale invasions. Every hundred years or so, some master spirit would weld the Mongol tribes into a conquering horde which, like a seething flood, would breach the Wall and roll over China. After much pillaging and destroying, the conquerors would settle down as masters.

But like the barbarian invaders of the Roman Empire, those rough Mongols would be ultimately subdued by the civilization of the vanquished. Within a few generations they would have lost their identity, swallowed up in the mass of the Chinese people. Yet by that time, another barbarian wave would have gathered in the north, and the process would be repeated.

The cumulative effects of this age-long process upon the Chinese temperament and attitude have been profound. Owen Lattimore rightly points out that the "Great-Wall tradition" colors every phase of Chinese foreign and domestic policy. "Barbarian invasion," he writes, "hung over China as a permanent threat, which was frequently realized in conquest. It therefore became a rule in Chinese history that the freedom of China did not depend on political unity and soundness of administration within China (as is usually assumed) so much as on disunity among the barbarians . . .

"There thus grew up inevitably a canon of statecraft and foreign policy based on the assumption that fighting the barbarians was less

4 Pearl S. Buck, "Communism in China," *The Nation* (N. Y.), July 25, 1928.

efficacious than promoting confusion among them—by intrigue, bribery, alliance, or other means.

"What has not been generally enough appreciated by Western students of Chinese history is the reverse application of this rule: that good government at home is less vital to the nation than successful intrigue abroad. The foreign and domestic policies of any nation are external and internal facets of a single phenomenon. If foreign policy is based on the assumption that courage and direct action are useless, then courage and initiative cannot be the guiding characteristics of internal policy . . .

"China has thrown off with astounding vitality the *individual* effects of many periods of subjection to foreign invaders. Nevertheless, the *general* effect has left a deep wound on Chinese life . . . For twenty centuries at least there has been no creative development within China. There have been only cycles, representing variable applications of a single cast of feeling, permanent in type, to problems that were treated as if they were eternal and unalterable. 'Whenever the Chinese were conquered, the normal reaction of their culture was to go underground until the conquerors had turned Chinese, when it came to the surface again, as Chinese as ever. Nor, when restored to freedom, did it take steps to solve the barbarian problem permanently and prevent future defeat. It simply repeated the rebirth, growth, and decay of similar periods in the past.

"Thus, generation by generation, the already established and unreceptive character of Chinese culture was confirmed and hardened into a quality of stubbornness, compounded of a superficial willingness to yield and a fundamental unwillingness to change."[5]

Such was the ossified, self-contained, utterly complacent China into whose southern ports the first pioneers of the expanding West came sailing, some four centuries ago. The Chinese were not greatly impressed. These strange white "sea barbarians" were ingenious, demoniacally energetic, and therefore possibly dangerous. But they were few in numbers and split into several tribes who cordially hated one another. Furthermore, they paid hard cash for teas and

5 Lattimore, op. *cit.*, pp. 22–25.

silks, or offered curious novelties in exchange. *Well*, let them land at a few specified ports, but under close scrutiny and strict regulation.

That was the situation regarding foreigners in China for more than three hundred years. Indeed, as time passed and sea barbarians gave offense, Chinese official restrictions grew more severe. Only through bribery of local mandarins did Western traders prevent their humiliating position from becoming intolerable. Meanwhile Western nations were founding colonial empires elsewhere in Asia and were hankering for more Far Eastern trade. Yet the august Son of Heaven and his mandarins rejected every diplomatic overture from the West with bland contempt. Rebuffed in diplomacy, the Western Powers long hesitated to try force; the Manchu Empire, though inwardly decadent, looked outwardly imposing. Not until well into the nineteenth century did an armed test come, when England resorted to arms in the so-called Opium War of 1839.

That armed test radically changed the whole situation. With ridiculous ease, British warships and British soldiers smashed the resistance of vastly larger Chinese forces. The entire Western world became aware that huge China was helpless against the military might of the West.

That knowledge was quickly applied. In a series of armed aggressions undertaken to enforce acceptance of demands for foreign privileges, China was opened wide to Western penetration. Indeed, the Westerner himself had suddenly vaulted from the status of a despised interloper to that of a superior being. "The Western resident in China, entrenched behind his new system of treaty rights, was looking down upon the Chinese as a mere 'native' in a China where the privileged foreigner had become the lord of creation."[6]

This state of affairs prevailed after 1860. Thenceforth China was steadily infiltrated by Western influences of every kind. At first it seemed as though the massive structure of Chinese society was little affected. Yet actually its foundations were being undermined. Expressed in Chinese terms, what was happening was a general and cumulative loss of "face." Not merely the Manchu régime but the

---

6 Arnold J. Toynbee, "The Far East's Reaction to Western Civilization," *Harpers Magazine*, September, 1927.

whole Chinese way of life was being discredited. For the first time in its history the Chinese people were confronted with an invasion of barbarians who were not merely better fighters but who were possessed of an advanced civilization of their own—a civilization with which the Chinese could not effectively cope. No use waiting patiently until the sea barbarians became Chinese, because *these* barbarians would never be assimilated. Here was a whole new situation calling for radically new treatment.

That was the logical conclusion to be drawn. When we turn to Japan we shall find that, under somewhat similar circumstances, the Japanese leaders read the signs of the times and acted accordingly. Not so old China. Its ingrained conservatism made voluntary adaptation impossible. Therefore it long persisted in the hopeless task of trying to apply old precedents to new circumstances, thus rendering ultimate failure more catastrophic and more complete.

The inevitable breakdown came toward the close of the nineteenth century. It began with the Chino-Japanese War of 1894. Humiliating defeat at the hands of the hitherto despised "island dwarfs" utterly discredited the Manchu régime in Chinese eyes and rendered its overthrow practically certain. Also this crowning revelation of Chinese weakness tempted the West to fresh aggressions. Convinced that the Celestial Empire lay on its deathbed, the Western Powers began to consider how its rich estate should be disposed of. European diplomats spoke of a "Chinese melon" almost ripe for slicing. A wild scramble like that for Africa, ending in a general partition of China, seemed to be on the cards.

That this partition did not take place was due, not to Chinese statesmanship, but chiefly to Western quarrels over the prospective spoils. John Hay's "Open Door" policy was an important, though secondary, factor. Contrary to popular notions, this American Secretary of State did not stand four-square against partition. What his famous diplomatic notes really meant was: "If you European Powers are going to carve up China, we insist that you respect American commercial rights in your various spheres." Possibly no one was more surprised than John Hay himself at the outcome. By obtaining "Open Door" promises from the European Powers, he so lessened the commercial value of a partitioned China that the job seemed no longer worthwhile. At least, the Powers, suspicious as they were of one another, no longer had a common incentive strong enough to sink mutual jealousies in common action.

China was thus destined to be saved. But the Chinese could not know this. They merely felt themselves in the grip of "foreign devils" who were squeezing them harder and harder. The result was an access of blind rage which exploded in the Boxer uprising of 1900. Boxerism was wholly reactionary; a fanatical revolt against everything foreign. As such, it was foredoomed from the start and merely brought down on China the wrath of the entire outer world—Japan included.

The Boxer fiasco and its disastrous aftermath convinced a minority of thinking Chinese that something new must be tried. However, this minority was not agreed upon what should be done. Some felt that moderate reforms along Western lines would suffice; others believed that wholesale Westernization was inevitable. These radicals, mostly young men educated abroad and typified by Sun Yat-Sen, hatched the revolution of 1911 which overthrew the Manchu dynasty and replaced it with a republic. So far as official proclamations went, China had been suddenly transformed into a Western nation-state.

As a matter of fact, this was all on paper. Old China having been neither a nation nor a state, such a transformation simply could not be improvised. Instead of forging Chinese unity, the Revolution merely shattered the old order without anything organic to take its place. This epoch-making upheaval overthrew far more than the Manchu dynasty. It also overthrew the class of civil-service officials who had administered China through every dynastic change for over two thousand years. These ultra-conservative mandarins, saturated with classical culture and hidebound by historic precedents, simply could not function in the new order of affairs. And this passing of the old officialdom was symptomatic of an even greater change—the passing of an entire traditional way of life based upon Confucian ethics and the clan-family. The Revolution had thus started a process of disintegration which was bound to spread from the political to the economic, social, and cultural sphere. Old China was headed for the melting-pot.

At the moment, these wider implications were not realized only the political consequences were apparent. Yet they were serious enough. For one thing, the overthrow of the Manchu dynasty logically broke the bonds between China and the "Outer Dominions"—Mongolia, Tibet, Eastern Turkestan, and even Manchuria. Historically, these vast regions had never "belonged" to China—the *real* China of the Eighteen Provinces inside the Great Wall. Indeed, it would be more accurate to say that China had "belonged" to Manchuria—or rather to the line of Manchu chieftains who had conquered their huge neighbor.

Of course, the Revolutionary leaders never admitted this. Applying Western ideas of state sovereignty and national unity, they proclaimed a federation including the Outer Dominions; and the West, misreading the situation, recognized the nationalist claim. Not so the Dominions. Inhabited by non-Chinese peoples jealous of Chinese encroachment, the Dominions regarded the Revolution as a strictly Chinese affair with which they wanted nothing to do. The Manchu dynasty having been, in their eyes, the sole link that bound them to China, its overthrow left them legally free to go their own respective ways—which the Republic was resolved they should not do.

This clash between the Republic's claim to full sovereignty and the Outer Dominions' claim to complete independence has been a chronic feud which, though ill-appreciated by the West, is big with future trouble. It largely explains the Japanese protectorate over "Manchukuo," the Russian protectorate over Outer Mongolia, the obscure struggles and foreign intrigues in Eastern Turkestan and Tibet. All the Dominions are rapidly slipping away from Chinese control. The situation throughout Eastern Asia thereby becomes increasingly precarious. And the outcome is not even remotely in sight.

The fiction of a Chinese nation-state which did not yet exist produced still other complications. In the first place, it has completely falsified China's foreign relations. The Western Powers have taken nationalist assertions at their face value and accord present-day China full diplomatic status. But when, for instance, the Chinese demand that the special privileges of resident foreigners be done away with, the Western Powers object, saying that China is not yet sufficiently stable. But if China is now really a nation-state, it is logically entitled to the rights of national sovereignty; hence, the "extra-territorial" status of foreigners, which was common practice in all the old Asiatic empires, no longer applies. The Western Powers, having technically admitted China's claims, now quarrel with the logical conclusions. Japan, better informed on Chinese affairs, takes a much more realistic attitude. Japanese statesmen say frankly that, in their opinion, China does not today possess a responsible government; consequently, China should not be dealt with according to the ordinary methods of international procedure. This does not mean that Japan's present policy toward China is either wise or just. It means, however, that Japan sees China as it is—which the West does not.

We need not tarry over the long welter of factional squabbles and civil wars that has cursed China for over twenty years. The thing to keep in mind is, not that Chinese politicians are corrupt and incapable, but that ever since the nationalist upheaval of 1911, the foundations of Chinese life have been crumbling and the whole situation has become more and more unstable. We should remember that the Republican leaders had to improvise a whole new régime of government. The task was stupendous. Perchance much abler men would not have done so very much better.

Another point to remember is that China's new rulers, despite their political shortcomings, have accomplished much along other lines. Already the basis of a new national culture has been laid. The "modern language movement" has made popular education possible. This new language, written in simplified characters, is the vehicle for a literature no longer confined to the elect few but reaching and molding the thought of the people as a whole. Although the peasant and coolie masses are as yet illiterate and hence not in direct touch with this literary renaissance, they are increasingly influenced by it. For the first time in China there is something like a "public opinion" in the Western sense.

Now all these are constructive forces, germinating even while the destructive process still goes on. Given time and opportunity, China may hope ultimately to stabilize herself in some way not yet apparent but which will embody a working compromise between her traditional genius and imported Western factors that have been genuinely assimilated.

Such is the hope; the prospect. Yet it is no certainty. Present conditions are so appalling that China may sink into utter chaos wherein her old culture would presumably be destroyed. Again, the inborn conservatism of the Chinese people may prevent the needed compromises between old and new. In that case, "by indefinite continuance of the present deadlock, the civilization of China may perish without coming to terms with Westernization. Such a catastrophe would mean a general spread of the so-called Communism already prevalent in parts of south-central China, which is neither textbook Marxism nor Russian revolution, but the violence of collapse and despair, destroying every system it can reach, Chinese or foreign. Its underlying feeling is one that seeks to level down, because of the hopelessness of leveling up. This would lay China open to conquest by all and any, Chinese or foreign, who had the power to take and to hold."[7]

China's greatest handicap is an ingrained attitude of passive inertia toward all matters of public concern. In his private business the Chinaman is usually energetic and resourceful. Yet the moment anything beyond the clan-family circle is involved, his initiative falters.

This is not due to lack of insight. Any well-informed Chinese will analyze to a nicety what is wrong with his country and will discourse intelligently on what should be done. But that is all there is to it; he rarely even dreams of supplementing talk with action. The normal Chinese attitude toward China's ills reminds one of Mark Twain's quip on the weather—something everybody complained of endlessly but never *did* anything about!

We saw that this mental habit springs from deep historic causes; that ages of recurrent barbarian invasion made the Chinese feel that action was useless against problems which time would automatically solve. We also saw that this applied to internal as well as to foreign affairs. That mental legacy from the past paralyzes the initiative of even the most high-minded Chinese and leads them merely to

7 Lattimore, *op. cit.*, pp. 35–36.

protest eloquently against evils which would stir Westerners to grim determination expressing itself promptly in decisive acts.

This explains why the Chinese submit so patiently to the grossest exactions of corrupt officials and racketeering "warlords." It likewise explains why the Chinese fail to resist foreign aggressions; and why, when they do resist, they do not keep it up until the aggressor is repelled. Instead of relying on themselves, the Chinese in such cases usually try to find allies who will do most of the fighting for them. Chinese policy toward Japan's Manchurian thrust is an excellent example.

The Nanking Government's best efforts were propagandist appeals to America, to the League of Nations, to anybody and everybody who might conceivably be induced to do something to stop Japan—everybody, that is, except the Chinese themselves. This, of course, is merely applying the ancient maxim of Chinese statecraft: "using barbarians to control the barbarians."

So long as this attitude prevails, there is no reason why China's present chaotic confusion may not go on indefinitely; no reason why the Chinese should meet foreign interference with anything more effective than bitter protests, punctuated by flare-ups of local armed resistance which, like straw-fires, will quickly die dawn.

The menace of foreign intervention indeed hangs over China today, and will presumably come to pass unless the Chinese soon set their house in some sort of order. Just how it will take place is uncertain. It might conceivably be a joint intervention, the result of a diplomatic bargain between Japan and one or more European Powers. More likely is Japanese intervention, single-handed and on a big scale. Should the pseudo-Communism which today ravages central China threaten to submerge the whole country, foreign intervention of some sort would be inevitable.

Japan certainly intends to keep a measure of control over the Chinese situation. But the precise moves in her Chinese policy are determined largely by factors outside China, including both Japan's general position in world-politics and her own internal affairs. We can thus more intelligently analyze Chino-Japanese relations as part of a survey of Japan herself.

PART II

CHAPTER III

JAPAN: AN AMAZING SYNTHETIC PRODUCT

MODERN Japan is one of the wonders of the ages. Eighty years ago, Japan was a hermit nation, leading a strange, self-centered life of its own almost as remote from the outer world as though set upon another planet. A few old men are still alive who recall days when knights in lacquer armor fought Homeric duels with two swords or stormed the crenellated walls of feudal castles defended chiefly by bowmen.

Only a trifle over sixty years have passed since Japan, having been forced reluctantly to open its gates, came fully to realize its weakness in face of an aggressively intruding world. Then it was that Japan's master-minds determined to Westernize their country. The result of this momentous decision was the most extraordinarily rapid transformation in all recorded history. Today Japan ranks as a "Great Power," dominating the Far East with her fleets and armies, capturing distant markets with the mass-production of her factories, vibrant with efficiently directed energy, bent on achieving a mighty destiny.

Yet this astounding record has its debit side. In the Westernizing process, Old Japan has almost vanished. What remains, survives mainly as a museum piece. The cherry blossoms are smutted with the soot of factory chimneys; they wither in the fumes belched from blast furnaces.

And even that is not the whole story. If Westernization had been complete, resultant gains would perhaps have offset the incidental loss. Westernization has, however, been incomplete. It has been a distinctly one-sided affair. The material aspects of our civilization have been taken over wholesale; our institutions and ideals have not been successfully transplanted. Yet here as elsewhere in the Orient, the impact of the West has shattered the traditional culture and ideals.

The result is that present-day Japan displays a lack of balance which is producing grave consequences. The Japanese people are neither contented nor happy. They are becoming aware of the heavy price exacted by a forced material transformation in so short a space of time. Japan advances rapidly along the Westernizing road, but her people show many signs of strain. The whole tempo of Japanese life is nervous, forced, exaggerated. Japan is feverish. She is running a temperature!

A major crisis, long latent, today seems clearly at hand. How will the Japanese people react thereto? The past may throw some light on that query, because this is not the first time Japan has sought to assimilate an alien civilization. Twice before, her rulers have tried to graft foreign ways upon a highly individualized yet rather fragile culture. And twice before, the disruptive effects of the experiment have caused a fierce revulsion against the intruding forces, ending in deliberate isolation. Will such a reaction again occur? Can it succeed this time? And what will be the consequences of a vain attempt?

These questions are of vital import, not only for the Far East but for the world at large. Should semi-Westernized Japan erupt or explode, the repercussions would shake the globe. Yet either alternative is possible. Japan's national temper is today ominously volcanic. Indeed, the volcanic nature of this island-chain seems reflected in the character of its inhabitants. Throughout history, Japan appears as something unique, dynamic—and dangerous.

The Japanese are racially the outcome of an ancient cross, blended by ages of inbreeding in unusual isolation. Thousands of years ago, migrating Malays entered the islands from the south and conquered the aborigines, known as Ainus. This folk were an eastern extension of the white race, tinged with Mongolian blood. The modern Japanese are thus a mixture of Malayan, Mongoloid, and Caucasian stocks—a unique racial combination. Time has harmonized these originally diverse strains into a unified people.

When the Malay migration occurred is unknown, but the invading bands seem presently to have been united under a series of forceful chieftains who are remembered as legendary heroes. About 660 B.C. one of these chiefs emerges as an historical personage named Jimmu Tenno, rated as the first Japanese "Emperor." That is our version of a title which has far more than a political meaning.[1] For Jimmu Tenno was the scion of a mythical line sprung from the Sun-Goddess Amaterasu; and this first Emperor was, in turn, the ancestor of a dynasty which has ruled Japan in unbroken succession for over twenty-five hundred years, right down to the present day. The reigning Emperor, Hirohito, is the one hundred and twenty-fourth of his line, and he has a son to succeed him. This divine dynasty, reigning eternally athwart the ages, is unprecedented. And, in Japanese eyes, its divinity is self-evident. Hirohito has the blood of the gods in his veins. He is the spiritual head of the whole "Yamato Race" which itself partakes of the nature of the Divine Ancestor in that it enjoys the lasting favor of the gods and is thus raised above the level of other mortals.

By the early centuries of the Christian era, the Japanese islands were the home of a people with a fairly stable government and the beginnings of a distinctive civilization. It was then that the Japanese first came within the cultural orbit of China, at that time especially flourishing under the great dynasty of Han. The brilliant Han civilization intrigued those early Japanese, who seem to have possessed a lively curiosity. Official missions were sent to China and doubtless brought back detailed reports of a highly favorable kind. In consequence, Chinese sages, scholars, and technicians were invited to teach the Japanese all about Chinese civilization. Things Chinese soon became the rage. Chinese ways, ideas, and culture were taken over bodily; that is to say, hastily and uncritically. Japan soon became outwardly Chinafied.

Then doubts began to arise. Those wholesale borrowings of a foreign culture and social order were not assimilated; they remained for the most part a surface veneer. Nevertheless, this veneer choked native developments and warped the normal line of evolution. Japanese life became perplexing and discordant.

1 The Japanese word is *Tenno.* Only foreigners make formal use of the title, *Mikado,* which in Japan is employed in a poetic sense.

Chinese political ideas were especially trouble-breeding. "In the end, the conflict between Chinese theory and Japanese sentiment resulted in disastrous civil wars and the establishment of a militant feudalism. The Feudal strife from 1100 to 1600 A.D. was, in essence, a revolt of the Japanese against Chinese civilization, as it had been transplanted to Japan—its formalism, its pedantry, its general unsuitability to their lively temperament . . . The medieval Japanese seem to have felt uneasily that they had swallowed more than they could digest . . . This means they no longer regarded China as the fount of civilization, and thought they could stand on their own cultural feet. The Japanese were attempting to develop in isolation; truly a bold experiment . . . Japan thus evolved, by turning in upon herself, a unique but extremely limited culture."[2]

During these centuries of isolation punctuated by civil strife, the unified government of earlier days gave place to a feudalism much like that of Europe during our Middle Ages. The imperial dynasty continued to be revered, but its political power was gradually lost to a rival authority known as the Shogunate. The Mikado retired from the world into mystic seclusion, while the Shoguns ran the state. But this change was never legalized; theoretically it remained a usurpation.

The Shogunate was indeed the football of politics; an office contended for among the great feudal lords, thereby provoking recurrent civil wars. Those rival grandees, the Daimyos, commanded the allegiance of a knightly fighting class known as Samurai, who held their lands from the Daimyos in return for military service.

About the middle of the sixteenth century a momentous event occurred—Europeans arrived in Japan. The first comers were Portuguese and Spanish, closely followed by English and Dutch. These strangers made a great stir in Japan. The Japanese soon became as curious about the West as they had been over China in former days.

Many Western novelties were keenly relished and quickly adopted. Japanese commanders instantly realized the possibilities of arquebuses and cannon. Japanese ship-captains re-rigged their junks on European models for longer voyages. Catholic priests and

---

2 "The Tragedy of Japan," *The Round Table*, September, 1932.

friars made so many converts that it looked as though Japan might soon be Christianized. Alongside all this, a series of strong Shoguns raised the power of the central government higher than it had been since the beginning of the feudal period.

Japan was indeed astir. By the year 1600, the Island Empire thrilled to new hopes and aspirations. "Expansion!" was then the watchword. In those days, Japan was full of ambitious soldiers, daring sailors, and enterprising merchants, whose vision looked eagerly abroad. Hideyoshi, a great commander sometimes called "The Japanese Napoleon," overran Korea and defeated a Chinese army. At the same time, Japan was grasping after sea-power. Japanese sailors were becoming the most adventurous navigators of the Far East. Fierce Japanese sea-rovers were the scourge even of Siam and the Dutch Indies. The Philippines were a center of Japanese trade, with a resident colony exceeding 1,000. Japanese merchants traded all over the Far East, and Japanese junks plied regularly to India. Those big junks were seaworthy craft, quite capable of crossing the Pacific to America. Indeed, we know positively that they did cross, for the Spanish records show that Japanese merchantmen reached the Mexican port of Acapulco on at least two occasions—in the years 1610 and 1613.

For a moment Japan stood on the threshold of empire. How extraordinary were her possibilities! Japan was in an expansive mood similar in many ways to that of Elizabethan England at that very period. If the Japanese had chosen the path of exploration, trade, and settlement, they could have colonized Australia, the South Sea Islands, and the Pacific coast of North America, quite unopposed. And for generations Japan's door of opportunity stood wide open. Down to about 1750, for example, there was nothing, absolutely nothing, to have prevented Japan from colonizing everything north of Mexico on the western shores of the New World.

Why did not this come to pass? Because a strong reaction against Westernism had set in at home. Those foreign importations were making trouble. The new religion, especially, gave deep anxiety to Japanese statesmen. Zealous converts tended to put their Christian faith above their political allegiance; they obeyed alien priests in defiance of solemn official warnings. This had to be looked into.

During the 1620's, the Shogun sent a mission to Europe in order to study the West. Its report was damning, especially on religious matters. That is not surprising, because Europe was then convulsed with religious strife and its very heart was being torn to pieces by the catastrophic Thirty Years War.

The climax came when Japanese Christianity got mixed up with politics. Some of the great nobles who had been converted used their Christianity to further their feudal ambitions. Intrigues against the central government led the Shoguns to repress the Christians as a seditious faction. But this led the native converts, through their Spanish priests, to seek aid from the mighty King of Spain—that arch-champion of the Catholic faith, whose armies had just conquered the nearby Philippines. That was the last straw! Alarmed and infuriated, the Shogun resolved to drive Christianity from Japan. A furious struggle ensued. The Japanese Christians resisted desperately, and only after terrible bloodshed and massacre were they rooted out.

Appalled at what had transpired, the Shogun and his counselors became convinced that the only way to ensure peace in the Island Empire and preserve it from the fate of the Philippines was to shut Japan off entirely from the outer world. And this was done in thoroughgoing style. By the Edict of 1654, no Japanese was allowed to leave the Empire on pain of death, and all sea-going ships were destroyed. The sole window on the outer world was through a lone Dutch trading-post where a few merchants, under humiliating conditions, were allowed to reside. Thenceforth, for two hundred years, the Japanese were almost as much cut off from the rest of mankind as though they had flown away to the planet Mars. Truly, the Japanese had made one of the supreme renunciations of history.

By its domestic results, the policy of deliberate isolation seemed to be justified. During this prolonged seclusion, Japan not merely enjoyed profound peace but also developed to the full her peculiar civilization. A series of able rulers, the Tokugawa Shoguns, patronized learning and the arts; even science and popular education. Within its closed economic circle the country maintained a steady though moderate level of well-being. The people knew next to nothing of what went on beyond their sea-girt horizon, yet the Shogun and his counselors kept in some sort of touch with world-affairs, largely through the Dutch who proved to be reliable and trustworthy.

It was toward the middle of the nineteenth century that the West again came knocking at the door. Long before the unwanted visit of Commodore Perry and his American squadron, signs of change were in the air. Several times European Powers had made diplomatic advances, which had been brusquely repulsed. Tidings of China's humiliating defeat in the Opium War and subsequent Western aggressions upon the Celestial Empire awakened a growing uneasiness in reflective Japanese minds. Could the encroaching Western Powers be kept forever at arm's length? Thus when Perry made his polite yet pointed request, Japanese statesmen had already done some hard thinking and reluctantly concluded to accept the inevitable in the shape of a treaty of amity and commerce with the United States, signed early in 1854. Within the next few years similar treaties were negotiated with the chief European Powers. Japan had opened her gates to the outer world.

These treaties were signed by the Shogun, whom the West naturally deemed the actual ruler of Japan. The dim figure of the Mikado was virtually ignored. Yet the Mikado's shadow-court was the focus around which was gathering an anti-foreign movement. Many of the great Daimyos, traditionally jealous of the Shogun, denounced his acts as unpatriotic extensions of a power which had always been legally a usurpation. The idea of restoring the Emperor to the plenitude of his authority was definitely broached.

Meanwhile, disgruntled Daimyos began anti-foreign agitation. Westerners entering Japan under the new treaties were insulted, and presently an Englishman was killed by some arrogant feudal retainers. The West, however, promptly showed the Japanese what that sort of thing would mean. A British squadron knocked the offending Daimyo's seaboard capital to bits and exacted an indemnity of $625,000 into the bargain. When another feudal lord fired on foreign merchantmen, a combined European and American fleet bombarded the port of Shimonoseki and imposed an indemnity of $3,000,000—a staggering sum for the Japan of those days.

These warnings were harsh but helpful. They opened the eyes of every thinking Japanese to the stern reality that resolute decisions and quick action could alone save their country from China's fate. The West clearly had neither respect nor mercy for weaklings. Therefore Japan must grow strong, and strength could come only through knowledge of the Western art of war. That meant going to the Western school. Very well; the Japanese would go, and would do their best to prove apt pupils. Even the reactionary Daimyos saw the error of their ways and fell in line.

Yet Japan's ablest minds saw that something more was needed than a mere copying of Western methods and Western ways. Little though they then knew about it, they realized that behind Westernism's brute strength must lie spiritual forces which furnished the driving-power. If, therefore, Japan was to remain essentially itself, the aggressive virility of the West could be countered only by mobilizing the spiritual forces latent in Japan itself. This is the deeper significance of the almost bloodless revolution engineered in 1868, when the Shogun was deposed and the Emperor restored to his ancient position as absolute head of the state. Then began that systematic cultivation of Emperor-worship symbolizing a religious patriotism which was to energize and fanaticize the Japanese people. Previously dispersed in a myriad feudal rills, the traditional sentiments of loyalty and devotion were henceforth carefully drained into a mighty river flowing without resistance along carefully planned channels.

Modern Japan is therefore due, not to a popular movement, but to a few master-minds. Faced with a supreme national crisis, these Elder Statesmen decided what should be done and embarked upon the hazardous experiment. Its success was assured by the docile obedience of a well-disciplined people who, having full confidence in their leaders, obeyed blindly every command. And, as time passed, the discipline inherited from feudal times was intensified by a new discipline springing from the official cult of Emperor worship and Shinto revived in modern guise. Of course the Westernizing process was furthered by the national traits of eager curiosity and liking for foreign novelties which the Japanese have always displayed. Nevertheless, mere curiosity and imitative ability are not the basic reasons for Japan's amazingly rapid material transformation—as is so often supposed.

What, then, are the emotional and spiritual foundations of the "Meiji Era," begun some sixty years ago? As already remarked, they are an interlocking duality: Emperor worship and Shintoism. Let us try to comprehend their significance, for upon them rests the whole ponderous superstructure of present-day Japan.

Shinto originated as a simple nature-worship in which the elements and the heavenly bodies were personified as gods. Homage was also paid to the spirits of certain mythological heroes, come to be regarded as semi-divine. When Buddhism appeared, by way of China, it partly absorbed Shinto; at least, the two cults got along amicably together. During the intense cultural development under the Tokugawa Shoguns, Shinto was revived as a separate religion, this being one phase of the trend toward emphasizing all that was purely Japanese which then prevailed. However, Shinto remained a simple, creedless nature and ancestor worship.

Such was the cult which the men of the Meiji Era chose as their instrument for spiritually energizing and disciplining the Japanese people for the great task which lay ahead. And they went about it in a very ingenious way. With their usual insight, the moulders of modern Japan saw that if they made Shinto the state religion they would offend a still-prevalent Buddhism, to say nothing of the small but growing Christian minority. Therefore they explicitly denied that Shinto was a religion; rather, was it the normal expression of Japanese national and racial unity. So Buddhists and Christians could bow before a Shinto shrine as conscientiously as, in the West, men of all faiths salute the flag. It was just the proper, patriotic thing to do. That was the official explanation. Meanwhile, Shinto was put wholly under official control—though in an entirely non-religious guise. In fact, all Shinto shrines are managed by a Bureau in the Department of Home Affairs.

Shinto's political usefulness lay in its being an ideal medium for Emperor-worship. We have already sketched the mythology of Old Japan and its intimate connection with the imperial dynasty. The Emperor had always been revered as of divine origin, but during the Shogunate, he was a remote, shadowy personage with little or no practical influence upon the popular consciousness. The Restoration of 1868 revived the Emperor's ancient political power, whilst Shinto exalted him to an almost boundless spiritual authority: Japan's legendary past was treated as historic fact. The Japanese people were bidden to revere their reigning Emperor as literally divine, sprung from the Sun-Goddess, whose immediate descendant, Jimmu Tenno, had founded the sacred dynasty to which the greatness and peculiar excellence of the Japanese people were primarily due.

This was amazingly clever politico-religious sleight-of-hand. As an English writer pungently remarks: "It is analogous to the situation which would exist if a European government officialized Genesis I, connected Adam and Eve by a genealogical tree to the Royal Family, and used this invention as a 'unificator for the thoughts of the people.'"[3]

No matter how absurdly unscientific all this may appear to Western eyes, the fact remains that *it worked.* More than half a century of intensive Shintoism and Emperor-worship has molded every phase of Japanese life and penetrated to the very marrow of the Japanese people. A patriotic devotion boundless in its loyalty and self-sacrifice; an exalted sense of national and racial greatness; an implicit faith in a divine mission, fanatically intense and kept ever at white heat—such have been the fruits.

These are strong statements on our part, yet a few excerpts from typical Japanese pronouncements on the subject[4] will show that we have not exaggerated. Here is how Japanese youth is indoctrinated. All Japanese school-teaching emphasizes the divinity of the Emperor, the peculiar wonders of Japanese patriotism, and "Yamato damashil"—soul of the Japanese or "Yamato" race. From earliest childhood, Japanese are taught to believe that they are the elect of

3 Stephen King-Hall, *Western Civilization and the Far East,* p. 287 (London, 1924).

4 Pronouncements, of course, by Japanese to a purely Japanese audience. Japanese statements for foreign consumption are, naturally, very different in tenor. The Japanese usually try to conceal or minimize Emperor-worship and other phases of their patriotic cult; and since the Japanese language is well known only to a few foreigners, concealment is easy. The quotations which follow in the text are taken from one of the few authoritative foreign works on the subject. This is a richly documented monograph by the Reverend D. C. Holton, entitled, "The Political Philosophy of Modern Shinto," and published in Volume 49, Part 2, of the *Transactions of the Asiatic Society of Japan.*

mankind: *The Yamato Race,* of divine origin; literally *Seed of the Sun*. The standard *History for Middle Schools,* for instance, descants upon "Our Empire of Great Japan, with an Imperial Line from above unbroken from time immemorial and with its subjects below matchless in loyalty and patriotism from ancient times down to the present"; and it concludes: "Such a national character is without parallel throughout the world."

Another educator writes: "The absolute authority of the Emperor constitutes the basis of our national system. It is the foundation on which the nation stands. If there were no Emperor, there would be no nation. Without him there would be no subjects, and our territory would cease to exist . . . He is god of light; he is manifest god. His authority is unique. He is the absolute ruler determined by the Divine Ancestor."

Still stronger meat is fed to the adult mind. Consider what the Japanese scholar, Doctor Kato, has to say: "Just as our country possesses in the towering peak of Mount Fuji a natural beauty unsurpassed in all the world, so this country . . . is not unworthy of the name, 'The Land of the Gods,' peerless on the earth."

The exalted mission of this peerless land and people is not left in doubt. As Doctor Kakehi puts it: "The Emperors of our country are equipped with qualities without parallel in the world . . .

"The center of this world is Japan. From this center we must expand this Great Spirit throughout the world. There are voices which cry: 'Great Japan is the Land of the Gods!' Nor is this to be wondered at. It is a true statement of fact. It is a matter of course. The expansion of Japan throughout the world and the elevation of the entire world into the Land of the Gods is the urgent business of the present, and again, it is our eternal and unchanging object."

In similar vein, Doctor Uesugi Shinkichi thus contrasts the post-war wreckage of the West with Japan's saving task: "It is now most clear that the salvation of the entire human race is the mission of our Empire. Nations are now in a condition of disorder . . .

"They are fallen into the pit. The hell of fighting and bloodshed has appeared on earth. When we observe such conditions, there is not one of our people who does not believe that, if they only had our Emperor as theirs, they would not come to such extremity.

Our people, through the benevolent virtue of the Emperors, have attained a national constitution that is without parallel in the world . . . Now, if all the human race should come to look up to the virtue of our Emperor and should come to live under that influence, then there would be light for the future of humanity. Thus the world can be saved from destruction. Thus life can be lived within the realms of goodness and beauty. Of a truth, great is the mission of our nation."

These words, so extravagant-sounding to Western ears, have been quoted, not in condemnation or ridicule, but in order to portray as vividly as possible the prevailing Japanese state of mind. They likewise render intelligible highly imperialistic utterances of Japanese writers or military men which find their way into Western print. What seem to us mere flights of jingo rhetoric may then be understood in the setting of their mental and emotional background.

This applies likewise to the founders of modem Japan. We must not regard them as cynical schemers, cunningly devising propaganda which they personally disbelieved. As a matter of fact, their faith in the greatness of Japan and the Yamato Race was as firm as that of their successors. What they did was to emphasize everything which might weld their countrymen m the bonds of an iron discipline and steel their souls to a tempered hardness fit for the ordeal which lay before them.

Therein the Elder Statesmen were not deceived, for Japan's position was then a terrifying one. Rudely shaken out of complete seclusion, this hermit-nation suddenly confronted an aggressive, predatory world equipped with irresistible power. Even the Chinese giant had just been beaten to his knees by the encroaching West. Above the sea-girt horizon, the Elder Statesmen could reach this warning, etched in letters of fire: *Adapt quickly, or suffer China's fate!*

That was the challenge flung in the teeth of a people who had never been conquered;[5] a people to whom an alien yoke would be worse than death. To avert that disaster, no measures were too drastic

5 The only serious attempt to conquer Japan was made by the Mongol Emperors in the thirteenth century. The repulse of the mighty Mongol army and fleet, and their subsequent destruction in a typhoon is a dramatic story strikingly like England's defeat of the Spanish Armada.

and any method was sanctified. So the Men of Meiji deliberately galvanized their people to frantic energy while controlling every move by exerting a power almost hypnotic.

Those were great men doing a great work. And they succeeded. Japan not only escaped the fate of China; she became a "Great Power"; respected—even feared, by the mightiest nations of the West. Within a trifle over half a century, Japan was transformed. Machine industry, world trade, science and technology, the art of war—every aspect of our mechanistic civilization, was eagerly seized upon. Japan was duly Westernized, on schedule and "according to plan." The Elder Statesmen might rest in peace. Their work was done.

Modern Japan presents the strange spectacle of a people trying hard to work the whole apparatus of a complex alien civilization while clinging resolutely to old institutions and ideals. This is an attempt to merge two radically unlike lines of development. The effort has been strenuous, but the results are far from satisfactory. In consequence, present-day Japan is caught in a series of dilemmas from which profound wisdom and deep insight can alone extricate her. Westernism must come to be understood in its essence as well as its externals.

That Japan's Elder Statesmen should have failed to grasp the inwardness of a hastily imported civilization is only what we might expect. But that their successors should have made so little headway is disturbing; it suggests a shortcoming in the Japanese make-up already indicated by earlier contacts with foreign cultures. As an English writer remarks: "The Japanese are not, as a people, given to philosophic speculation. They are sharp observers, deeply interested in the outward shape of things, so that all the external manifestations of Western civilization filled them, in the sixteenth century, and again in the nineteenth, with a restless curiosity and a determination to master the new knowledge. But they have felt no keen desire to explore the intellectual dominions of the West. Their minds never seem to have had a metaphysical bent."[6]

The unfortunate consequences produced by such lack of deeper understanding are set forth by the same observer, when he says:

6 "The Tragedy of Japan," *op. cit.*

"This explains much in Japanese life today. There is little or no blending of civilizations; but a confusion, even a conflict. The result is a kaleidoscopic mixture which, even among so hardy a people, produces an almost intolerable strain.

In the home, there is the struggle between the family system and the individualism which is encouraged by competitive industry and trade. In school and university, there is a struggle to reconcile the claims of the native culture with Western learning; and the burden upon students has tragic consequences. In government, there is the perpetual difficulty of getting results out of a machine on the Western model run by operatives whose life has a predominantly Eastern background."[7]

The most ominous aspect of the matter is that these strains and stresses, instead of lessening, grow more and more acute with the passage of time. The fundamental disharmony between Shinto and science, between Emperor-worship and parliamentary government, between the "world-mission" of the Yamato Race and a normally conducted foreign policy, becomes more strident with each succeeding decade.

The vast majority of Japanese believe that to renounce even partially the legacy of the past would fatally weaken the foundations of their national life and bring down the whole edifice of modern Japan in crumbling ruin.

Yet this same edifice already creaks and groans so distressingly from the reciprocal tensions of its ill-assorted materials that it threatens to break asunder even though the foundations remain untouched. Here is the spiritual and cultural dilemma behind those obvious problems which are usually considered by themselves instead of in connection with the root-problem from which they all arise. Bearing this in mind, let us survey Japan's present situation at home and abroad.

From the very start, Westernism upset Japan's former economic equilibrium. Old Japan was quite sufficient unto itself. Save for a trickle of foreign commerce through a single Dutch trading-post, Japan lived in a closed economic circle, on an agricultural basis with a small volume of fine quality goods produced by handicraftsmen.

---

7 *Ibid.*

This nicely adjusted balance Westernization promptly 'shattered. One of the first things the Meiji régime did was to bring in machine industry. Textile factories soon dotted the landscape. Industrial centers sprang up like magic, crowded with a new working class mobilized from ex-craftsmen or peasants lured from the land.

Like everything else, this rapid industrial development was planned and directed by a few master-minds, molding a disciplined and docile people. There were no waste motions; no hit-or-miss experiments. The government either financed industry itself or enlisted the wealth of a few merchant families already grown rich in feudal times. That is why modern Japan's economic life has always been dominated by a handful of merchant-clans like the Mitsui and Mitsubishi. Japanese industry at once acquired a surprising degree of efficiency. The scanty store of native capital was used to the best advantage, and foreign borrowings were thereby kept within safe bounds. As for organization methods, they leaped ahead of the times. "Before cartels were ever heard of, Japan had them. Before rationalization became a new word in the language, the lexicon of Japanese business had a place for it. Before the state began to dominate the economic life of the West, the Japanese Government, with its subsidy system, was at the head and front of Japan's economic life. Japan, in the words of Mr. Arno S. Pearse, head of the Lancashire Cotton Federation, developed into one huge trust."[8]

Foreign critics often assert that this highly centralized industrial system rests upon the backs of oppressed, "sweated" workers. Now it is true that Japanese wage-scales are very low, judged by Western standards. It is likewise true that bad working conditions and abuses exist. Japanese labor leaders have long agitated for reforms, and bitter strikes have taken place. Nevertheless, the labor situation must be understood in Japanese terms.

The Japanese worker is content with very little and has an ingrained aptitude for continuous labor which amazes foreign observers As a French resident of Japan puts it: "Even in the enervating heat of summer the industrious Japanese keep on working. Their life is regulated by a slow but constant rhythm that would exhaust a European in a few days.. . . Rising at the break of dawn, the Japanese

8 From an editorial in *The Christian Science Monitor,* May 8, 1932.

work far into the night without stopping. Labor and life are so intimately interwoven that they can never be separated."[9]

Relations between workers and employers are still tinged with the old feudal attitude of mutual loyalties and responsibilities, while capital and labor are alike inspired by a common devotion to "Great Japan." Not long ago, as part of the great drive to capture world trade, the Japanese textile workers were officially informed that it was their patriotic duty to take a drastic wage-cut. The cut was taken without a murmur.

The importance of such "moral imponderables" in Japanese trade is set forth by, a prominent Osaka textile manufacturer, who writes: "One of the fundamental factors which enabled the Japanese cotton industry to carry out substantial improvements is spiritual. It can be described as the Nippon Spirit. And this spirit is peculiar to Japan alone."[10] He goes on to tell how this Nippon Spirit is maintained and refreshed by systematic instruction. In his own factory, for instance, he gives operatives free lessons in feudal ethics, together with "music, religion, and etiquette."

All this proves that Japan's commercial successes are due to several factors, only one of which (her recently depreciated currency) is a temporary advantage, the rest being long-term or even permanent in character. Certainly, "cheap labor" is far too simple an explanation for the amazing growth of Japanese foreign trade during the last three years. At the very depth of the world-depression, when other nations saw their exports dwindle away, Japan launched an intensive, world-wide sales-campaign.

Practically every land on earth was bombarded with Japanese products—mostly consumers goods of the cheaper grades. Japan did not hesitate to "carry coals to Newcastle." For that was just what she did by underselling home-made electric-light bulbs in the U. S. A., watches in Switzerland, and cotton goods in Britain. Imagine the consternation at Manchester, England, the old textile citadel, when its own retail shops displayed Japanese socks at thruppence (six cents) a pair—much less than the same articles could be

9 Helene Iswolsky, "Everyday Japan," *La Correspondant;* translated in *The Living Age,* September, 1932.

10 Koyata Yamamoto in the *Osaka Mainichi,* May 31, 1934.

manufactured and sold on the spot! No wonder that a French textile manufacturer exclaimed: "Even if I stole my raw material and did not pay my employees anything, I could not compete at such prices!"[11]

These commercial attacks on the industrialized nations of Europe and America were, of course, limited to certain lines of trade. In low-standard lands, however, Japan delivered a grand assault all along the line. In our survey of Latin America we noted impressive Japanese commercial victories as the climax of plans laid many years before; and throughout Asia and even Africa it is much the same story. One or two examples of Japanese sales-technique in the Orient will reveal the resourcefulness of their methods.

Two years ago, India was suddenly scoured by a corps of Japanese peddlers, selling their wares from village to village and from door to door. Peddlers deluxe they were, too; for they wore neat khaki uniforms, spoke several Indian languages, and proved to be college men specially trained for their jobs. Naturally they could sell much cheaper than British or even native Indian storekeepers could possibly do, while no ordinary trade restrictions could touch them because they were dealing, not with jobbers or retailers, but directly with the ultimate consumer—the common peoples.

Equally striking are Japanese sales-tactics in the Philippines. Here they turned a trick on redoubtable old John Chinaman himself. For generations most of the small storekeepers in the Philippines have been Chinese. There prices were reasonable, but the improvident Filipinos usually had no ready money and the Chinese extended credit only at usurious rates—which made them heartily disliked. Along came the Japanese and established chain-stores combining still lower prices with easier credit-terms. Result: the Chinese storekeepers are being driven out wholesale, while the Japanese have captured Filipino trade and Filipino goodwill for good measure.

Japan's world-wide trade offensive in depression times naturally aroused furious protests on every side. Manufacturers and merchants everywhere demanded that tariffs be raised and quotas stiffened against Japanese goods. Parliamentary chambers rang

---

11 Quoted by Max Rudert in his article, "The Yellow Trade Menace," Prague, *Neue Weitbuchne;* translated in *The Living Age,* February, 1934.

with speeches against the "Commercial Yellow Peril," and measures were drafted to hinder Japanese trade.

But Japan had an ace up her sleeve. When Britain, for instance, undertook to curtail Japanese trade throughout the Empire, Japan threatened to take no more Indian cotton or Australian wool, buying in South America instead. This proved to be a trump card. Australia and India begged Britain to call off the trade-war. Also, Hindus, Africans, and other low-standard colonial populations pointedly remarked that they saw no reason why they should be forced to buy British goods when Japanese goods were so much cheaper. The upshot has been a series of compromises like that whereby Japanese trade with India is liberally ratioed and Japan agrees to take a generous amount of Indian raw cotton. Anglo-Japanese trade relations are thus at least provisionally regulated. Elsewhere, however, trade conflicts arising from Japan's export campaign go on unchecked. Careful analyses of the situation[12] lead one to think that Japan's great trade-offensive has not yet reached its climax, and that so long as she continues to undersell all competitors her foreign trade will expand.

Yet these commercial triumphs may be dearly bought in the long run. Ruthless undercutting spells terrific effort and stern self-sacrifice, especially on the part of the Japanese working classes. It is one more phase of that cumulative overstrain visible for many years. Japan's urban population has long shown signs of physical deterioration; a constant stream of industrial recruits from the countryside is needed to furnish enough healthy, vigorous workers. Furthermore, Japan is fast depleting her slender reserves of coal, iron, and copper, thus becoming increasingly dependent upon imported raw materials.

"This," maintains an economic analyst, "will weaken Japan in the long run, just as its excessive exports will weaken it. Germany and England never exported more than a quarter of their total products even in periods of the most intense competition, while the U. S. A. never exported more than 10 or 12 per cent. How long will it be before the foundations crumble beneath such an excessive

12 See especially *Foreign Policy Reports*, Volume 10, Number 16; dated October 20, 1934, and containing detailed statistical analysis entitled "Japan's Trade Expansion."

export trade, which can be maintained only by the most fantastic exploitation of the native population and the destruction of their own best powers? Such a mass-attack on world trade contains the seeds of its own destruction. Trouble also threatens in the political and military sphere . . . Yet can Japan draw back? It is like a boiler in which the pressure is constantly rising. In ten years its population has increased from 56,000,000 to 66,000,000. With the aid of the state, a huge industrial plant is being built up and fantastic exports are being promoted. What will happen when Japan must stop? Can she stop without having a social earthquake shatter the overpopulated island? An old Japanese legend reads: 'He who rides a tiger cannot dismount.'"[13]

Overpopulation! That is the driving-force behind Japan's frantic quest for foreign markets, just as it lies behind her heavy armaments and her aggressive foreign policy. Japan is a relatively small country. Its total area[14] is slightly less than that of the State of California and only half as large again as that of the British Isles. Furthermore, Japan is a mountainous land, poor in natural resources. Yet this island-group is today literally jammed with people breeding at a phenomenal rate.

This is directly due to Westernization. In our general survey of the Orient[15] we saw that the impact of the West everywhere tended to increase the population. In Japan this trend has gone farthest. Self-contained old Japan had a population stabilized at about 30,000,000, its naturally high birth-rate being balanced by an equally high death-rate due to frequent epidemics, periodic famines, and the widespread practice of abortion supplemented by infanticide.

Westernization radically altered this situation by enabling a vastly larger number of persons to make a living. "New Japan was a land where two people could live better than one had lived before, and live better. Cities grew and factories multiplied. No longer had the farms to provide for every child born on them.. . . The new industries were employing the new millions as fast as they left

13 Rudert, *op. cit.*

14 That is to say, the area of Japan proper, excluding recent territorial acquisitions such as Formosa and Korea, inhabited by non-Japanese populations.

15 Part II, Chapter I, of this book.

school. The new industrial system needed millions of workers and the workers were born.. . . Up until now, with all respect to the writers who for twenty years have been predicting an explosion, the population problem of Japan has been an academic one. By three good tests—food, employment, and savings—the wealth of Japan has been increasing more rapidly than population."[16]

Today, however, the Nemesis of overpopulation stares Japan in the face. Japan is literally "full-up." Despite intensive agriculture, her countryside is saturated. Immigration is a dead issue; no foreign country will accept Japanese by the million—and nothing less would suffice. The colonial dependencies have likewise proved a vain hope; Koreans and Chinese under-live Japanese settlers—and, anyhow, Korea and Manchuria are too cold, and Formosa is too hot for the nicely adjusted Japanese climatic taste. One major outlet alone remains—more industrialization. The machine must, somehow, be made to ensure the rising generation its daily bread; or, rather, its daily fish and rice.

The newcomers are so many—and so many, many more are destined to come! From a base-line of approximately 30,000,000, the population-curve has shot up to dizzy heights. As late as 1880, the graph showed only 36,000,000. By 1914, an ever-quickening birth-rate combined with the life-saving efforts of modern science had brought the population up to nearly 50,000,000. What was to be done? The Japanese could not live by taking in one another's washing. They had to look abroad for the means to support even those then alive. So Japan continued to industrialize herself and became increasingly dependent upon foreign trade.

The Great War was a godsend. Japan's foreign trade grew by leaps and bounds. When peace ended the war-time boom, Japan concentrated on China, logically her chief market. How vital that had become to Japan's economic life was seen in 1931, when the great Chinese boycott temporarily disrupted Chino-.Japanese commercial relations. Then it was that Japan went off the gold standard and, using her devalued yen as the spearhead, launched her world-wide export drive.

16 Hugh Byas, "Japan's Record Crop of Babies," *New York Times Magazine*, December 10, 1933.

By almost superhuman exertions, Japan just manages to give a meager living to her present population—now swollen to 66,000,000. But how about the future?—perhaps the very near future? The Japanese are now spawning at the rate of over 1,000,000 per year. That is unheard of. Even "Mother India" cannot beat that record. Japan's present death-rate is lower than that of many Western nations. Indeed, her birth-rate also begins to fall, for the Japanese are commencing to restrict their families through later marriage and to some slight extent by contraceptive birth-control. Yet the restrictive process will presumably be so gradual that it looks as though the population cannot be stabilized much under twenty years, by which time the Japanese should number somewhere between 90,000,000 and 100,000,000. How are all those extra millions to be taken care of through further extensions of foreign trade in a world ridden by economic nationalism; threatened with new wars and revolutions?

Yet unless those coming millions can gain a livelihood, Japan must either suffocate or explode—with the betting-odds heavily on the latter alternative, because the Japanese are not minded to lie down and quietly starve. "A flood of babies, with insufficient food and work, will be a social tidal wave, and our Kellogg Pacts, Geneva Covenants, and Nine-Power Treaties so many King Canutes. A nation of 66,000,000 people; literates, voters, newspaper readers, already partly organized for capitalist production, cannot be figuratively assigned to a cell, on bread and water. If existing economic frontiers are closed to her goods, Japan will burst open others There is no way of providing for these children except by employing them to manufacture goods and selling them, chiefly in Asia. If economic nationalism means that the outlets will be blocked, then it is scarcely worthwhile troubling the Disarmament Conference further."[17]

Such is Japan's dilemma of overpopulation. And it is a problem, not of the future, but of the here and now. Its most pressing aspect, however, is visible, not in the cities but over the countryside. Japan's export drive has temporarily given the industrial workers jobs. Those jobs are, for the most part, so poorly paid that the laboring masses live on a sub marginal scale which threatens to undermine their health and vigor. Nevertheless they eat—after a fashion.

17 *Ibid.*

Japan's rural population presents the real difficulty. With few new factory jobs for the rising peasant generation, population literally piles up on the farms. In consequence, "the economic plight of the Japanese farmer has become intolerable. You see him these summer days, in a temperature above ninety degrees, toiling from dawn till dark in stinking mud to rear by hand the rice which, because of its high value, is the only crop he can afford to grow on his minute patch of land. The social problem in Japan is not found in the cities, but on those tiny green farms, cultivated to the last inch like gardens, where 48 per cent of the population live. The French peasant is thrifty, but the Japanese farmer has less than one-sixth of the land the French peasant has, and he has four or five children instead of the Frenchman's average of two."[18]

How bad conditions have become in parts of rural Japan is revealed by the following poignant lines: "In several prefectures, peasants are living on roots and herbs. There is wholesale selling of girls; in some districts there are many villages with no more girls of marriageable age. Before reaching that point, some peasants burn their houses in the secret hope of collecting insurance, but there have been so many fires that the insurance companies refuse to pay. Families are dissolving. Husbands and wives are separating; children are abandoning their parents."[19]

Present-day Japan is thus stung to action by the sharpest of life's instincts—that of self-preservation. Now add to this primeval urge a burning faith in "Great Japan" and the peculiar excellence of the Yamato Race; add to that again the Bushido code glorifying self-sacrifice and welcoming heroic death, and we can realize the fierce longing in Japanese hearts to cut the Gordian knot of their difficulties and hew out a great destiny with the Samurai sword. Against that grim emotional background, the trend of Japanese foreign relations can best be appreciated.

The Yamato Race, led by its God-Emperors, should surely be designed for a glorious future. That future is variously glimpsed according to the fertility of Japanese imaginations. Mastery of China, overlordship of Asia, even "world-dominion"—such are the

18 "Unrest in Japan," *New York Times,* September 18, 1932.

19 Japonicus, "Will Japan Crash?" *Le Suis Partout* (Paris); translated in *The Living Age,* September, 1932.

ascending flights of fancy in which many sons of Nippon indulge. No one can justly accuse the Japanese of reticence in these matters. So often have they discussed them, so frankly are their grandiose ambitions set forth in print, that the goals are clearly revealed. The library of Nippon's imperialist literature is large, and constantly increases.[20]

Yet those ambitious goals are, for the most part, distant possibilities, realizable only under favorable circumstances which may never come to pass. That much, all Japanese save a few jingo hot-heads will readily admit. To be sure, with characteristic thoroughness, Japan makes ready to grasp contingent opportunities. We saw this in our survey of Latin America, and the same is true of the Philippines, the Dutch Indies, Eastern Siberia, and China's crumbling borderlands through Mongolia clear to Turkestan. But those are side-issues. Of themselves, they will not lead to decisive action.

The keynote of Japan's foreign policy is her relations with China. That huge neighbor is at once a potential Nemesis and the gateway to boundless opportunity. A truly strong China would automatically dwarf Japan into a mere satellite, dependent in every way. On the other hand, a China dominated and exploited by Japan would multiply the scope of Nippon's power.

Acutely conscious of these alternatives, every Japanese, high or low, is inflexibly determined to forge over China not necessarily complete domination but at least an effective measure of control. In Japanese eyes, such control appears from every angle to be a vital necessity. Take the economic aspect alone. "China is Japan's greatest potential market. It is nearby, and with its vast population has the possibility—although not the certainty—of developing almost limitless purchasing power. Anyone with pad and pencil can figure out the astonishing totals in trade with 450,000,000 people. An enthusiastic Californian recently showed that prosperity could be well-nigh restored to the Pacific coast if every Chinese could be persuaded to buy just one California prune each week!

20 The earlier phases of this imperialistic literature are to be found analyzed, with outstanding citations, in the author's book, *The Rising Tide of Color*, Chapter II. For similar treatment of more recent aspects, see his book, *Lonely America*, Part 2, Chapter V (New York, 1932).

Although China will develop factories of its own and will gradually manufacture such goods as cheap-grade cotton cloth in increasing volume, there will still be an ample basis for Japanese trade, provided China should not attempt to exclude Japanese goods by boycotts, quotas, or prohibitive tariffs. In competition with Western countries, Japan will have the advantage of nearness, similarity of language, acquaintance with the needs and tastes of the Chinese, and the ability to manufacture cheaply and efficiently."[21] Even if Japan should lose most of her foreign markets through the rise of economic nationalism, a stable, prosperous, friendly China might well prove to be Japan's commercial salvation.

A stable, prosperous, friendly China. That is what Japan wants. She has no idea of "conquering" China, still less of trying to turn its people into imitation Japanese. But Japan does not intend to see China sink into chaos or become the cat's paw of other Powers; neither will she tolerate the establishment of a Chinese Government definitely anti-Japanese in character.

If this last statement seems to imply an unwarranted interference with China's national sovereignty, remember that Japan denies that China is as yet truly a nation, capable of conducting itself in a normal way. In Japanese eyes, China is little more than an amorphous mass whose future evolution is highly uncertain. And the Japanese are resolved that China shall not develop into something which would spell Japan's ruin.

So much for the long-term factor. Meanwhile, China seems likely to go to pieces. Therefore, no matter what happens in China proper, Japan keeps tight hold on China's outlying dependency, Manchuria—a vast region which Japan regards as vital to herself for both economic and strategic reasons. On that, all Japanese are whole-heartedly agreed. Viscount Ishii announced a basic principle of Japanese foreign policy when he stated: "Today, as thirty years ago, Manchuria is the key to our security."

The Japanese viewpoint regarding both the Manchurian issue and the larger Chinese problem has never been more ably set forth than in an official memorandum drafted by Yosuke Matsuoka, Japan's leading spokesman at Geneva during the great diplomatic

21 George H. Blakeslee, *Conflicts of Policy in the Far East, p. 55* (New York, 1934).

controversy which ended in Japan's withdrawal from the League of Nations in the spring of 1933. The outstanding portions of this Memorandum read:

"That China needs reorganization, we entirely agree. But we know better than to think that the task of bringing order out of chaos in a country larger than all Europe can be accomplished by any means within the scope and power of the League of Nations. Force, and only force, can bring such a project to fruition. And we have little hope that any Power or group of Powers is ready to undertake the first essential; namely, the suppression of the powerful and numerous semi-bandit war-lords, whose armies total between 2,000,000 and 3,000,000 men . . . The Lytton Commission's proposal of an international gendarmerie for the suppression of banditry and the restoration of order in Manchuria was only less visionary . . . Japan could not and would not countenance any internationalization of Manchuria. The solution we have found is a better one.

"The National Government of China is a name and an aspiration; not an existing, controlling authority. The National Government controls but a few of the eighteen provinces of China proper, and holds them only by force. Remove that force, and the civil officials flee for their lives for the safety of the foreign-controlled treaty ports. The Communist hordes control a greater extent of territory. The remaining provinces are ruled by independent war-lords. China is not a nation, in the sense that you and I understand the meaning of that word . . .

"In Manchuria, we have taken nothing from the Chinese people that they ever possessed . . . Manchuria was never, in all history, governed by China . . . Manchuria was brought into the Chinese Empire by the Manchus, who crossed the Great Wall and conquered China about three hundred years ago. From that time down to the beginning of the present century it was kept as a Manchu domain, a private estate appanage of the Manchu dynasty. Migration into Manchuria was denied to the Chinese. Only a few succeeded in crossing the Wall and penetrating the sparsely settled territory. Not until sometime after Russia had obtained, in 1898, from the Manchus what were, in fact, dominating rights in Manchuria, were Chinese permitted to enter freely.

"To the rights which Russia held, . . . Japan succeeded seven years later. As a result of Japan's, and not China's sacrifices, the sovereignty of the territory was returned to the Manchu dynasty in 1905. But even the Manchus did not subsequently govern it. The ruler of the land was Chang Tso-lin . . . a bandit chief who rose to power by superior military and political acumen . . . The old Chang Tso-lin had twice proclaimed the independence of Manchuria. He dealt with foreign Powers as an independent authority. The younger Chang continued to maintain this independence. He made an alliance, however, with Chiang Kai-shek, the chief of China's so-called National Government, and agreed to fly the national flag in Manchuria.

"Both Changs, father and son, and some of the generals under them, were Chinese and not Manchus. But that a group of Chinese bandits became so powerful that they could make themselves masters over Manchuria does not mean that China ruled Manchuria. Nor do the people of Manchuria want their former Chinese rulers to return."

This excellent statement deserves our close attention. It sets forth matters often ignored or never known in the West. Of course, Mr. Matsuoka is making Japan's case, so he leaves out certain items—notably the fact that Manchuria's population is today nine-tenths Chinese. Nevertheless, his interpretations of Manchuria's historic relation to China and of the present state of China itself are both substantially correct. We Westerners, and especially we Americans, must try to understand the realities of the Chinese situation; therefore we must stop taking at face-value the assertions of Western-educated Chinese who, when they use words like "Republic" and "Nation," merely parrot lessons learned from ourselves.

Japan has followed a consistent policy in China for the past twenty years. Basically this policy has never varied since the outbreak of the Great War spelled a permanent weakening of Western power in Asia and thereby gave Japan a golden opportunity to establish her primacy over the Far East. From the Twenty-one Demands to the conquest of Jehol, Japan's attitude toward China has been one of forceful insistence on certain essentials, coupled with conciliation in other matters. Just now it looks as though this policy would succeed—at least for a time. Caught between the Communist devil and Japanese pressure from beyond the sea, Chiang Kai-shek and his colleagues of the National Government, including the big treaty-port bankers, seem to be getting ready to make a deal with Japan. They apparently believe that China's supreme need is the establishment of at least a measure of internal peace and order. This cannot be even attempted in face of Japanese hostility and can succeed only with Japanese backing. Therefore it would not be surprising to see a definite Chino-Japanese understanding, including official recognition of Manchukuo and tacit acceptance of Japanese political and economic leadership. Whether the National Government could hold the nationalist-minded elements throughout China to this bargain remains to be seen.

Let us assume for the sake of argument that the bargain is made and lived up to. For the time being, Japan will have triumphed. But in the long run her prospects are not so bright. China's fundamental grievances will remain, while the stronger and more unified she becomes, the faster will nationalistic feeling grow amongst her people. Only by the most tactful, considerate diplomacy can Japan avoid affronting this rising nationalism and focusing it against herself. But those are precisely the qualities in which Japanese foreign policy has always been conspicuously lacking. Sharp observers, the Japanese can size up correctly a given situation, but long-range estimates based on a comprehension of alien states of mind are quite another matter. Japanese cannot put themselves mentally in the other fellow's place—very possibly because the average Japanese is so utterly devoid of a sense of humor. And lack of such comprehension breeds impatience, inclining them to compulsion instead of persistence in conciliatory methods. Their record in Korea shows this. Materially they have done a great deal for Korea, just as they are now doing in Manchukuo. But they have not won the hearts of the Korean people, who remain chronically refractory to Japanese rule.

These temperamental shortcomings will tend to array against Japan a whole series of moral "imponderables." The farther Japanese arms and diplomacy extend her supremacy, the graver the problem of subject yet unreconciled populations will become. The Japanese do not seem to possess the subtle genius for empire. The long-headed tolerance of the Romans and the British instinct for illogical compromise are alike lacking. On all sides Japan inspires fear and distrust. How egregiously she has failed to win the confidence of other Asiatic peoples! Her preferred championship of the "Pan-Asia" movement leaves them cold; they have scant wish to be freed from Western tutelage, only to be subjected to the harsher domination of a Great Japan. If the Yamato Race be indeed destined to attain world-dominion, it must do so virtually single-handed, without the backing of loyal allies or faithful friends. And that is a deed which has never yet been done.

Even to dominate the Far East, Japan needs a high degree of domestic harmony and stability. Yet we have seen that present-day Japan betrays an increasing unbalance and disharmony which, in turn, cause all sorts of internal stresses and strains.

It comes down to this: Modern Japan is not an organic growth; it is a magnificent synthetic product. In contact with it, one has a perpetual sense of tension; an intuition of subterranean forces, held down, yet always there. An explosion is possible—and such a cataclysm would presumably be as volcanic as one of the frightful earthquakes to which this geologically unstable country is perpetually exposed. For all its imposing appearance, present-day Japan may suddenly and dramatically pass away.

Unbalance; sharpened tensions caused by maladjustment between old and new factors, have long revealed the approach of a major crisis in Japan's national life. So deep-going are present disharmonies, so widespread current unrest, that the climax of this waxing crisis seems at hand. Unless the situation unexpectedly eases, the breaking-point cannot be far away.

What form the climax will take is as yet uncertain. It may be a foreign war. Again, it may be revolution, not merely political but also economic, social, even idealistic and cultural in character. One thing is sure: Japan is stirred to the depths; the soul of its people cries out for a solution of those varied dilemmas and contradictions which have plagued it for so many years. It demands either the fulfillment of hopes inspired by the Meiji Era or a second transformation, equally sweeping but on other lines. Once more we should emphasize that, though the coming climax may be precipitated by some political or economic happening, the real issue lies in the realm of ideas and ideals.

Japan's present abnormal condition is strikingly shown by the state of its business and domestic politics. These conditions hark back to the Westernizing transformation begun some seventy years ago.

Old Japan was agricultural and feudal—much like Europe in our Middle Ages. The social structure was topped by an aristocratic noble and knightly class. Beneath them stood the peasantry—but a peasantry enjoying a considerable measure of economic security and social esteem. The Japanese peasant was not a serf; he was an upstanding man pursuing an honorable calling. Far lower in the social scale were the merchants and traders. A peasant, if sufficiently brave and intelligent, might become a Samurai and wear two swords. A merchant, with much gold but scant dignity or sense of honor, could not aspire to such an elevation.

The Meiji Era opened to the merchant class the door of opportunity. Yet they entered with due humility. When the Emperor, deeming them the fittest instruments, commanded them to head new financial and industrial developments, they loyally placed their talents and their wealth at his service. Great was their reward. Economic power and business profits remained concentrated in a relatively small group of mercantile clan-families. This group, headed by those financial-industrial giants, Mitsui and Mitsubishi, today own or control most of Japan's fluid capital and a large proportion of the national wealth in every form. Thus the humble merchant class of old Japan has blossomed forth into a proud plutocracy.

The rising plutocracy long since discovered useful allies and servitors in another new class—the politicians. An Imperial grant of parliamentary institutions as a logical part of the Westernizing process naturally required men to work them. They were staffed mainly by townsmen, especially by young men trained on Western lines for new professions like the law. These youngsters were ambitious but usually short of cash, and parliamentary politics was an expensive game. What more natural than that High Finance and Big Business should graciously aid those whose friendship might be very worthwhile? So relations between plutocrats and politicians became ever closer, until it was common knowledge that the two major parties in Parliament were subsidized—the Seiyukai Party by the Mitsuis and the Minseito Party by the Mitsubishis, respectively. In the present House, for instance, those two parties hold 415 of the 458 seats, the overwhelming majority of the legislature thus being clearly under plutocratic control. Furthermore, Japanese politics are notoriously corrupt. Jobbery, bribery, and a series of nasty scandals have discredited the politicians as a class in public estimation.

So long as Japan was gaining in wealth and general wellbeing, plutocratic encroachments and political corruption might regretfully be tolerated. When, however, poverty began to stalk in town and country, and when the nation's future was gravely beclouded, many Japanese asked themselves how much longer such things should be endured.

These critics were of two kinds. One variety consisted of "liberals," sincere converts to Westernism, who proposed a reform program along conventional Western lines typified by phrases like "more democracy." Yet these liberals were a very small minority, mostly "intellectuals." Back of them stood no solid, prosperous middle class, because wealth and commercial opportunity had been so restricted to the plutocracy that such a middle class had not come into being. Thus the Japanese liberals awakened scant popular echo. Indeed, their program of thoroughgoing Westernization In spirit as well as in externals affronted not merely plutocrats and politicians but likewise that other body of critics who proposed a very different cure for Japan's ills. To Westernize the mind and soul of the Japanese people would apply a drastic revamping of its old ideals. How, pray, could Shinto and Emperor-worship be reconciled with the critical skepticism of "advanced" liberal thought? How would a vigorous policy of national expansion, political and economic, backed by military and naval preparedness, square with plans for international co-operation looking towards the goal of a cosmopolitan world-order?

The answer is: they were not reconciled. A Japan thus Westernized would be a Japan utterly transformed. And any such mental and spiritual regeneration could be accomplished only after a prolonged transition period during which Japan would be riven by internal disputes and correspondingly weakened abroad. In the perilous post-war world, dare Japan risk so crucial an experiment even if it were theoretically worthwhile.

Indeed, was it worthwhile? What about those wondrous Western ideals? How had the West put them into practice? In the Great War? How about Communism and Fascism? Was not the West itself in revolt against its vaunted ideals—Liberty, Democracy, et cetera? By their fruits ye shall know them!

Those were the queries flung at the Japanese liberals, and their answers did not satisfy. Wherefore liberalism in Japan is today decidedly in eclipse. It may revive sometime, but just now it is a minor factor. Of course, we refer to genuine liberals—sincere idealists like Yukio Ozaki. Most of the so-called liberal opposition consists of plutocrats and professional politicians who seek to protect their vested interests by mouthing liberal slogans which, in the past, have served them well.

So much for the liberals. Now a word or two about the Japanese "radicals"—another minority group of Western derivation. Radical ideas, like all Western novelties, aroused the eager curiosity of the Japanese mind. As early as 1882, a tiny Socialist Society led a brief existence, while Anarchism and Syndicalism enjoyed a passing albeit extremely limited vogue. These passing fads, be it noted, were confined almost entirely to intellectual circles. The working classes tended to follow Anglo-Saxon precedents by forming trades-unions and a moderate Labor Party, seeking to better the workingman's lot by collective bargaining and the ballot-box; not by bombs or barricades. This is not surprising, because the Japanese industrial workers, though poor, are for the most part orderly, neat, literate, and self-respecting. They are in no sense a benighted "proletariat."

The Communist phase of Japanese radicalism began soon after the war, when certain radical leaders headed by Sen Katayama went, to Moscow for a conference of the Third International. Converted on the spot, they were the link by which Communist propaganda entered Japan. Numerous agents, well equipped with funds, were especially successful among university students. Much alarmed, the Japanese Government started an intensive campaign against "dangerous thoughts." Yet the most brutal police methods seemed to kindle radical enthusiasm rather than damp it down. Throughout the 1920's, Communism was a bogey forever haunting the bureaucratic mind.

Then Japanese Communism declined as rapidly as it arose. The reason is plain. Like Japanese Liberalism, it was overwhelmed by the general revulsion against Westernism; by the great upsurge of traditional ideals and loyalties which dominates Japanese national life today. This is the movement variously termed "Fascism," "Japanism," "Back to Asia!" and more besides.

What it is doing to Communism; why; and what it portends, are strikingly set forth by an American observer, who writes:

"A true Communist puts his Communism first and his nationality second. But a true Japanese, even though he be a Communist, is first and always a Japanese. And Japanese students have come to recognize this . . . Now those who are in jail are recanting and those out of jail are coming to police headquarters to announce their change of belief. Out of more than 30,000 Communists arrested since 1928, it is expected that all but perhaps 200 will have renounced their faith. Two hundred remaining true out of 30,000! Since two arrested leaders, Sano and Nabeyama, belied their faith recently, recanting has been the order of the day. Sano, sitting in jail awaiting trial, decided that the world-revolution aim of the Communists did not take into account the peculiar needs and character of the Japanese people.

Another Communist leader, Tanaka, decided that the Emperor meant more than Karl Marx to Japan. He came to court in a white kimono (white being the mourning color), in tribute to his mother, who had committed suicide because of his disgrace, and as evidence of the purification of his ideas . . . There have been many suicides of the disillusioned and conscience-stricken.

"Now this is most significant—that persons are willing to go to death for the wrong they have done their families, but not willing to go to death in the cause of Communism. Do Japanese lack the courage of martyrs? . . . No people on earth court death as do the Japanese . . . No, Japanese do not lack the courage to die. Nor are they easily shaken from a purpose. Then why do they not hold to Communism? Because Communism in Japan is a conceit, not a conviction. Doubtless there are some insincere recanters. But in most cases the recanting is probably genuine. It was the Communism that was insincere.

"The red weed comes up with one good jerk on the Japanese conscience. It has never been able to take firm root because the soil is already full of the black, staunch, all-absorbing roots of Japanese nationalism. So the radical who must eat fire is changing his diet from Communism to an intense patriotism which would, if necessary, assassinate corrupt politicians, abolish political parties, and unite the nation under control of the one force that still represents the old samurai spirit of Bushido—the Japanese army.

"Numerous proletarian societies have abandoned their anti-war slogans and turned reactionary. The movement to 'restore Japan to ancient and better ways' is sweeping through the schools. In the universities, groups have been formed under the military instructors to read old novels, practice the manly art of *judo* (jujitsu), and study ways to make the Island of Japan truly insular; secure against the world that she has too much imitated. And reactionaries do not recant. Of all the patriotic assassins brought to trial during recent months, not one has been penitent . . . The chief rite in all reactionary groups is the prayer meeting. Beware of a movement that centers around the prayer meeting! Communism has no prayer meeting. It lacks the religious fervor of the new nationalism which has all the fire of a Methodist revival."[22]

So tremendous an emotional upsurge must spring from causes deep and enduring. They do, indeed, run back to the Meiji Era. What we now witness is a cumulative reaction against the Westernization then inaugurated—a reaction gathering strength in proportion to the failings which the Westernizing process has displayed.

We saw that, by the Meiji Era the old merchant class and the new political and professional elements were big gainers. Other classes, however, were less fortunate. This was notably true of the great feudal lords who, at the Emperor's bidding, renounced their ancestral privileges but got little save patriotic satisfaction in return.

22 Willard Price, "Japanese Lean to Fascism," *The Sunday Star* (Washington, D. C.), October 7, 1934.

Some of these ex-grandees subsequently allied themselves by marriage or otherwise with the rising plutocracy, just as members of the old European nobilities did after the Industrial Revolution. Others, however, scorned to demean themselves by money-making, continuing the feudal tradition by devoting themselves to public service.[23] This was also true of the Samurai, who naturally gravitated to the officers-corps of the army and navy—branches where much honor but no wealth was to be gained. Since the rank-and-file are mainly peasants, both services are strongholds of conservatism, though caste feeling is slight because men of peasant origin can, and often do, rise to the highest grades. All ranks are therefore closely united by common bonds of patriotic devotion, keen sense of honor, and thirst for glory. Lastly, both services have close, sympathetic connections with the peasantry and, in somewhat lesser degree, with the people at large.

Conservative, patriotic elements, wherever found, naturally watched with aversion tinged by waxing indignation the new-won power and pomp of the plutocracy. The corrupt misuse of imported political institutions by Big Business and its henchmen discredited the whole parliamentary régime in conservative eyes. The last straw seems to have been when the much-vaunted grant of manhood suffrage turned out to be a "joker," because campaign expense-accounts often run as high as 50,0000 yen. Under these circumstances, how many men could enter Parliament untarred by the plutocratic brush? And, in consequence, how was it possible to redress popular grievances by parliamentary means?

Constitutional reform being impracticable, other methods were employed. Patriotic youths began to commit *harakiri*[24] before the doors of prominent persons become unpopular through acts or policies deemed against the public interest. Such ceremonial suicide brings deep disgrace upon him who has caused this agonizing sacrifice.

Other super-patriots took more positive action; they formed secret societies whose members pledged themselves to kill those in authority whose conduct might merit an extra-legal doom. Then

23 Before its recent devaluation, the yen had a value of approximately fifty cents or two shillings, one-half pence, gold.

24 Literally: *belly-cutting.*

occurred the series of political murders whereby several of Japan's leading political lights were violently extinguished. These deeds were not popularly regarded as ordinary crimes. In fact, on more than one occasion, judges burst into tears when learning of the assassins' lofty ideals and pure motives.

The popular mood was vividly displayed in the extraordinary scenes following the death of Admiral Togo, the victor over the Baltic Fleet in the Russo-Japanese War. *Togosan,* as the people called him, was the incarnation of Old Japan—a Samurai, born in feudal times. Reared by a stern mother in the strictest tenets of Bushido, he never swerved from his Spartan code. Scorning luxury and distinctions, he lived a frugal old age in a simple home, his chief pleasure being the care of a tiny garden. His last wish was that a favorite pair of pruning-shears be laid in his plain coffin of unpainted hinoki-wood. When the venerable hero passed 'away, all Japan mourned, and millions made pilgrimage as to a holy shrine. The spirit of Old Japan was aglow once more.

That enkindled spirit is fast engendering ideas; some shallow, others fantastic, yet all boding ill for the semi-Westernized political and economic structure built up since the Meiji Era. Fanatical voices call the people back to the past—or rather to an idealized version of the olden time. Peasant leaders denounce Big Business, anathematize the City, and preach an extravagant sort of Populism. Various "Fascist" groups evolve a characteristically Japanese brand of National-Socialism, according to which the plutocrats must surrender their wealth as the feudal lords did their privileges at the Meiji Era. Thereafter, the Emperor, as the Father of the Yamato Race, will administer everything in the interests of the entire nation. Parliament and politics will, of course, be abolished.

All these apostles of drastic change look to the army as the instrument of salvation. And the army obviously listens. Although no formal revolutionary stroke has as yet been delivered, the army has been very much in politics these past two years, notably in its insistence upon a Coalition Government, "above party." For a time, this government included a soldier, General Araki, who typifies the still un-crystallized yet rapidly developing movement of protest and revolt.

Sadao Araki certainly owes nothing to the Meiji dispensation. Like many of the Samurai, his family was thereby condemned to poverty and obscurity. His mother worked as a kimono seamstress in a dry-goods establishment in order to bring up her children, and his younger sister could not afford to go to school. Such domestic privations have not heightened his regard for Westernism, in Japan or elsewhere.

His views are set forth in a pamphlet entitled: *The Mission of Present-Day Japan.* Its keynote is an uncompromising belief in the supreme importance of Nationality and Race, for he says: "In a very thorough discrimination lies the salvation of mankind. Each race must work out its own natural destiny according to its own qualities. To know the world, you must know yourself. To deal with our present difficult situation we must start with the consciousness that we are Japanese and no other." China's disrespect for Japan's rights, the League's disparaging attitude, and other unfortunate happenings are due to Japan's departure from "Japanism." As Araki puts it: "Things have come to this pass because the Japanese themselves have forsaken their pride, faith, and self-consciousness, and have become immersed in frivolity of thought and life."

Labor tends to speak in the same strain. The platform of the new National-Socialist Party states: "A socialistic Japan must be founded on our own principles. We can follow neither Comintern nor the English Labor Movement." A Nationalist leader draws the logical conclusion by asserting: 'Back to Asia!' is our watchword. We should part company with the materialistic civilization of the Occident which we have followed blindly for sixty years, and return to the old spiritual life of Japan."

A striking picture of Japan today is painted by the French publicist, Maurice Lachin, who has just published a book based on first-hand studies and observations.[25] He comes to the startling conclusion that Japan stands on the verge of a social revolution uniquely Japanese in character, since it will be made in the name of the Emperor, whose godlike powers would be enhanced rather than diminished in consequence. This revolution is apparently inevitable.

25 Maurice Lachin, *Japan, 1934* (Paris, 1934). The passages here cited are taken from a summary of the book translated from the French in *The Living Age*, October, 1934.

"Half Japan yearns for it today, passionately and completely." The present semi-Western economic and political regime benefits, at most, two millions of the population. Besides the poverty-stricken working class and peasantry, the great mass of middle-class Japanese—intellectuals, teachers, clerks, minor officials, and army or navy officers are wretchedly paid and have no cause to support the existing régime. For instance:

"From childhood, the future army officer is brought up with the idea that he has been plundered by the capitalist or that the capitalist has delivered his parents over to poverty. He never, or almost never, frees himself from this condition . . . and must lead an extremely meager life in the Japanese fashion. Everything that suggests European luxury is forbidden to him."

Lachin quotes a Japanese journalist as saying that an officer who recognized a member of the Mitsui family on the street, went up to him and boxed his cars. Nobody intervened. The Mitsui no longer dare venture forth without guards. "You could never imagine,' explained the journalist, 'how we hate the Mitsuis. I myself, if I met a Mitsui in some place where there were no police, would not hesitate to kill him.'"

Such is the ominous tumult of Japan today. But, as an English observer justly remarks, "The dominant motif, running through all the confused, fermenting ideas of 'Back to Asia!,' is a loss of faith in 'Western civilization, both as to its social morality and as to its economic sufficiency.

The war, so purposeless and destructive, shattered the claim of the West to a superior morality; the present depression, fantastic as a nightmare in its spectacle of a world reduced to poverty amid superabundance, has demolished belief in our economic infallibility. At the subconscious roots of 'Back to Asia!' is a profound feeling that Japan has gone too far toward the West and must hark back to native ideas more congenial to the character and capacities of her people."[26]

Disregarding the rant of its "lunatic fringe," the program of Japanese Fascists boils down to State Capitalism of a peculiar kind;

---

26 Hugh Byas, "'Back to Asia!' Japan's New Cry," *New York Times Magazine*, October 2, 1932.

a curious blend of radical Western ideas and the theocratic principle of a God-Emperor inspiring and directing everything.

Now this may come to pass. And it might work. The shift from private to public ownership could apparently be made in Japan with comparatively little disturbance. Capital is concentrated in so few hands that its transfer to the state would vitally concern only a small group of bankers and big business men. And they probably would not make much trouble. An Imperial Edict voicing the popular desire would presumably silence their protests and cause them to hand over their wealth as meekly as the Daimyos did their feudal privileges in the Meiji Era. The Japanese are not individualists. So strong is their group-consciousness that it is almost impossible for a small minority to go counter to the general trend. Furthermore, the economic system of modern Japan has never been on a truly individualistic basis. In the beginning, it was decreed and fostered by the state. The government has always been in business, while business has, in turn, always sought official backing. Avowed State Capitalism in Japan would, therefore, be more a shift in emphasis than something radically new.

The real issue is, not the possibility but the effectiveness of such a change. In the first place, it certainly would not abolish poverty in Japan, for the simple reason that the sum-total of the national wealth is so small in proportion to population that no redistribution of the national income would, of itself, make an appreciable difference to the average peasant or town worker. What, for instance, would the Mitsui and Mitsubishi millions amount to when spread thin over 66,000,000 people?

Japan's basic economic problem is, not how to divide what she has but how to multiply the present total. The only practicable way to do that is by expanding her foreign trade. But this means increasing her industrial efficiency. How far would State Capitalism do it? We know that private management is already extremely efficient, no matter how unevenly dividends may be distributed. Would national planning and official administration effect economies in production, distribution, and management great enough to offset possible debit items due to loss of personal initiative and individual enterprise?

Indeed, it is not merely a question of balancing gains against losses; State Capitalism must show a large, sustained favorable balance if economic conditions in Japan are not soon to become intolerable. Somehow or other, already overcrowded Japan has got to provide for an extra 15,000,000 or 20,000,000 people during the next twenty years. Otherwise, Japan must either suffocate or blow up, no matter what her political, economic, or social arrangements may be. There is no way of escaping that grim alternative.

But that raises another question: How does the "Back to Asia!" slogan square with this economic dilemma? If it be anything more than an emotional outcry, "Back to Asia!" means not merely a revival of old ideals and customs but also at least a partial abandonment of Western ways in favor of traditional ways and living-standards. This, however, at once raises a whole series of highly specific choices which would be very hard to make. No other Oriental people has so enthusiastically adopted the myriad comforts and conveniences of our mechanistic civilization. The existence of the Japanese city-dweller is amazingly Westernized. How is he going to cut out of his daily life a thousand and one things to which he has become accustomed—not to mention many Western things he has not yet got but ardently wants?

Getting down to cases, therefore, the real question is: "*How* far back to Asia?" And, judging by present conditions, the distance traveled will not be great. That, however, means that the Japanese cannot, or will not, notably reduce their present standard of living; a standard which, although it looks to Western eyes, is far higher than the Chinese or Hindu coolie level.

But even if the Japanese should scrap everything Western and start living like back-country Chinese coolies, they simply could not feed themselves out of their own resources. The self-sufficient Old Japan had approximately 30,000,000 inhabitants. The impact of the West started a prodigious population-growth which has already reached 66,000,000, and which will ultimately attain a height of between 80,000,000 and 100,000,000 before the impetus is fully spent.

Japan's attitude towards Westernism must, in the last analysis, be one of adjustment; not of rebellion or renunciation. A British thinker well says: "The burden which Japan shouldered at the Meiji Era was heavier than she knew. Once before, in the seventh century, she had taken over the apparatus of a foreign social order, and had found by experience that she could not make it work. That failure did not seem disastrous, because she was then able to cut loose from her teachers, digesting such lessons as she could, and rejecting the remainder. But when she adopted a Western way of life, the choice was final; she was bound to keep it up."[27]

Westernism has, for Japan, proved to be a sort of Nessus' shirt. It slipped on readily enough. To doff it, however, Japan would have to tear the living flesh from her bones.

27 "The Tragedy of Japan," *The Round Table*, September, 1932.

PART II
CHAPTER IV
INDIA: A SUB-CONTINENT IN TRAVAIL

INDIA is a land of paradox. Geographically a unit, India has never known real political union save that recently imposed from without by the British "Raj." Full of warlike stocks, India has never been able to repel invaders. Inhabited by many races, these races have never fused, but have remained distinct and mutually hostile, sundered by barriers of blood, speech, culture, and creed. Thus India, large and populous as Europe or China, has neither, like China, evolved a generalized unity; nor has it, like Europe, become a specialized diversity. Instead, India has remained a formless, unstable indeterminate, with tendencies in both directions which were never carried to their logical conclusion.

Now this paradoxical condition still prevails. The impact of the West, though it wrought momentous changes, has complicated rather than clarified the situation. Every West-era importation has been subtly warped or perverted. The result is a state of affairs which, to Westerners, does not make sense.

The Westerner, for example, sees a "nationalist" movement that on closer scrutiny turns out to be, not nationalism but a religious reaction directed both against Westernism and against much that is native to India itself. This is merely a sample of India's deceptive appearance. Unless we get behind what *seems to be* to what *is,* we shall view India as Hindu sages claim man sees the world— through a "Veil of Maya." The realities of the situation will be hidden from our eyes.

Indian history has been determined by three great invasions: the Aryan, occurring about 1500 B.C.; the Mohammedan, running intermittently from 1000 to 1700 A.D.; and the English, beginning about 1750 A.D. and culminating a century later in full ascendancy.

The Aryans were a fair-skinned folk basically akin to ourselves. Pouring through those northwestern passes which alone give land-access to India, elsewhere impregnably guarded by the mountain wall of the Himalayas, the Aryans conquered the dark-skinned Dravidian aborigines and settled down as masters.

This conquest was, however, superficial and partial. The bulk of the Aryans remained in the northwest, the more adventurous spirits scattering thinly over the vast peninsula. Even in the north, large areas of hill-country and jungle remained in the hands of the aborigines, while very few Aryans ever penetrated the south. Over most of India, therefore, the Aryans were a small ruling class superimposed upon a much more numerous native population.

Fearing to be swallowed up in the dark Dravidian ocean, the fair Aryans tried to preserve their political mastery and racial purity by the institution of "caste," which has ever since remained the foundation of Indian social life.

Caste was originally a "color line." But it was enforced not so much by civil law as by religion. Society was divided into four castes: Priests, Warriors, Artisans or Farmers, and Menials. The first two orders were monopolized by the Aryans. This was especially true of the priestly or Brahmin caste, which acquired a position of leadership that it has always maintained. The lowest or Sudra caste consisted of the subject Dravidian masses.

The castes were kept apart by a system of religious taboos. Intermarriage, partaking of food and drink, even physical approach, entailed ceremonial defilement which sometimes could not be expiated. Disobedience to these taboos was punished by the terrible penalty of "outcasting," whereby the offender did not simply fall to a lesser caste but sank even below the Sudra and became a "Pariah," or man of no-caste, condemned to the most revolting occupations and with no rights which even a Sudra need respect.

Thus Indian society rested, not on civil but on ceremonially religious law. Furthermore, the Indian religion ("Hinduism") became social rather than moral in character. Indeed, concerned as it is with ritual and caste observances rather than with conduct and ethical ideals, Hinduism is not a "religion" in the sense of the other great human faiths—Christianity, Islam, Judaism, and Buddhism in its original form.[1]

India's unique social and religious system had momentous, and in the main disastrous, consequences. As a color-line, caste worked very imperfectly. Despite its prohibitions, even the Brahmins ultimately became more or less impregnated with Dravidian blood.[2] But as a social system, caste continued to function in ways peculiar to itself.

The four original castes gradually divided into hundreds and even thousands of sub-castes. These had little or no racial significance. Yet they were all just as exclusive as the original four. The outcome was a shattering of Indian society into an intricate mosaic of rigid social atoms, between which co-operation or even understanding was impossible.

The results upon Indian history are obvious. In the words of a British authority: "The effect of this permanent maintenance of human types is that the population is heterogeneous to the last degree. It is no question of rich and poor, of town and country, of employer and employed, the differences lie far deeper. The population of a district or town is a collection of different nationalities—almost different species—of mankind that will not eat or drink or intermarry with one another, and that are governed in the more important affairs of life by committees of their own. It is hardly too much to say that by the caste system the inhabitants of India are differentiated into over 2000 species, which, in the intimate physical relations of life, have as little in common as the inmates of a zoological garden."[3]

1 Confucianism, like Hinduism, cannot be classified as a "religion"—but *for* just the opposite reason. The teachings of the great Chinese sage are a code of common-sense ethics, with neither ritual nor theology.

2 According to some historians, this race-mixture occurred almost at once. The theory is that the Aryan conquerors, who outside the northwestern region had very few of their own women with them, took Dravidian women as wives or concubines, and legitimatized their half-breed children; the offspring of the conquerors, both pure-bloods and mixed-bloods, coalescing into a closed caste. Further infiltration of Dravidian blood was thus prevented, but Aryan race-purity had been destroyed.

3 Sir Bampfylde Fuller, *Studies of Indian Life and Sentiment,* p. 40 (London, 1910).

A land thus socially atomized and politically split into many principalities was clearly predestined to fall before the first strong invader. This invader was Islam. Beginning with border raids, Moslem attacks culminated in *a series of* great invasions. Coming through the northwestern passes as the Aryans had done ages before, the Mohammedans first conquered the border region of the Punjab; then, from this well-established base, they spread gradually eastward until most of northern India was under Moslem rule.

The Moslem invaders enjoyed two notable advantages: they were fanatically united against the Hindus whom they loathed as worshippers of idols, and they made many converts among the native populations. The very opposite of Hinduism, Islam, with its doctrine that all Believers are brothers, could not fail to attract multitude of low-castes and out-castes, who by conversion to Islam might rise to the status of the conquerors. This is the chief reason why the Mohammedans of India today number nearly 78,000,000—well over one-fifth of the total population These Indian Moslems are descended, not solely from Afghan, Arab, Turkish, and Persian invaders, but far more from the millions of Hindu converts who embraced Islam at one time or another.

The flood-tide of Moslem expansion came in the sixteenth century, when the great Turko-Mongol chieftain Baber entered India and founded the "Mogul" Empire. Baber and his successors overran even the south and united India politically as it never had been before. Yet even this conquest was superficial. The Brahmins, threatened with destruction, preached a Hindu revival; the Mogul dynasty petered out; and early in the eighteenth century the Mogul Empire collapsed, leaving India a welter of warring principalities, Mohammedan and Hindu, fighting one another for religion, for political advantage, or for sheer lust of plunder.

Out of this anarchy the British rose to power. The English were at first merely one of several other European elements—Portuguese, Dutch, and French—who established small settlements along the Indian coasts.

These Europeans never dreamed of conquering India whilst the Mogul Empire endured. In fact, the British connection with India began as a purely trading venture—the East India Company. But when India sank into chaos the Europeans were first obliged to acquire local authority in order to protect their "factories," and were later lured into more ambitious policies by the impotence of petty rulers.

Then the Europeans fought amongst themselves; the British ousted their white rivals; the East India Company was abolished, and India came directly under the British Crown. Britain's political ascendancy went hand-in-hand with Western penetration in all its phases. Roads, railways and canals opened up and commercially developed India; the Suez Canal brought India effectively closer to Europe, whilst education on Western lines broadcast new ideas.

Over this rapidly changing India stood the British *Raj*—a system of government unique in the world's history. It was the utterly alien government of a few hundred highly skilled administrative experts backed by a small professional army, ruling a vast collection of subject peoples. These new rulers governed as they saw fit, with no more legal responsibility to the governed than the native despots whom they displaced. But the British governed well. In efficiency, honesty, and sense of duty, the Government of India is probably the best example of benevolent absolutism that the world has ever seen. The British *Raj* gave India profound peace. It played no favorites, holding the scales even between rival races, castes, and creeds. Lastly, it made India an administrative whole—something that India had never been before. For the first time in its history, India was firmly united under one rule.

Yet the very virtues of the British *Raj* sowed the seeds of future trouble. Generations grew up forgetful of past ills, seeing only European shortcomings, and, above all, familiar with Western ideals of self-government, liberty, and nationality. In India, as elsewhere in the East, there was bound to arise a growing discontent against Western rule.

Down to the last quarter of the nineteenth century, organized political agitation against the British *Raj* was unknown. The Indian masses, preoccupied with the ever-present problem of getting a living, accepted passively a government no more absolute, and infinitely more efficient, than its predecessors. Of anything like self-conscious Indian 'nationalism" there was virtually no trace.

The first sign of organized discontent was the formation of the "Indian National Congress" in the year 1885. The name itself showed that the British *Raj,* covering all India, was thereby evoking amongst some of India's diverse elements a common viewpoint and aspiration. However, the early Congresses were very far from representing Indian public opinion, in the general sense of the term. On the contrary, they represented merely the views of a small professional class, mostly journalists, trained in Western ideas and methods. The European type of education introduced by the British had turned out an Indian *intelligentsia,* conversant with the English language and saturated with Westernism.

This new *intelligentsia,* convinced as it was of the value of Western ideals and achievements, could not fail to be dissatisfied with many aspects of Indian life. In fact, its first efforts were directed, not to politics, but to economic and social reforms like the suppression of child-marriage and broader education. But, before long, political matters came to the fore. Well-read in English history, the Indian intellectuals felt keenly their lack of self-government. Soon a vigorous native press developed, preaching the new "home-rule" gospel and welding the *intelligentsia* into a self-conscious unity.

Down almost to the close of the nineteenth century Indian discontent could hardly be termed "nationalist." With a few exceptions, the small group of Europeanized intellectuals aimed neither at independence nor at the ending of British control, but rather the reforming of Indian life along Western lines, including a progressive extension of self-government under British paramount authority.

But with the turn of the century there came a sudden change in the situation which radically altered the character of Indian unrest. India, like the Orient at large, was stirring to a new self-consciousness. True nationalist symptoms appeared. Indian scholars delved into their musty chronicles and sacred texts, and rediscovered India's historic past. Reformed Hindu sects like the Arya Somaj lent religious sanctions. The little band of Westernized intellectuals was swamped by other elements thinking, not in terms of piecemeal Western reforms, but of a new India, rejuvenated from its own vital forces and free to work out its own destiny in its own way. From the nationalist ranks now arose the challenging slogan: *Bandemataram!* ("Hail Motherland!")

This movement was of a peculiar character. It was a restricted sort of nationalism, less Indian than Hindu in spirit and purpose. That, however, made it gravely suspect to the large Mohammedan minority. And, from their standpoint, the Moslems were fully justified; because the new nationalist ideal was Aryan India; the India of the legendary Golden Age before the invading Moslem came. *Back to the Vedas!* was a nationalist watchword, and this veneration for the Hindu sacred books implied a revival of aggressive Hinduism.

That was just what was taking place. An extraordinary change had come over even the Western-trained intellectuals. Men who, a few years before, had vaunted the superiority of Western ideas and had openly flouted "superstitions" like idol-worship, now denounced everything Western and reverently sacrificed to the old gods. The "sacred soil" of Hindustan must be purged of the foreigner. But the "foreigner," as these nationalists conceived him, was not solely the Englishman; he was the Mohammedan as well.

This was stirring up the past with a vengeance! For centuries the great Hindu-Moslem rift had split India. The rift had never been closed, but it had been veiled somewhat by the neutral overlordship of the British *Raj*. Now the veil was torn aside, and the Mohammedans saw themselves threatened by a rebirth of militant Hinduism like that which had shattered the Mogul Empire two centuries before.

The Moslems were not merely alarmed; they were infuriated as well. Recalling the glories of the Mogul Empire just as the Hindus did those of Aryan India, the Moslem deemed themselves the rightful lords of the land and had no mind to fall under the sway of despised "Idolaters."

The Mohammedans did not love the British, but they hated the Hindus, and they saw in the British *Raj* a bulwark against the rising menace of hereditary foes who outnumbered them nearly four to one. To be sure, the Indian Moslems were not unaffected by the general spirit of unrest which was sweeping over the East. They, too, felt a quickened self-consciousness. But, being a minority in

India, their feelings took the form of a rather sentimental sort of Pan-Islamism.[4]

Returning to our consideration of Indian nationalism: it was not only Hindu but also distinctly Brahminical in character. More and more the Brahmins became the driving-power, seeking to perpetuate their supremacy in the India of the morrow as they had in the India of the past. But this neo-Brahminism aroused apprehension within the body of Hindu society itself. Many low-castes and Pariahs began to fear that an independent or even a self-governing India might be ruled by a tyrannical Brahmin oligarchy which would deny them the benefits they now enjoyed under British rule. Also, some of the Hindu princes disliked the thought of a theocratic régime that might sharply curtail their authority. Thus "Indian nationalism" was really an alliance between the Brahmins and the Western-educated intellectuals, who had pooled their ambitions in a program for jointly ruling India.

Quickened by this ambition and fired by religious zeal, the nationalist movement rapidly acquired a fanatical temper characterized by a mystical abhorrence of everything Western and a ferocious hatred of all Europeans. Japan's victory over Russia in 1904 acted like a spark to a well-laid train of powder. The very next year, nationalist fanatics embarked on a campaign of terrorism. Its leading spirit was one Bal Gangadhar Tilak, often called "the father of Indian unrest."

Tilak typified nationalist fanaticism. A Brahmin with an excellent Western education, he was the sworn foe of British rule and Western civilization. An able propagandist, his harangues roused audiences to frenzy, while his newspaper, *Yugantar*, preached systematic hate, assassination, and rebellion. For instance, it once stated editorially: "The only subscription required is that every reader shall bring in a European head." On another occasion, commenting on the murder of an English lady and her daughter, *Yugantar* exclaimed exultantly: "Many a female demon must be killed in course of time, in order to extirpate the race of *Asuras* from the breast of the earth!"

4 It is interesting to note that the last census (1931) showed that during the previous decade the Moslem element increased by 13 per cent, whereas the Hindu population increased by 10.4 per cent. This Moslem increase may be due partly to conversions from Hinduism.

These atrocious words were being translated into equally atrocious deeds. Many English officials, soldiers, and civilians were murdered by nationalist fanatics, often mere youths, who, when caught and convicted, went to their deaths glorying in deeds done for the cause. The government of course answered terrorism by stern repression. The native press was muzzled, agitators were imprisoned or executed, and the hands of the authorities strengthened by punitive legislation. For several years, India seethed with an unrest which jailings, hangings, and deportations did not succeed in stamping out.

Presently, however, the situation took at least a temporary turn for the better. The extremists were, after all, a small minority, and cool heads, both British and Indian, sought a way out of the mess. Indian conservatives condemned terrorism and besought their nationalist fellow countrymen to seek the realization of their aspirations by peaceful means.

On the other hand, liberal-minded Englishmen, while refusing to be stampeded, evolved a program of conciliation. The upshot was the Indian Councils Act of 1909. Thereby, Britain acknowledged in principle the nationalist claim to self-government, and actually handed out a first installment in the shape of local elected assemblies, with scant legislative powers yet with plenty of scope for debate, criticism, and advice.

These timely concessions acted like oil poured on troubled waters. Terrorism waned. Sedition went underground. India enjoyed some years of relative tranquility. Thus began the see-saw between Indian demands and British conciliation which has gone on for the past twenty-five years. During this quarter-century the British *Raj* has weathered two big nationalist storms—one immediately after the war and the other in recent years.

Western observers are apt to attach vast importance to the details of nationalist tactics on the one side and of British concessions on the other. In fact, neither are of primary importance. What really matters are the relative attitudes of the three main driving-forces in India itself—the Hindu nationalists, the Moslem anti-nationalists, and the increasingly self-assertive low-caste or Pariah elements collectively known as "The Depressed Classes."

Were it possible for that redoubtable trio to get together on a common program of action, the British would have to assent to almost any demand, because their united power would be irresistible. And the reason for this is that the *Raj* today rests, as it always has rested, far less on brute force than upon a balance of mutually antagonistic native forces.

The peculiar character of British rule in India is seldom appreciated. Therefore we tend to consider it as normal and natural. Yet the mere existence of the *Raj* is amazing. Surely, nothing like it has happened before. Beside it, the Roman Empire was a commonplace. Think of a sub-continent, large as all Europe and inhabited by 350,000,000 people, governed by a handful of avowed aliens hailing from a small island thousands of miles away! This alien handful surely cannot govern India against its will.

However great their skill and prestige, continuance of their rule must mean that Indians do not emphatically wish their rule to end; have not resolved to throw them out. The British *are* in India, not because of superhuman power or ability, but because they have thus far filled a need there which Indians are as yet unable to supply.

The basic fragility of the *Raj* was strikingly analyzed many years ago by that wise student of the Orient, Meredith Townsend.

Writing away back in the Gay Nineties,[5] when the West stood at the height of its power and when Indian unrest was scarce more than a name, Townsend boldly asserted: "The English think they will rule India for many centuries or forever. I do not think so, holding rather the older belief that the empire which came in a day will disappear in a night. . . . Above all this inconceivable mass of humanity, governing all, protecting all, taxing all, rises what we call here 'The Empire,' a corporation of less than 1,500 men, who are set to govern, and who protect themselves in governing by finding pay for a minute white garrison of 65,000 men; one-fifth of the Roman legions—though the masses to be controlled are double the subjects of Rome. That corporation and that garrison constitute the 'Indian

5 Meredith Townsend, *Europe and Asia,* pp. 82–87. Though the citation which follows in our text above is taken from the fourth edition of his book, issued in 1905, the first edition was published at the turn of the century, and consisted for the most part of reprints from magazine articles which had appeared over a period of years during the nineteenth century.

Empire.' There is nothing else. Banish those 1,500 men in black, defeat that slender garrison in red, and the Empire has ended, the structure disappears, and brown India emerges, unchanged and unchangeable. To support the official world and its garrison there is, except Indian opinion, absolutely nothing. Not only is there no white race in India, not only is there no white colony, but there is no white man who purposes to remain . . . There are no white servants, not even grooms, no white policemen, no white postmen, no white anything. If the brown men struck for a week, 'The Empire' would collapse like a house of cards, and every ruling man would be a starving prisoner in his own house He could not move or feed himself or get water."

This basic weakness of British rule was put to a searching test by the widespread boycotts of everything British first proclaimed by the nationalists soon after the war and later revived in somewhat different form. In both cases the moving spirit was the world-famous Mahatma Gandhi. The career of this extraordinary man clearly reveals the workings of the Hindu mind. In his youth, Gandhi drank deeply from the fount of Western learning. As a young man he was an excellent type of the Westernized *intelligentsia* which we have already observed. In fact, he became a highly successful barrister, qualified to practice law in England as well as in India.

Gandhi's revulsion against the West began some years before the war when he went to South Africa to champion the cause of Indian immigrants there, whose situation under the restrictionist regulations of the Union Government had become difficult. Gandhi's nationalist leanings were intensified by the repressive measures adopted by the Government of India to combat a wave of violent unrest at the close of the Great War. From that moment he came out whole-heartedly for *su'araj*—full self-government for India.

But Gandhi aimed at something which went far beyond freedom from British political control. He sought emancipation from Westernization as well. Condemning Westernism, root and branch, Gandhi had, in fact, renounced the world and adopted a life of extreme religious asceticism. In short, he had become a "holy man" with a high reputation for sanctity. As such, his influence over the

Hindu masses was potentially enormous, for throughout Indian history the Hindu saint has often wielded a power more impressive than that of emperors and kings.

Such a man was just the leader for a daring experiment. Not only Gandhi but also those mysterious Brahminical personages who determine nationalist policies behind the scenes, decided that the time was ripe to launch a new kind of attack against the British *Raj.* Terrorism having failed and armed rebellion being practically impossible, the *Raj* might still be brought to terms by boycotting on a gigantic scale. This was the scheme known as "non-co-operation."

Politically, non-co-operation meant that no good nationalist would have anything to do with the new legislative bodies decreed by the British Government as part of its latest concession to Indian discontent. Therefore, voters should stay away from the polls, the elections would be farcical, and the new legislatures would prove unworkable. But that is only the beginning of the story. Lawyers and litigants were to avoid the courts, taxpayers refuse to pay imposts, workmen were to go on strike, shopkeepers refuse to buy or sell British-made goods, and even pupils to leave school or college. This wholesale "outcasting" of everything British would render the English in India a new sort of Pariah—literally "untouchables"; the British Government and the British community in India would be left in complete isolation, and the *Raj,* rendered unworkable, would have to capitulate to nationalist demands for full self-government.

Such was the non-co-operation scheme, led and directed by the dynamic personality of Mahatma Gandhi.

The nature of his popular appeal can be gauged by the following extract from one of his speeches: "It is as amazing as it is humiliating that less than 100,000 white men should be able to rule 315,000,000 Indians. They do it somewhat, undoubtedly, by force, but more by securing our co-operation in a thousand ways . . . The British cannot rule us by mere force. And so they resort to all means, honorable and dishonorable, in order to retain their hold on India. They want India's billions and they want India's man-power for their imperialistic greed. If we refuse to supply them with men and money, we shall achieve our goal: namely, *su'araj,* equality, manliness."

This characteristically Indian enterprise was a more formidable threat to British rule than might off-hand be supposed. An "outcasting" boycott was congenial to the Hindu mind. The fact that it was a passive-resistance movement held in line many moderates who would have refused to embark upon a campaign of terrorism or upon armed rebellion.

Furthermore, though essentially a Hindu movement, the nationalist cause could now count upon the sympathy of some Mohammedans. At the moment, the Indian Moslems were wrought up over the harsh treatment meted out to Turkey in the recent peace-settlement, and they were even more indignant at the way Britain had let down her Arab allies, especially in Syria. So embittered was Moslem feeling that, for the time being at least, many were glad to see the British authorities in difficulty of any sort. For that matter, the aftermath of the war was disturbing India in so many ways that the country seethed with general dissatisfaction and vague discontents. The nationalist leaders had picked a good moment to deliver their stroke.

The non-co-operation campaign was in full swing by 1921, and certainly made plenty of trouble. Some provinces were badly disorganized, while here and there passive resistance turned into rioting and bloodshed.

The British *Raj* met the challenge firmly. Thousands of nationalists, including Gandhi himself, were jailed; the native press was muzzled, and the whole official technique of repression was put in force. This stern conflict of wills dragged on for several years, interrupted by interludes of negotiation. But, in the larger sense, the movement failed. The English community was not "outcaste." The *Raj* was not beaten to its knees; it controlled the situation.

Britain still ruled India. Why? Because the Indians were not generally resolved that the British should get out. Despite much zeal and devotion, the nationalists were still a minority even of the Hindus. The bulk of the Moslems remained suspicious and aloof. Lastly, the nationalists themselves tended to split over the thorny problem of the Depressed Classes. That amazing controversy, so incomprehensible to most Westerners, illustrates clearly what we have already remarked—that the course of events in India is determined less by what Britain does than by what Indians do amongst themselves.

Under Hinduism, the lot of low-castes and outcastes or Pariahs is a dreadful one. So far as religious observances and personal relations are concerned, the coming of British rule made no difference, because the British maintained strict neutrality in such matters. But the *Raj* did protect the life and property of the lowliest Pariah against the lordliest Brahmin—a tremendous change since the old days. The *Raj* has therefore proved a sure bulwark against the return of ancient abuses.

So long as the *Raj* ruled absolutely over all, the Depressed Classes (popularly known as "Untouchables") might rest secure. However, the rise of a strong Brahmin-led nationalist movement demanding self-government for India made the Untouchables ask themselves what their fate would be in an India where impartial British rule had been replaced by a regime under high-caste direction and control.

Fear of future exploitation at the hands of a tyrannical Brahmin oligarchy soon led the Untouchables to organize on their own account. Shortly before the war, an Untouchable association known as the *Namasudra* appeared, with a big membership and capable leaders. How great were its possibilities can be judged by the fact that the Untouchables total well over 50,000,000!

The Namasudra viewpoint is clearly set forth by its first President, Doctor Nair. "Democracy as a catchword," he says, "has already reached India and is widely used. But the spirit of democracy still pauses east of Suez, and will find it hard to secure a footing in a country where caste is strongly entrenched . . . I do not want to lay the charge of oppressing the lower castes at the door of any particular caste. All the higher castes take a hand in the game. The Brahmin oppresses all the non-Brahmin castes. The high caste non-Brahmin oppresses all the castes below him.

"We want a real democracy; not an oligarchy, however camouflaged by high-sounding words. Moreover, if an oligarchy is established now, it will be a perpetual oligarchy. We further say that we should prefer a delayed democracy to an immediate oligarchy, having more trust in a sympathetic British bureaucracy than in an unsympathetic oligarchy of the so-called high castes who have oppressed us in the past and will do so again but for the British Government. Our attitude is based, not on 'faith' alone, but on the instinct of self-preservation."[6]

The Namasudra Association was an event of deep significance. It meant the emergence of a wholly new factor in the Indian situation. The Untouchables, hitherto mere ciphers in Indian affairs, were becoming self-conscious. Soon they would become self-assertive. A well-organized block of over 50,000,000 people must markedly alter the previous balance of forces. It would naturally strengthen the *Raj*, because the Untouchables were automatically loyalist. It would correspondingly weaken the nationalist cause because it would break the traditional solidarity of Hinduism—the real driving-force behind the nationalist movement.

Nationalism's astute Brahmin leaders instantly saw the danger. They first tried to crush it by intimidation. In many local elections, for example, the Brahmins threatened to outcaste all low-caste voters who did not support nationalist candidates—surely an emphatic Oriental touch to Western electoral procedure!

However, these dictatorial tactics merely intensified the fears of the Untouchables and hardened their resolve to protect themselves from Brahmin domination. Indeed, the vanguard of the Untouchables has gone so far as to consider seceding from Hinduism altogether.

Their present leader, Doctor Ambedkar, asserts that, by its very nature and because of the iron grip of its Brahmin hierarchy, Hinduism cannot be reformed. Since, therefore, the Untouchables have no hope of an honorable place within the Hindu fold, Doctor Ambedkar proposes that they seek new spiritual pastures. He and his colleagues are at present seriously considering the comparative merits of Buddhism, Islam, and Christianity. The Doctor is said personally to favor Buddhism.

Of course these extreme views are as yet confined to a relatively small group. The Untouchable masses, ignorant and illiterate, hold no such ideas. Still, the trend is there, and to orthodox Hindus the bare possibility that their ancient system may be disrupted is

6 Doctor T. Madavan Nab, "Caste and Democracy," *Edinburgh Review,* October, 1928.

appalling. Yet the issue cannot be ignored or evaded. It has been thrust dramatically to the fore by a political controversy between the Untouchables and Hindu Orthodoxy.

In the course of a slow yet steady policy of concession to Indian political aspirations, the British Government recently provided for the establishment of provincial parliaments enjoying a considerable measure of power. This at once raised the question of how the membership should be elected. The British asked what electoral method the Indians themselves wanted. The Hindus answered, in effect:

"A general popular vote, just as in England, without distinction of race or creed." This sounds very liberal and democratic, but other Indians promptly pointed out the "joker." Since the Hindus outnumber all the other elements put together, and since Indians think primarily in terms of their religious allegiance, the Hindu proposal would result in legislatures overwhelmingly composed of Hindus who could (and undoubtedly would) legislate chiefly in their own special interest. That, said all the non-Hindus, would be intolerable; something they simply would not stand for. They therefore proposed a system of proportional representation which would protect their interests against Hindu domination. In this connection it must not be forgotten that, though the Mohammedans are far-and-away the largest single non-Hindu group, other important minorities exist—notably Buddhists, Christians, and Sikhs. Nevertheless, including the Untouchables, the Hindus outnumber the combined minorities almost two to one.

Including the Untouchables! There's the rub. The nationalists might have brought themselves reluctantly to proportional representation if they had been sure of controlling the solid Hindu vote. But the Untouchables demanded that a fixed percentage of the Hindu seating quota be reserved for them. When this demand was rejected by the orthodox leaders, the Untouchables informed the British Government that, for electoral purposes, they were not to be classed as Hindus but as another minority, entitled as such to separate representation.

This would, indeed, be a body-blow both to the nationalists and to Hinduism Yet it was apparently going to happen. The British

Government maintained an attitude of strict neutrality. It was ready to do anything on which the Indians might agree. However, *something* must be done; otherwise elections could not be held, and the promised legislatures would not come into being. When Hindus and minorities continued at loggerheads, the British Government broke the deadlock by itself fixing the quotas. In this award the Untouchables were naturally assigned legislative seats of their own. Great was the joy of the Untouchables. But even greater was the horrified wrath of orthodox Hindus, nationalist or otherwise.

It was at this crucial moment that Gandhi leaped dramatically into the breach. Having been sentenced to a long jail term for civil disobedience, he had not been politically active for some time. The Mahatma now come back into the limelight by announcing that he would "fast unto death" if the Untouchables continued to stand apart from the orthodox Hindus. At the same time, however, Gandhi told his orthodox brethren the Untouchables' demand for reserved seats must be granted, and that the harsher religious and social discriminations should be done away with.

Gandhi's grim ultimatum proved to be a veritable bombshell. Every one realized that Gandhi would certainly starve himself to death unless his terms were met; also, that there was no time to lose, because the frail little man could not survive prolonged privation. As the days passed, a wave of popular emotion swept all India and compelled both factions to get together in conference. So the world soon witnessed the extraordinary spectacle of leading Hindus and Untouchables squatting down together in the Poona jail yard around the Mahatma's cot and in his presence signing an agreement that at least patched up their quarrel. The Pact of Poona was immediately cabled to the British Government which gladly modified its arbitrary award by including the Untouchables in the Hindu quota.

Gandhi had achieved an amazing personal triumph. Yet, just because it was personal, it did not prove lasting. The Poona Pact had been signed under duress. Neither side had dared incur the odium of having caused the Mahatma's death by standing out. The leaders on both sides, however, continued to dislike and mistrust one another. As soon as the wave of popular emotion subsided, the opposing battle-lines began to re-form. Ere long, orthodox Hindu discontent rallied around the Brahmin hierarchy led by Pandit Malaviya, a stately, white-haired personage of the old school. To him and his colleagues Gandhi's concessions to the Untouchables meant little less than the ruin of Hinduism. They certainly did spell a notable lessening of Brahmin power; for, entirely aside from politics, the admittance of Untouchables to anything like religious equality flouted the Brahmins' vast discretionary authority. Incidentally, we may remark that Gandhi, though belonging to one of the higher castes, is not a Brahmin. Thus the subtle caste-bond, so tremendously strong in Hinduism, was always lacking between him and the Brahminical order.

Pandit Malaviya and his fellow-zealots are naturally allied with the extreme nationalists who quarrel with Gandhi on two counts: because he made terms with the Untouchables, and because he advocated giving the provincial parliaments a trial. The ultra-nationalists condemn any dealings with the government until the British yield to their demand for full self-government amounting to independence. They prefer, therefore, to continue seditious tactics.

As if those two irreconcilable factions were not enough, Indian nationalism has developed a third type of extremists who can be termed radicals in the Western sense. The Indian radicals look on political agitation as only the means to a larger end—social revolution. Yet here, as elsewhere, the radical wing is split into Socialists and Communists. The best-known Socialist leader is Pandit Jawaharlal Nehru. Since the Communist Party is outlawed by the government, it has "gone underground" and its real leaders are virtually unknown.

The nationalist movement thus seems to be splitting three ways, while its organized nucleus, known as the Congress Party, appears to be badly disrupted. Gandhi's recent resignation from the office of Party President removes a vital link that held it together. The Mahatma probably realizes that his political authority is on the wane. Curiously enough, his religious prestige is still as high as ever. The Hindu masses revere him as almost divine. But in India, as in other parts of the Orient, the masses have little to say. It is the religious and political leaders who have the last word; and the big-wigs of

Hinduism think Gandhi has ceased to serve their purposes. Such being their opinion, he is probably "through" politically—though his name may still be used. Gandhi's exact status is merely one of many current uncertainties. Indeed, the whole political situation in India becomes so increasingly confused that even the near future is problematical.

* * *

We have summarized India's political tangle less for its intrinsic importance than because of its bearing upon India's larger problems. Why, for instance, has the first notable installment of self-government offered by Britain become a veritable apple of discord which has set all India by the ears and aroused such bitter domestic controversies that the project may prove unworkable before it is even tried? If Indians cannot agree amongst themselves as to how local legislatures should be elected and how seatings of members shall be apportioned, what are the prospects for a still more important move that Britain has formally promised as soon as the Indians have taken certain steps to bring it about? We here refer to a proposed All-India Federal Parliament endowed from the start with powers and prerogatives whose eventual culmination is intended to be full self-government. This project has been definitely set forth by the British Government. The idea is explained in an official pronouncement which reads: "It is explicit in the Declaration of 1917 that the natural issue of India's constitutional progress, as there contemplated, is the attainment of Dominion status."[7]

The Federal Parliament project involves the relation of "British India" to the native states—one of the thorniest problems in India's political evolution. Interspersed among the areas under direct British rule are many districts ruled by native Princes according to native laws and customs. Some of these autonomous states are as large as European nations;[8] the smallest are tiny enclaves surrounded by territory under British rule. Great or small, however, each native state has its own legal status, carefully defined in a special treaty between the reigning Prince and the British Crown.

7 Announcement by the Viceroy of India in a Gazette Extraordinary on October 25, 1929.

8 The largest is Hyderabad, in south-central India, with an area of 82,000 square miles and a population of over 12,000,000.

Now it is obvious that any general scheme of self-government for India must include the native states. This is insisted upon by nationalists of all shades in British India, and the British Government admits that they are right. Accordingly it has announced that one of the pre-requisites to the setting up of a Federal Parliament is the assent of a majority of the Indian Princes to the arrangement. The Princes, however, demand certain guarantees before entering the proposed Federation. Many of them distrust the nationalists, especially the radical nationalists who would like to abolish the Princes altogether. Princely reluctance, together with certain financial provisions, still prevents the Federal Parliament from getting beyond the blue-print stage.

Such difficulties, however, are in themselves not insuperable. And that, together with the enormous benefits which would result from a stable, contented India grappling wholeheartedly with its economic and social problems, furnish the stock arguments of Indian nationalists and British liberals or radicals, alike, when they maintain that self-government for India is a supreme necessity.

This viewpoint is clearly stated by a well-known English thinker of somewhat radical tendencies. Says Harold J. Laski: "The big Indian problem is poverty. The reorganization of the agrarian system, the development of Indian industry, a comprehensive effort to deal with the problems of public health and education; these, with such other problems as child-marriage and the Depressed Classes, ought to be the real material of public discussion. Yet no Indian politician can be persuaded to face them seriously until responsible government is in being. Until then, he will pursue the ostrich policy of attributing all evils to foreign domination. There will be a continuation of that listless inertia in the face of momentous social difficulties which is the curse of India. Rhetoric will occupy the place of thinking; denunciation will comfort those who ought to be busy with constructive effort. Enthusiasm will be concentrated on the shadow, instead of on the substance, of the larger problems.

The lines of division in Indian public opinion will be unreal, because they will not be set by the material with which it is urgent to cope. India is the outstanding proof of the fact that only in self-government can the means of social regeneration be found.

Deprived of that, the Indian lacks that sense of responsibility which is the condition of social progress."[9]

All very sensible and very logical, Mr. Laski. Yet may you not be putting the cart before the horse? Does not the decision really lie more with the Indian people than with the British Government? Assume for the sake of argument that all Britain is desperately eager to establish self-government in India forthwith; just *how* is it to be done? Should the British Government accept the nationalist method? But that would mean coercing stubborn non-Hindu minorities which, in British India alone, total nearly 100,000,000; or, if we include the Depressed Classes among the Hindus, almost 150,000,000. On the other hand, should the government give consideration to these minorities? That apparently means a continuation of the nationalists' refusal sincerely to play the game. There is the deadlock which Indians themselves must break before the problem of self-government can genuinely be solved. No matter how much Indians *ought* to think economically and sociologically, the hard fact is that they *do not* think that way at the present time. Instead, they continue to think basically as they have always done—in terms of religious and social differences which root in the very fiber of their being. Until Indian thinking and feeling are notably changed, self-government for India on Western lines will be difficult, if not impossible.

Indeed, the prospects of harmonizing Western institutions, methods, and ideas of all sorts with the native genius are probably less bright in India than anywhere else in Asia. Despite prolonged and complex "Westernization," India displays not merely a tendency toward blind reaction but a conscious, purposeful hostility to the very spirit of the West.

This intense, deep-seated antagonism to all things Western springs from Hinduism itself. The Hindu religion, together with the social system which is its logical expression, stands unique and apart in human history. As already remarked, Hinduism is essentially non-ethical in character.

Its higher side consists chiefly of subtle metaphysical speculation infinitely remote from mundane affairs, while its practical side is

9 Harold J. Laski, "India at the Crossroads," *Yale Review*, March, 1932.

concerned almost wholly with ceremonial observances regardless of their moral significance. As a result, Hinduism is perhaps the most depressing, hidebound cult that has ever afflicted mankind. That eminent student of human ideas, the late William Archer, does not seem to have pronounced too severe a criticism when he wrote:

"Hinduism has a marvelous gift for extracting bad effects from good intentions, actual ugliness from potential beauty. It is always washing and never clean . . . Hinduism is, in short, the great anachronism of the modern world . . . It is a wholly unfiltered religion—a paganism which has resolutely declined filtration. If it includes in its pantheon any personage holding a position in the least analogous to that of Gautama Buddha or Jesus, it can only be Krishna—and what a difference is there! It is this tendency towards pollution rather than purification that assigns it its place—incomparably the lowest—in the scale of world-religions. Until Hinduism has somehow got itself filtered, India cannot reasonably claim fellowship on terms of equality with the civilized nations of the earth."[10]

Yet this "great anachronism" is no outworn or dying creed. It is very much alive; its vitality is great, and it intends at all costs to survive. Furthermore, it sees in 'Westernism a deadly foe with whom no real compromise is possible. Here is the explanation for the seeming contradictions in the Indian nationalist movement. Hinduism, which inspires that movement, possesses, as Lord Meston well says, "a reality, an intensity, a dominion to which there is nothing at all comparable in the modern world."[11]

Hence, this Brahmin-led "nationalism" aims at a goal utterly different from what we deem in any sense nationalist. Indian nationalism is, at heart, "rather the revolt of a privileged class against modern influences which threaten its social predominance; it is the struggle of an ancient civilization to stem the advance of its most dangerous rival, the power of Western civilization."[12]

This likewise explains the anti-Western crusade preached by Gandhi, a man of high intelligence who knows so intimately the West and its ideals. Here is how the Mahatma condemns Westernism,

10 William Archer, *India and the Future,* pp. 86–87 (New York, 1928).

11 Lord Meston, *Nationhood for India,* p. 68 (New Haven, 1932).

12 *Ibid.*

root and branch: "It behooves every lover of India to cling to the old Indian civilization even as a child clings to its mother's breast . . . In order to restore India to its pristine condition, we have to return to it. Machinery is the chief symbol of modern civilization. It represents a great sin . . . Railways accentuate the evil nature of man . . . If India would discard modern civilization, she can only gain by so doing."[13]

Gandhi's strange career shows how Hindus apparently Westernized can zealously participate in Kali's dark and bloody rites, or in disgusting ceremonies like those daily performed on the Ganges river-bank at Benares. Hinduism's mysterious hold on even its most seemingly enlightened votaries led a thoughtful German observer to remark of the civil disobedience campaign: "In India today a great struggle is on to expel the English. India's best men are being imprisoned or martyred. But are they doing this for the sake of India's freedom or are they sacrificing themselves to the old, bloody gods whose power is as strong as ever? . . . A highly intelligent Hindu politician once said that the first thing the Indians would do when they had thrown out the English would be to permit once more the burning of widows . . . The holy river Ganges and the magic that flows therein are stronger than all Western ideas The most Europeanized Indians still remain Indians; that is to say, men who may have assimilated a complete European education, but who none the less remain utterly foreign."[14]

Of course this refers to Hindus and Hinduism. It does not necessarily apply to all India—certainly not to the great Mohammedan minority. Hinduism is fundamentally as alien to Islam as it is to the West. This, however, merely intensifies India's truly tragic situation, in travail as she is today with the clash of mighty forces that seemingly cannot be reconciled.

Despite its amazing vitality, Hinduism is not powerful enough to expel Westernism, crush Islam, and lead India back to some revived version of ancient times. Yet Hinduism may be strong enough to block constructive progress and perpetuate the present deadlock.

---

13 Quoted from Robert E. Speer, *Race and Race-Relations,* p. 62 (New York, 1924).

14 Cohn Ross, "The Paradox of India," *Pester Lloyd* (Budapest); translated in *The Living Age,* November, 1931.

In that case India would get nowhere in particular; she would just mill around in chronic turmoil.

We here refer not only to politics but to Indian life in general. For instance, take the matter of Westernization. In our preliminary survey of the Orient[15] we saw how widely Westernism had permeated India, and how vain were mystic dreams that the India of railways, motor buses, moving pictures, and smoking factory chimneys would revert to the bullock cart and the spinning wheel. That is not the alternative. The real issue is, not whether Westernism may be uprooted, but whether Westernism can become effective. The moral and spiritual *sabotage* (instinctive as well as deliberate) which Hinduism inflicts on the Westernizing process is only too plain. That is the chief reason why, despite incredibly low wages and bad working conditions, factory workers are not usually efficient, manufactured goods from what we deem in any sense nationalist. Indian nationalism is, at heart, "rather the revolt of a privileged class against modern influences which threaten its social predominance; it is the struggle of an ancient civilization to stem the advance of its most dangerous rival, the power of Western civilization."[16]

This likewise explains the anti-Western crusade preached by Gandhi, a man of high intelligence who knows so intimately the West and its ideals. Here is how the Mahatma condemns Westernism, root and branch: "It behooves every lover of India to cling to the old Indian civilization even as a child clings to its mother's breast . . . In order to restore India to its pristine condition, we have to return to it. Machinery is the chief symbol of modern civilization. It represents a great sin. . . . Railways accentuate the evil nature of man . . . If India would discard modern civilization, she can only gain by so doing."13

Gandhi's strange career shows how Hindus apparently Westernized can zealously participate in Kali's dark and bloody rites, or in disgusting ceremonies like those daily performed on the Ganges river-bank at Benares. Hinduism's mysterious hold on even its most seemingly enlightened votaries led a thoughtful German observer to remark of the civil disobedience campaign: "In India

15 Part II, Chapter I, entitled: "Asia's Five-Fold Revolution."

16 *Ibid.*

today a great struggle is on to expel the English. India's best men are being imprisoned or martyred. But are they doing this for the sake of India's freedom or are they sacrificing themselves to the old, bloody gods whose power is as strong as ever? . . . A highly intelligent Hindu politician once said that the first thing the Indians would do when they had thrown out the English would be to permit once more the burning of widows . . . The holy river Ganges and the magic that flows therein are stronger than all Western ideas The most Europeanized Indians still remain Indians; that is to say, men who may have assimilated a complete European education, but who none the less remain utterly foreign."[17]

Of course this refers to Hindus and Hinduism. It does not necessarily apply to all India—certainly not to the great Mohammedan minority. Hinduism is fundamentally as alien to Islam as it is to the West. This, however, merely intensifies India's truly tragic situation, in travail as she is today with the clash of mighty forces that seemingly cannot be reconciled.

Despite its amazing vitality, Hinduism is not powerful enough to expel Westernism, crush Islam, and lead India back to some revived version of ancient times. Yet Hinduism may be strong enough to block constructive progress and perpetuate the present deadlock. In that case India would get nowhere in particular; she would just mill around in chronic turmoil.

We here refer not only to politics but to Indian life in general. For instance, take the matter of Westernization. In our preliminary survey of the Orient[18] we saw how widely Westernism had permeated India, and how vain were mystic dreams that the India of railways, motor buses, moving pictures, and smoking factory chimneys would revert to the bullock cart and the spinning wheel. That is not the alternative. The real issue is, not whether Westernism may be uprooted, but whether Westernism can become effective. The moral and spiritual *sabotage* (instinctive as well as deliberate) which Hinduism inflicts on the Westernizing process is only too plain. That is the chief reason why, despite incredibly low wages and bad working conditions, factory workers are not usually efficient,

17 Cohn Ross, "The Paradox of India," *Pesier Lloyd* (Budapest); translated in *The Living Age*, November, 1931.

18 Part II, Chapter I, entitled: "Asia's Five-Fold Revolution."

manufactured goods do not average high in quality, and Indian industry fails to keep pace with that of other Oriental countries like China, to say nothing of industrially advanced Japan So competent an authority on Indian affairs as Lord Ronaldshay believes that Western industrialism in India is still an exotic growth and agrees with a nationalist spokesman that it is as yet "a foreign wen on the face of India." Lord Ronaldshay points out that nearly all the important native manufacturers are Parsis—a small non-Hindu community centering in Bombay.[19]

Elsewhere, Indian industry is chiefly due to British capital and management. These facts lead him to say: "I find it difficult to escape from the conclusion that the organization of industries on the lines evolved by Western nations is something which is altogether alien to the genius of the Indian people. Western industrialism is, indeed, regarded by a not inappreciable section of educated public opinion not merely with indifference but with deep-rooted aversion. And the modern factory is as uncongenial to the Indian workman as the industrial system is to the educated Indian idealist."[20]

The most serious consequence of this seemingly innate aversion is that it may render impossible an easing of India's most pressing economic and social problem—overpopulation. In India, as in Japan, the impact of the West stimulated a prodigious upsurge of population. In the old days, before the Raj had imposed the *Pax Britannica* and had introduced Western life-saving methods, India's population did not average much over 100,000,000. Today it is 150,000,000, breeding up to the very margin of subsistence. The only way in which this rapid increase can be even temporarily taken care of is through further industrialization coupled with scientific agriculture in Western lines. Should India take Gandhi's advice, scrap the whole paraphernalia of Westernism, and go "back to the

19 The Parsis are descended from Persian refugees who fled to India in the seventh century, A.D., when their country was conquered by the Mohammedans. They have retained their ancient Zoroastrian fire-worshipping faith and are still a distinct group, racially and temperamentally. Their high average financial ability has rendered them vastly more influential than their small numbers would statistically indicate. According to the last census (1931), the Parsis number a trifle under 800,000.

20 Earl of Ronaldshay, *India: A Birds-Eye View*, p. 180 (London and Boston, 1924).

Vedas," untold millions would be doomed to speedy death from sheer starvation.

Yet even with the aid of Western science and technique, India's population problem looks almost hopeless in the long run. And the reason for that is undoubtedly Hinduism, which makes any adequate measures of birth-control impossible. Hinduism's responsibility for the intensification of this problem in a peculiarly deplorable form has never been more trenchantly exposed than by a Hindu. Nearly twenty years ago, a little book appeared from the pen of one P. K. Wattal, a native official in the Finance Department of the Government of India. Obscurely published at the height of the Great War,[21] this modest volume has never attracted a tithe of the attention it deserves—certainly not in India, where its author remains a lone voice crying out in the philoprogenitive wilderness.

Though obviously seeking to avoid giving undue offense to his co-religionists, Mr. Wattal does not evade the issue or gloss over ugly facts. He begins by asking his fellow-countrymen to look at the population problem rationally and without prejudice. "This essay," he says, "should not be construed into an attack on the spiritual civilization of our country, or even indirectly into a glorification of the materialism of the West. The object in view is that we should take a somewhat more matter-of-fact view of the main problem of life, viz., how to live in this world. We are a poor people; the fact is indisputable.

"Our poverty is, perhaps, due to many causes. But I put it to every one of us whether he has not at some of the most momentous periods of his life been handicapped by having to support a large family, and whether this encumbrance has not seriously affected the chances of advancement warranted by early promise and exceptional endowment. It is a physical fact, and has nothing to do with political environment or religious obligation."[22]

After this appeal to reason in his readers, the bold pioneer develops his thesis. The primal cause of over-population in India, he asserts, is early marriage. Contrary to Western lands, where

---

21 *The Population Problem In India A Census Study*, P. K. Wattal. Bombay, Bennett, Coleman & Co. Ltd, Calcutta and London, 1916.
22 *Ibid.*

population is kept down by prudential marriages and contraceptive measures, "for the Hindus marriage is a sacrament which must be performed, regardless of the fitness of the parties to bear the responsibilities of a mated existence. A Hindu male must marry and beget children— sons, if you please—to perform his funeral rites lest his spirit wander uneasily in the waste places of the earth. The very name of son, *putra,* means one who saves his father's soul from the hell called *Puta.* A Hindu maiden unmarried at puberty is a source of social obloquy to her family and of damnation to her ancestors. . . .

"The worst of the matter is that, despite the efforts of social reformers, child-marriage seems to be increasing." The upshot is a tremendous birth-rate, but this is "no matter for congratulation. We are paying the inevitable penalty for bringing into this world more persons than can be properly cared for."

Mr. Wattal then goes on to describe the cruel items in India's death-rate: the tremendous female mortality, due largely to too early childbirth, and the equally terrible infant mortality, nearly 50 per cent of infant deaths being due to premature birth or debility at birth. These are the inevitable penalties of early and universal marriage.

For, in India, "everybody marries, fit or unfit, and is a parent at the earliest possible age permitted by nature." This process is highly dysgenic; it is plainly lowering the quality and sapping the vigor of the race.

The baser elements of the population—the negroid aboriginal tribes, and the Pariahs or outcastes—are gaining the fastest. Also, the vitality of the whole population seems to be lowering. The census figures show that the number of elderly persons is decreasing, and that the average statistical expectation of life is falling.

"The coming generation is severely handicapped at start in life. And the chances of living to a good old age are considerably smaller than they were, say thirty or forty years ago.

"Have we ever paused to consider what it means to us in the life of the nation as a whole? It means that the persons who alone by weight of experience and wisdom are fitted for the posts of command in the various public activities are snatched away by death; that the guidance and leadership which belong to age and mature judgment in the countries of the West fall, in India, to younger and hence less trustworthy persons."[23]

After warning his fellow-countrymen that neither improved methods of agriculture, the growth of industry, nor emigration can afford any real relief to the growing pressure of population on means of subsistence, Mr. Wattal concludes with a plea to face the situation frankly and strive to cope with it promptly. "We can no longer afford to shut our eyes to the social canker in our midst. In the land of the bullock-cart, the motor has come to stay. The competition is now with the more advanced races of the West, and we cannot tell them what Diogenes said to Alexander—'Stand out of my sunshine!'"

So ends this striking little book—which has produced no appreciable effect. A modern Ephraim, Hinduism is indeed joined to its idols Unhappily, the stern processes of our world will not let this idolater alone.

* * *

India's future is not bright. And this seems to hold irrespective of the British connection. If the *Raj* endures, order will presumably be maintained, but the *Raj* cannot cure India's basic ills. Furthermore its continued tenure will be due chiefly to a deadlock of rival native factions none of which has any special fondness for the *Raj,* as such. British rule in India is, and must continue to be, alien and aloof. As William Archer humorously puts it: "The Briton comes to India to govern, governs, and goes away again. His relations with a few Indians may be more or less friendly; but he no more enters into the national life of the country than the plumber who puts in your water-pipes, or the electrician who 'wires' your house, becomes a member of your family."[24]

Should the British quit India or be expelled, the prospect would be dark indeed. Even under the *Raj,* ugly flare-ups reveal the lava-floods of religious fanaticism that simmer and surge beneath the thin crust of a superimposed authority. Were Indians suddenly left to their own devices, it is a practical certainty that they would soon

---

23 *Ibid.*

24 Archer, *op. cit.,* p. 10.

stage a colossal dog fight beside which the Chinese fracas would look like child's play. Hindus, Moslems, Sikhs, Gurkhas, native Christians, and some minor elements would be at one another's throats for supremacy or bare survival. In short, India would revert to anarchy even worse than that which followed the collapse of the Mogul Empire two centuries ago and went on interminably until the imposition of British control.

The tragic aspects of present-day India are vividly portrayed in a recent book by an English couple who "went out" ready to do their bit for India but presently returned home, saddened and disillusioned.[25] The man, Edward Charles, was principal of a large Hindu-Moslem college in Central India. His father had spent a lifetime in the Indian Civil Service, and the son inherited high ideals of duty and self-sacrifice. The "white man's burden," however, proved to be a harrowing one. Shortly after his arrival at the college, he found a cobra in his private bathroom and knew beyond doubt that it had been put there to kill him. This grisly episode heralded a strike of all the Hindu students. The Moslem students, however, not only refused to walk out but tried to make the Principal their champion. The strike threw the adjacent city in an uproar, with religious riots impending and the small British community fearful least this might be the spark that would set all India aflame. Later on, Principal Charles learned that the strike had been instigated and engineered by two apparently loyal Hindu members of his own faculty.

Both Mr. Charles and his wife stress the virulent hatred, deceit, and loathing felt by the Hindus both toward their white rulers and toward their Moslem fellow-countrymen. Their poignant narrative, in diary form, reads like a nightmare, and they left India convinced that a century and a half of British efforts in India had wrought only futility and failure. Mary Charles quotes the pungent comment of a local English official, which rather typifies such remarks on the Indian situation when the conversation is "off the record." The gentleman's words were: "Home rule is coming, and it'll be like hell let loose when it comes, and while it's coming we're going to have a *bloody* time!"

---

25 Edward and Mary Charles, *Indian Patchwork* (New York, 1934).

PART II
CHAPTER V
ISLAM: A WORLD IN TRANSFORMATION

THE Near East is well named. More than geography is involved. Compared with the rest of Asia, the Near East is culturally and spiritually *closer* to the West. Of course there are marked distinctions between them. Distance is relative; it depends on the point of view. Entering the Near East direct from Europe, the differences seem enormous. If, however, we come upon the Near East after having traversed the vast breadth of Asia, our perspective alters and familiar landmarks begin to appear. We are no longer among peoples like those of the Far East whose historic evolution has been wholly apart from ours; neither do we encounter phenomena such as Hinduism, profoundly alien to our mental and spiritual bent. Both in religion and culture, the West and the Near East are basically akin. However widely these may have diverged through the ages, they spring from the same root.

This being so, the impact of the West upon the Near East has produced effects quite different from those elsewhere in the Orient. The results have been less shattering and the possibilities of genuine assimilation are better.

The tremendous difficulties inherent in thoroughgoing Westernizations of Eastern lands have already been glimpsed, alike in the Far East and in India. Even modern Japan, for all its disciplined aptitude, is as yet essentially an artificial product. After some seventy years of strenuous, purposeful endeavor, Japan's Westernization remains something superimposed upon an older order—with most unpleasant consequences. Compare this with the modernization of Turkey, and the distinction between the two processes becomes clear. The Near East's problems are thorny enough, yet they are not so difficult as those further to the eastward, nor is the outcome so dubious.

Broadly speaking, the Near East possesses a fundamental unity—that of Islam. The native Christian and Jewish[1] minorities are local survivals from long-past times. Now Islam is more than a creed; it is a culture and a way of life. However radically it may be modified by Westernism, Islam will remain the basis upon which new developments will repose. Also, Islam is not ossified or decadent, as many Westerners assume. It is very much alive, and it has long been in genuine evolution. The Islamic world touched its lowest depth of decrepitude two centuries ago. Thereafter began the movement known as the Mohammedan Revival[2]—a spiritual leaven which has never ceased to work and which continues to produce important effects.

This revival, be it noted, was not due to Western impacts; it sprang from Islam's own vitality. Here, then, we have a new factor, not present elsewhere in the contacts of East and West. This further marks the difference between the current transformation of the Near East and that of other Oriental regions.

Today, as always, Arabia is a land of mystery. Aloof and impenetrable, this huge block of a million square miles lies, a world apart. Yet, ever and anon, its vast expanse is swept by a mighty wind. The serried dunes of the desert, sucked upward by furious eddies, darken the sky with curtains of sand. Resistless, remorseless, the *simoon* or desert wind sweeps out of Arabia, overwhelming all that stands in its path.

As with nature, so with man. Arabia, itself unconquerable, breeds mighty conquerors. Now and then a great spirit arises, welds scattered tribes with the fire of fanaticism, and launches a human

---

1 We here refer to the old 'Sephardic" communities of Turkey, Arabia, and North Africa; not to the recent Zionist colonization of Palestine, which is a European importation.

2 The author has described this movement and has traced in detail its subsequent phases, together with the interaction between them and Western influences, in a book entitled *The New World of Islam,* first published in New York and London in 1921, and subsequently translated into French, Arabic, and Turkish. As a general survey it is still fairly adequate down to its date of publication, though of course it should be read in the light of subsequent developments.

simoon upon the neighboring lands. Thus does Ibn Saud weld Arabia at this very hour. And thus, in infinitely greater measure, did Mohammed the Prophet, thirteen hundred years ago.

The rise of Islam is perhaps the most amazing event in human history. Springing from a land and a people alike previously negligible, Islam spread within a century over half the earth, shattering great empires, overthrowing long-established religions, remolding the souls of peoples, and building up a whole new world—the world of Islam.

This whirlwind conquest was the prelude to a brilliant cultural flowering throughout the Near East. The Arabs were an innately gifted race, eager to learn and appreciative of the gifts which older civilizations had to bestow. The result was a new civilization—Saracenic civilization, in which the ancient cultures of Greece, Rome, and Persia were revitalized by Arab vigor and the Islamic spirit. Down to about 1,000 A.D., the realm of Islam was the most civilized and progressive portion of the world.[3] Studded with splendid cities, gracious mosques, and quiet universities where the wisdom of the ancient world was preserved and appreciated, the Moslem East offered a striking contrast to the Christian West, then sunk in the night of the Dark Ages.

The quick-flowering Saracenic civilization presently declined. For this there were several reasons. In the first place, the mushroom Arab Empire stretching from Spain to the borders of India was a haphazard creation. The Prophet himself had no hand in it. His ministry was so brief that before Islam's career of conquest had more than started, he bad passed from the scene.[4] Mohammed's

---

3 The only parallel civilization at all comparable was that of China. During the seventh century, A.D., China produced the brilliant Tang period—a veritable Golden Age of literature and art. But this was soon interrupted by internal troubles and by barbarian invasions from the north.

4 In the year 622 A.D., Mohamed fled from Mecca, his birthplace, which had rejected his teachings, to the city of Medina, where he had made many converts and where he soon became supreme. This shift, known as the *Hegira* marks the establishment of Islam, and from it the Moslem calendar is calculated. Mohammed died ten years later. By that time Mecca had submitted to him and most of Arabia had been unified under his rule, but the first Moslem foreign enterprise, the invasion of Syria, did not begin until 635, three years after Mohammed's death.

death gave the signal for factional quarrels characteristic of the Arabs, which soon deepened into bloody civil wars.

In these sordid struggles the unity and simplicity of early Islam were alike lost. Islam started out as a theocratic democracy known as the Caliphate. Mohammed proclaimed that all Believers were brothers—a doctrine congenial to a free desert people. His immediate "successors"[5] were austere, God-fearing men who governed in most democratic fashion. But the capital was soon moved from Medina to Damascus in Syria, and thence to Baghdad in Mesopotamia, where the democratic simplicity of Arabia gave place to traditions of Oriental despotism. The freedom-loving Arabs retired to their deserts, leaving the Caliphate to be run by Syrian and Persian converts or persons of mixed blood. Presently, political unity was disrupted, with rival Caliphs at Baghdad, in Egypt, and in Spain.

The triumph of political despotism eventually sealed the doom of progressive thought and creative culture as well. The Arabs of Mohammed's day were a fresh, unspoiled people inspired by a high ideal. They had their full share of Semitic fanaticism; but, though fanatical, they were not bigoted; that is to say, they possessed not closed but open minds. They held firmly to the tenets of their religion, but this religion was extremely simple. The core of Mohamed's teaching was theism *plus* certain practices. A strict belief in the unity of God; an equally strict belief in the divine mission[6] of Mohammed as set forth in the Koran, and certain clearly defined duties—prayer, ablutions, fasting, almsgiving, and pilgrimage—these, and these alone, constituted the Islam of the Arab conquerors of the Eastern world.

So simple a theology could not seriously fetter the Arab mind—alert, curious, eager to learn, and ready to adjust itself to conditions ampler and more complex than those in the parched environment of the desert. The resulting adjustment spelled Saracenic civilization.

5 That is the translation of the Arabic word Khaiija—Anglicized into *Caliph*.

6 To be carefully distinguished from divinity. Mohammed not only made no pretensions to a divine origin, but specifically disclaimed any superhuman attributes. He regarded himself as the last of a series of divinely inspired prophets, beginning with Adam and extending through Moses and Jesus to himself, the mouthpiece of God's latest and most perfect revelation.

For a time, thought was relatively free, producing a wealth of original ideas and daring speculations. In time, however, reactionary forces gained in strength. The liberals, known as Motazelites, upheld the doctrinal simplicity of Islam and also contended that the test of all things should be reason. On the other hand, the conservative schools asserted that the test should be precedent and authority. These men, many of them converted Christians imbued with the traditions of Byzantine orthodoxy, undertook an immense work of Koranic interpretation. As the result of these labors there gradually arose a Moslem theology and scholastic philosophy as rigid, elaborate, and dogmatic as that of the Medieval Christian West.

Though the intellectual struggle was long and bitter, the outcome was a foregone conclusion. Everything conspired to favor the triumph of dogma over reason. At length, the despotic Caliphs came out decisively for religious absolutism. Standards of dogmatic orthodoxy were established, Motazelites were persecuted, and the last vestiges of Saracenic liberalism were extirpated. The standards of Moslem thought were fixed. All creative activity ceased. The very memory of the great Motazelite doctors faded away. The Moslem mind was closed, not to be reopened until our own days.

This ossifying civilization was subjected to a series of alien impacts more or less destructive in character. Having lost their early vigor, the Arabized peoples of the Near East presently passed under the rule of Turkish nomads from Central Asia. Although they soon became Mohammedans, these primitive tribesmen were slow to acquire more than a veneer of Saracenic culture. Also they had a strong racial consciousness which hindered fusion. Indeed, the Turkish and Arabic temperaments are so unlike that the two stocks have never understood each other or gotten along well together.

Barely had Turkish rule been stabilized when down on the Near East came a frightful visitation in the shape of the Mongols. Of all the barbarians who have afflicted civilized men, the Mongols were the most terrible. We noted their blighting effects on Russia and on China; yet neither suffered so atrociously as did the Near East. That whole region, to the borders of Egypt, was ravaged time and again by those appalling barbarians, whose object seems to have been not so much lasting conquest or even loot as a sheer satanic lust for blood and destruction. The Mongols reveled in butchering whole populations, laying waste entire countrysides—and then passing on to fresh fields. All Persia was stamped flat under the Mongol hoofs, while great cultural centers like Ispahan and Baghdad were literally wiped off the map, their smoking ruins surmounted by gleaming pyramids of human skulls. When the Mongol invasions finally ceased, the ravaged and depopulated Moslem East fell under the sway of the Ottoman Turks.

Amongst the Turkish tribes which had established themselves athwart the Near East, the Ottomans or *Osmanli,* as they called themselves, were the best disciplined and produced the most able leaders. In consequence they gradually extended their sway from a small district in Asia Minor to a mighty realm in three continents. We should remember that while the Ottoman Sultans were driving up through the Balkans toward the heart of Europe they were likewise subjugating Hither Asia and Northern Africa, until the Near East was politically unified as it had not been since the time of the early Caliphate. Indeed, by assuming the title of Caliph, the Ottoman Sultans proclaimed their ambition to bring the whole Moslem world under at least their spiritual authority.

In its heyday, the Ottoman Empire was an imposing structure possessing tremendous power. It was strictly a military empire, fashioned for conquest. The art of war was fostered; everything else languished. So the Near East ignored the sweeping changes then occurring in the neighboring West.

Contemptuously indifferent to the doings of *Giaours,*[7] the Moslem East wrapped itself in the tatters of Saracenic civilization and continued to fall behind. Even its military power presently vanished, for the Turk sank into lethargy and ceased to cultivate the art of war.

By the eighteenth century the Moslem world had sunk to the lowest depth of its decrepitude. Manners and morals were alike execrable. The last vestiges of Saracenic culture had vanished in a barbarous luxury of the few and an equally barbarous degradation of the multitude. Learning was virtually dead. Government had become despotism tempered by sedition and assassination. Ground

7 Infidels; misbelievers—the Turkish word usually applied to Christians.

down by misrule, peasant and townsman had alike lost all incentive to labor or initiative, so agriculture and trade fell to the lowest level compatible with bare survival.

As for religion, it was as decadent as everything else. The strict monotheism of Mohammed had become overlaid with a rank growth of superstition and puerile mysticism. The mosques stood unfrequented and ruinous, deserted by the ignorant multitude which, decked out in charms and amulets, listened to squalid fakirs or ecstatic dervishes, and went on pilgrimages to the tombs of "holy men," worshipped as saints and "intercessors" with that Allah who had become too remote a being for direct devotion.

As for the moral precepts of the Koran, they were ignored or defied. Even the holy cities, Mecca and Medina, were sinkholes of iniquity, while the *Ha* or pilgrimage ordained by the Prophet had become a scandal through its abuses.

In short: the life had apparently gone out of Islam, leaving naught but a dry husk of soulless ritual and degrading superstition behind. Could Mohammed have returned to earth, he would unquestionably have anathematized his followers as apostates and idolaters.

Yet, in this darkest hour, a voice came crying out of the vast Arabian desert, the cradle of Islam, calling the faithful back to the true path. This puritan reformer, the famous Abd-el-Wahab, kindled a fire which presently spread to the remotest corners of the Moslem world, purging Islam of its sloth and reviving the spirit of olden days. The great Mohammedan Revival had begun.

Mahommed ibn Abd-el-Wahab was born about the year 00 A.D. in the heart of the Arabian desert, the region known as the Nejd. Yet even to this remote spot came tales of the moral and spiritual decadence rampant in the outer world. These tales so troubled the conscientious soul of young Abd-el-Wahab that he resolved to see with his own eyes what was amiss.

Sojourning in many lands, he found all in the same evil plight. Only in his homeland, the Arabian desert, were manners still simple and religion a living thing. The Bedouin tribes were as yet unspoiled. They, the Prophet's own blood-kin, should be the Chosen Remnant by whom Islam would be restored and purified! Such was the vow of Abd-el-Wahab. Thenceforth he ranged the desert, preaching his mission. It was no easy task. Though the simple folk heard him gladly, those in authority for the most part turned a deaf ear. Then, one day, he came upon the tents of a tribe whose Sheikh listened—and was converted. Thereupon, he and Abd-elWahab made a solemn covenant to regenerate Islam.

That compact, made in a remote oasis almost two centuries ago,[8] has had momentous consequences. Amongst other matters, it bears directly upon the current political situation in the Near East. For that old-time desert sheikh was the head of the clan of Saud, and from him descends the present master of Arabia, Abdalaziz ibn Saud, whose amazing success seems largely due to a profound conviction that he is destined to fulfill the mission begun by his remote ancestor.

The original covenant between Sheikh Saud and Abd-elWahab started the militant movement known as Wahabism. Its joint authors proclaimed what amounted to a holy war, their aim being the creation of a theocratic state on the model of the early Caliphate. Islam was preached in all its pristine purity: a fervent belief in God, almost devoid of ritual and loathing aught savoring of idolatry. The "simple life" was insisted upon. Wine, opium, tobacco, silken raiment—all were sternly taboo. Shrines and veneration of saints were roundly condemned. "Back to the Koran!" was the watchword of these austere puritans.

The zeal engendered was astonishing. These Wahabis displayed a militant fanaticism that was irresistible. Tribe after tribe was annexed to the growing Wahabi state. Often it was done without striking a blow, because Wahabi missionaries would have so persuaded the people that the tribal sheikh found himself bereft of followers and thus forced tamely to submit.

The new realm was no loose tribal confederacy; it was a tightly organized state. Everywhere brigandage was put down, blood-feuds were forbidden, and perfect order established. The wildest of the Bedouins were tamed and puritan orthodoxy enforced. It was nothing short of a miracle.

In time, the two Mahommeds passed from the scene, but their work, in able hands, went steadily on. When Desert Arabia had

8 The precise date was 1747 A.D.

been measurably unified, the Wahabis felt ready for the next big step. The holy cities were their logical goal. These sacred spots were then outlying possessions of the decadent Turkish Sultans. But early in the nineteenth century, the Wahabi hosts burst forth from their deserts and swept the Turks away. Then began a great cleansing of the holy places. This greatly edified the puritan elect but infuriated the ruling and priestly classes elsewhere in Islam. Helpless himself, the Ottoman Sultan called upon his powerful Egyptian vassal, Mehemet Ali, to drive these mad fanatics from the holy cities and restore Ottoman authority.

Mehemet Ali was nothing loath. He had just built up a fine army of hard-fighting Albanians and Circassians, smartly drilled by European instructors and well equipped with artillery. The clash which followed was terrific. The Wahabi cavalry raced headlong upon belching batteries and solid infantry squares, perishing joyously in thousands with full assurance of Paradise. But at length this wild frenzy bowed before the military science of the West. The holy cities were retaken, and the broken remnants of the Wahabi hosts retired sullenly into the deserts whence they came. There, to be sure, Wahabism survived. But its military power was crippled and its political authority gradually loosened. That phase was over.

Wahabism's spiritual role, however, had only just begun. The Nejd remained a focus of puritan zeal whence the new spirit radiated in all directions. Soon the Wahabi leaven began working in the most distant quarters. In fact, within a generation, the strictly Wahabi movement had broadened into the larger development known as the Mohammedan Revival, and this in turn was developing numerous phases of the most varied character.

Wahabism was an ultra-puritan reformation. The Wahabis, despite their moral earnestness, were excessively narrow-minded, and it was perhaps fortunate for Islam that they soon lost their political power and were compelled thenceforth to confine their efforts to moral teaching.

As time passed, the Mohammedan Revival broadened along more constructive lines. Moslem reformers had not dug very deeply into their religious past before they discovered—Motazelism. Liberal-minded reformers were indeed delighted to find such striking confirmation of their ideas, both in the writings of the Motazelite doctors and in the sacred texts themselves.

The founder of Islam had a practical mind, great respect for learning, and an almost rationalistic bent These qualities are revealed by his own words. Here are some of Mohammed's sayings:

"Seek knowledge, even, if need be, on the borders of China."

"One word of knowledge is of more value than the reciting of an hundred prayers."

"The ink of sages is more precious than the blood of martyrs."

"One word of wisdom, learned and communicated to a Moslem brother, outweighs the prayers of a whole year."

"God has created nothing better than reason."

"In truth, a man may have prayed, fasted, given alms, made pilgrimage, and all other good works; nevertheless, he shall be rewarded only in the measure that he has used his common sense."

Sayings like these had furnished the old Motazelite doctors with strong texts in their brave fight against encroaching obscurantism. They served the modern reformers equally well by giving them good Koranic backing for their liberal attitude.

Of course their numbers were at first small, and of course they drew down upon themselves the anathemas of fanatic Mullahs[9] and the hatred of the ignorant multitude. Yet by the middle of the nineteenth century, every Moslem land had its group of broad-minded, forward-looking men. These groups were important in more than a purely religious sense. They likewise furnished minds receptive to Western ideals and capable of appreciating the many good things the West had to offer. Such minds were fitted to interpret Westernism to their fellow-countrymen and thus to lay the intellectual foundation for its genuine assimilation. Their

9 The Mullahs are the Moslem clergy, though they do not exactly correspond to the clergy of Christendom. Mohammed was averse to anything like a priesthood, and Islam makes no legal provision for an ordained priestly class or Caste, as is the case in Christianity, Judaism, Hinduism, and other religions. Theoretically any Moslem can conduct religious services. As time passed, however, a class of men developed who were learned in Islamic theology and law. These ultimately became practically priests, though technically they should be regarded as theological lawyers. There likewise developed religious orders of fakirs and dervishes; but primitive Islam knew nothing of them.

mental attitude is well expressed by a leading Indian Moslem liberal reformer, who wrote as early as 1867: "We must study European scientific works, even though they are not written by Moslems and though we may find in them things contrary to the teachings of the Koran. We should imitate the Arabs of olden days who did not fear to shake their faith by studying Pythagoras."[10]

This constructive trend was not solely religious and cultural; it wrought fruitfully in the political field as well. We have seen that in the Islamic world political freedom, like religious freedom, was soon crushed and almost forgotten Almost—not quite; for memories of the Meccan Caliphate, like memories of Motazelism, remained in the back of men's minds, ready to come forth again with better days. No court theologian could entirely explain away the fact that the Prophet had said: "All Moslems are free." No court chronicler could entirely expunge from Islam's annals the story of its early days, traditionally known as The Age of Blessedness. The Mohammedan Revival, though primarily a puritan reformation of religion, was also in part a political protest against the vicious and contemptible tyrants who misruled the Moslem world.

This internal movement of political reform springing from purely Islamic sources was soon cross-cut by another political current flowing in from the West. Comparing the miserable decrepitude of the Moslem East with Europe's prosperity and vigor, thinking Moslems began to realize their shortcomings, and they could not avoid the conclusion that their woes were in large part due to their wretched governments. Indeed, a few even of the Moslem princes came to realize that there must be some adoption of Western political methods if their countries were to be saved from destruction.

Of course none of these reforming princes had the slightest idea of granting their subjects constitutional liberties or of transforming themselves into limited monarchs. They intended to remain absolute, but absolute more in the sense of the "enlightened autocrat" of eighteenth-century Europe and less in the sense of the purely Oriental despot. What they wanted were true organs of government—army, civil service, judiciary, et cetera—which

10 The writer in question was Sir Syed Ahmed Khan, the founder of the celebrated Moslem college of Aligarh, India.

would function efficiently and semi-automatically as governmental machinery, and not as mere formless masses of individuals who had to be continuously prodded and punished by the sovereign himself in order to get anything done.

As time passed, reformers of quite a different sort began to appear; men demanding Western novelties like constitutions and parliaments. Their numbers were rapidly recruited from the widening circles of men acquainted with Western ideas through the books, pamphlets, and newspapers which were being increasingly published, and through the education given by schools on the Western model that were springing up. In 1876, Turkish liberals actually wrung from a weak Sultan the giant of a parliament.

This premature triumph was, however, followed by a period of reaction. Turkey's quick relapse into Oriental despotism under Sultan Abdul Hamid was paralleled by similar repression in Persia and in North Africa. Down to the Young-Turk revolution of 1908 there were few outward signs of liberal agitation in Moslem lands. Nevertheless, the agitation was there, working underground. Therefore the Young-Turk revolution and the kindred Persian movement in the same year were really a bursting forth of pent-up forces that had long been gathering strength. One of the best informed Western students of Islamic conditions wrote at the time: "Turkey was not so unprepared for parliamentary institutions as might at first sight appear. There lay hidden some precedent, much preparation, and a strong desire, for parliamentary government."[11]

In our survey of the complex movement termed the Mohammedan Revival we must remember that its forward-looking phase was offset by much narrow-mindedness, and blind fanaticism, while all types of reformers, liberal or puritan, were outnumbered by self-seeking reactionaries and by the ignorant, unthinking masses. The true significance of the Mohammedan Revival is that it arose spontaneously; that the Islamic world displayed of its own accord the will to self-regeneration.

This is what differentiates the Moslem East from the rest of the Orient. Here, then, the impact of the West acted not upon a rigid

---

11 Professor A. H. Lybyer, "The Turkish Parliament," *Proceedings of the American Political Science Association,* Volume VII, page 66 (1910).

social order but upon one whose traditional inertia was already being shaken by self-engendered factors. The inpouring tide of Westernism of course sharply deflected the course of Islamic evolution. Nevertheless, Islam *was* evolving. Whither? We cannot tell. So deeply has Westernization cross-cut native trends that the goal which Islam might have attained by itself has now vanished beyond recall.

The interplay of native and Western factors is most strikingly seen by the reactions of two outstanding forces in the modern Islamic world. These great dynamics are Pan Islamism and Nationalism; the former characteristically Moslem, the latter a distinctively Western importation. In order to understand their mutual interaction, we should consider what each means in Near Eastern life.

Pan-Islamism, which in its broadest sense is the feeling of solidarity between all "True Believers," is as old as the Prophet, when Mohammed and his few followers were bound together by the tie of faith against their pagan compatriots who sought their destruction.

To Mohammed the principle of fraternal solidarity amongst Moslems was vital, and be succeeded in implanting this so deeply in Moslem hearts that thirteen centuries have not eradicated it. The bond between Moslem and Moslem today remains much stronger than that between fellow-Christians. To be sure, Moslems fight bitterly amongst themselves, but these conflicts never quite lose the aspect of family quarrels and tend to be adjourned in presence of infidel aggression.

Pan-Islamism, in its modern phase, began with the Wahabi movement. The state founded by Abd-el-Wahab in the Nejd was modeled on the theocratic democracy of the Meccan Caliphs, and the Wahabi dream was a puritan conquest of the whole Moslem world, culminating in a revival of the Caliphate in its original form. Foiled in this grandiose design, Wahabism soon caused political disturbances throughout Islam which were essentially protests against the political decadence of Moslem states and the moral decadence of Moslem rulers. These outbreaks were not inspired by any special fear or dislike of the West, since Europe was not yet seriously assailing Islam except in outlying regions like European

Turkey or the Indies, and the impending peril from the West was consequently not appreciated.

By the middle of the nineteenth century, however, the situation had gravely altered. The French conquest of Algeria, the Russian conquest of Transcaucasia, and the British mastery over virtually all India, convinced thoughtful Moslems everywhere that the Islamic world was in danger of falling under Western domination. It was at this time that Pan-Islamism assumed that distinctly anti-Western character which it has ever since retained.

Failure of the most desperate local resistance to halt European encroachments showed that long preparation and skillful do-ordination of effort were needed if the Western advance was to be stayed. The wiser Pan-Islamic leaders also realized that they must study Western methods and adopt much of the Western technique of power. Above all, they felt that the freeing of Islam from Western control must be preceded and accompanied by a profound spiritual regeneration, thereby engendering the moral forces needed both for the war of liberation and for the fruitful reconstruction which was planned afterwards. At this point the ideals of Pan-Islamists and liberal reformers approach each other. Both recognize Islam's present decadence; both desire its spiritual regeneration. It is on the nature of that regeneration that the two parties are opposed. The liberals believe that Islam should really assimilate Western ideals. Many Pan-Islamists, however, still believe that primitive Islam contains all that is morally necessary, and contend that only Western methods and material achievements should be adopted by the Moslem world.

Self-conscious, systematic Pan-Islamism dates from about the middle of the nineteenth century. The movement crystallized about two distinct factors: new-type religious fraternities like the Sennussiya, and the concerted propaganda of a group of powerful personalities headed by the celebrated Djemal-ed-Din.

Religious fraternities have existed in Islam for centuries. They all possess the same general type of organization, being divided into lodges *(Zawiac)* headed by Masters known as *Mokaddem,* who exercise a more or less extensive authority over the *Khouan* or brethren. Until the foundation of the new-type organizations best exemplified by the Sennussiya, however, the fraternities exerted little practical influence. Mystical and devotional in character, such political influence as they did exert was casual and local, while joint action was impossible owing to mutual rivalries and jealousies. Many of these old-time orders still exist, but they have no political significance save where they have been leavened by the new-type fraternities.

These latter date from the mid-nineteenth century, the Sennussiya being in every way the most important. Its founder was a powerful personality whose early career is much like that of Abd-el-Wahab. An Algerian by birth, his reformist efforts were devoted to North Africa. Making the *Hall* or pilgrimage to Mecca, his zeal was further quickened by Wahabi teachers. It was then that he seems to have definitely formulated his plan for a militant puritan order. Establishing his headquarters in the Libyan desert, he soon attained great power and wide spiritual authority. A series of able Grand Masters have upheld the prestige of the Order, and after some ninety years of existence the Sennussiya is a notable factor in Islam. Its formal independence has been lessened by recent Italian occupations of several Libyan desert oases formerly Sennussi strongholds. Its political influence and spiritual power, however, remain seemingly unimpaired. All North Africa, from Morocco clear across to Somaliland, is dotted with Zawias or lodges, all absolutely dependent upon the Grand Lodge, headed by the Grand Master, El Sennussi, who sits serenely apart, sending his orders throughout his Invisible Empire.

Those orders are of more than religious import. The local Zawias have many duties. Besides the Mokadden or Master there is also a *Wekil* or civil governor, who has discretionary authority over the whole local community; at least, so great is the prestige of the Sennussiya that a word from Wekil or Mokadden is always listened to and is usually obeyed. Thus, side by side with the various European colonial authorities, British, French, or Italian, as the case may be, there exists an occult government with which the colonial authorities are careful not to come into conflict.

The Sennussi, on their part, are equally careful to avoid an open breach with the European Powers. Their long-headed, cautious policy is truly astonishing. For nearly a century this militant order has bided its time. Locally, the Sennussi have often been involved in military operations, especially against the Italians in Libya; but the Order itself has never officially thrown down the gauntlet.

These Fabian tactics do not mean that the Sennussi are idle. Far from it. On the contrary, they are ceaselessly at work with the spiritual weapons of teaching, discipline, and conversion. The Sennussi program is the welding, first of Moslem Africa and later of the entire Moslem world into much the same theocratic state as that aimed at by the Wahabis of Arabia. But they believe that Islam's political liberation from Western domination and the subsequent realization of the Pan-Islamic dream must be preceded by a profound spiritual regeneration. Toward this end they strive ceaselessly to improve the manners and morals of the populations under their influence. They likewise seek to better material conditions by encouraging improved cultivation of oases, digging new wells, building rest-houses along the desert caravan routes, and promoting trade.

All this explains the Order's remarkable self-restraint. So, year after year, and decade after decade, the Sennussi advance slowly, calmly, coldly; gathering great latent power, yet avoiding the temptation to expend it one instant before the proper time. Meanwhile they are covering North Africa with their lodges and schools, disciplining the people to the voice of Mokadden and Wekil. Lastly, their missionaries range ever further to the southward, converting multitudes of pagan Negroes to the faith of Islam.

The other nucleus of modern Pan-Islamism is the propagandist movement intimately associated with the dynamic personality of Djemal-ed-Din. This remarkable man had a stormy and checkered career. He was a great traveler, knowing intimately both the Moslem world and parts of Europe as well. Unlike Abd-el-Wahab and El Sennussi, be paid scant attention to theology, devoting himself to politics. Although born early in the nineteenth century,[12] Djemal-ed-Din fully grasped the impending Western peril; therefore, at a time when few Moslems realized the danger, he was busy concerting plans of defense. European colonial authorities soon singled him

12 He was born in Persia, but was of Afghan blood.

out as an especially dangerous agitator. The English, in particular, feared and persecuted him. Ultimately, his wanderings led him to Constantinople, where he found a generous patron in Sultan Abdul Hamid, who was then beginning to evolve his own Pan-Islamic policy. Thenceforth these two congenial spirits worked together and conducted a campaign which had notable results.

Abdul Hamid is one of the strangest personalities of modern times. A man of unusual intelligence, his mind was warped by odd twists which went to the verge of insanity. Nursing grandiose projects, he sought to realize them by dark and tortuous methods. The Pan-Islamic idea caught his imagination, and he promptly tried to bend it to his own purposes. Unlike his immediate predecessors, Abdul Hamid determined to use his titular position as Caliph for far-reaching political ends. Emphasizing his spiritual head-ship of the Moslem world rather than his political headship of the Ottoman Empire, he endeavored to win the active support of all Moslems and, thereby, to intimidate European Powers who threatened Turkey. He certainly did impress Europe, which took his Pan-Islamic propaganda seriously and came to look upon Abdul Hamid as a sort of Mohammedan Pope.

That, however, was far from being the case. Abdul Hamid never won the support of either the Wahabis or the Sennussi, whose leaders suspected his motives and questioned his judgment. Furthermore, Moslem liberals everywhere disliked him for his despotic, reactionary rule. On the other hand, thirty years of unremitting propaganda brought many Moslem princes and notables to acknowledge his spiritual authority, while the unthinking masses tended to regard the mighty Caliph in Istanbul as the Defender of the Faith and his empire as the bulwark of Islam. The real test of his Pan-Islamic efforts would have been if Turkey had been assailed by a European Great Power and the Sultan-Caliph had issued a general summons to the *Jehadd* or Holy War against the infidel. That test was never needed, because Abdul Hamid's tortuous diplomacy succeeded in averting the danger throughout his long reign.

The Young-Turk Revolution of 1908 is a momentous date in Moslem history. Not only did it drive Abdul Hamid from his throne; it was also a triumph for Western ideas, especially for that

Western principle, Nationalism, whose effects upon the Moslem East we shall presently discuss. However, the disasters which soon overtook the Young-Turk régime caused a sharp revival of Pan-Islamic feeling. In four short years (1908–12) the Moslem world was buffeted by a whole series of European assaults. Britain and Russia jointly strangled the Persian nationalist revolution; France closed her grip on Morocco; Italy seized Tripoli; and, to cap the climax, the confederated Christian Balkan States sheared away Turkey's European possessions to the very walls of Constantinople.

Upon Islam the effect of these cumulative disasters was tremendous. A wave of mingled despair and rage swept the Moslem world from end to end. This was precisely what Pan-Islam's spokesmen bad been prophesying for half a century—a Crusade of the West bent upon Islam's destruction! Was this not bitter confirmation of the warnings of Djemal-ed-Din? The outbreak of the Great War in 1914 thus found Islam everywhere deeply stirred against European aggression and keenly conscious of its own solidarity against the West.

Under these circumstances it may seem strange that no general explosion occurred when Turkey soon entered the fray and the Sultan-Caliph issued a formal summons to the Holy War. Of course this summons was not the flat failure which Allied reports led the West to believe at the time. The British Government subsequently admitted that the Allies' Asiatic and African possessions stood within a hand's breadth of cataclysmic insurrection. The cataclysm certainly would have come to pass if Islam's accredited leaders had everywhere spoken the fateful word. But the word was not spoken. Instead, Moslem leaders outside of Turkey either kept silent or did their best to calm the passions of the fanatic multitude.

The attitude of those leaders did credit to their discernment. They realized that this was neither the time nor the occasion for a decisive struggle with the West. They were not yet materially prepared, nor had they perfected their mutual understandings. Above all, the moral urge was lacking. They knew that athwart the Caliph's writ was stenciled *Made in Germany.* Far-sighted Moslems had no intention of pulling Germany's chestnuts out of the fire; no wish to aid in building up a Teutonic Empire in the East which might spell for themselves a mere change of masters. Far better to let the West fight out its desperate feud, weaken itself, and reveal its future intentions. Meanwhile Islam could bide its time, grow in strength, and await the morrow.

Such was the prevailing Moslem attitude at the opening of the post-war period which ushered in a complex crisis understandable only in the light of that nationalist factor which we will now analyze.

Nationalism in the Moslem East is a Western importation—and a recent one, at that. Down to the middle of the last century the Islamic world was virtually devoid of true national feeling. To be, sure, there were strong local and tribal loyalties. There was intense dynastic sentiment like the Turks' devotion to their *Padishas,* the Ottoman Sultans. There was also marked pride of race such as the Arabs' conviction that they were Allah's "Chosen People." Here, obviously, were potential nationalist elements. But those elements were as yet dispersed and uncoordinated. They were not yet fused into the new synthesis of self-conscious nationalism. The only Moslem people that could be said to possess anything like real nationalist feeling were the Persians, with their traditional devotion to their plateau-land of Iran.

The various peoples of the Moslem world had thus, at most, a rudimentary national consciousness; a dull, inert unitary spirit; capable of development, perhaps, but as yet scarcely perceptible even to outsiders and certainly unperceived by themselves.

Furthermore, Islam was in many respects hostile to nationalism. Islam's insistence upon the brotherhood of all True Believers and its political ideal of the Caliphate naturally tended to hinder the formation of sovereign, mutually exclusive national units; just as the budding nationalities of Renaissance Europe conflicted with the medieval ideals of universal papacy and "Holy Roman Empire."

Given such unfavorable surroundings, it is not strange to note Moslem nationalist tendencies germinating obscurely and confusedly until relatively recent times. It was in Turkey that a true nationalist consciousness first appeared. Working upon the Turks' devotion to their dynasty and pride in themselves as a ruling race lording it over many subject peoples both Christian and Moslem, the Turkish nationalist movement made rapid progress.

Precisely as in Europe, the nationalist movement in Turkey began with a revival of historic memories and a purification of the language. Half a century ago, most Turks knew next to nothing about their origins or their history. Religious discussions and details of the life of Mohammed or Islam's early days interested men more than the spread of Ottoman power in three continents. The nationalist pioneers taught their fellow-countrymen their historic glories, awakening both pride in the past and confidence in the future. At the same time, the neglected Turkish tongue was modernized until it became a fitting vehicle for popular literature and journalism.

The chief stimulus to Turkish nationalism was, of course, Western political pressure. The more men came to love their country and cherish its future, the more European encroachments spurred them to defend their threatened independence. At first, the nationalist ideal was "Ottomanism," the welding of a real nation in which all citizens, whatever their origin or creed, should be "Ottomans," inspired by an Ottoman patriotism.

This, however, conflicted sharply with the rival nationalisms of the Christian minorities within the empire, to say nothing of the new Arab nationalism which was taking shape at that very moment. Turkish nationalism was also frowned on by Sultan Abdul Hamid, who had an instinctive aversion to all nationalist movements.

The revolution of 1908, however, suddenly brought nationalism to power. Whatever their differences on other matters, the Young-Turks were all ardent nationalists. Indeed, the very ardor of their nationalism was their undoing.

With the rashness of fanatics the Young-Turks tried to "Ottomanise" the whole empire at once. That enraged all the other nationalities, alienated them from the revolution, and gave the Christian Balkan States their chance to smash disorganized Turkey in 1912.

Thus, on the eve of the Great War, the Ottoman Empire seethed with conflicting nationalist ferments which were fast disrupting its political unity. And elsewhere the new spirit was rising fast, especially in Egypt, where a violent nationalistic movement had arisen against British rule. Nationalism in the Moslem East was, in fact, a two-edged sword striking both at Western domination and at princely absolutism in lands not yet under Western control.

The Great War did more than embitter the relations between Moslem East and European West; it likewise precipitated an acute crisis within Islam itself. During the prewar decade the Near East had been torn between rival tendencies toward Pan-Islamism or Nationalism.

We saw that the various Pan-Islamic movements all aimed at a regenerated Moslem world, freed from Western control and at least loosely unified in some modern version of the old Meccan Caliphate. Opposed to this essentially internationalist ideal stood the new nationalism, which implied the break-up of Islam's traditional solidarity into peoples so intensely self-conscious that their particular interests would increasingly outweigh religious and cultural matters held in common.

Now, remembering that Islam is perhaps even more a way of life than it is a creed, we can see that the Pan-Islamic program might have been realized, especially if Moslem puritans and liberals could have worked together. A liberal solution of the problem was actually tried by the Turkish leaders who, back in the 1870's, framed a constitution and a parliament for the Ottoman Empire. That experiment was quickly killed by Abdul Hamid, and its attempted revival by the Young-Turks forty years later was foredoomed to failure because, in the interval, nationalism had permeated every sizeable group in the polyglot empire and made all the non-Turkish minorities, Moslem or Christian, reject the "Ottoman" compromise which the Young-Turks offered.

However, the Moslem East still had one common bond—fear of European domination. We saw that during the prewar years a series of European aggressions inflamed the Islamic world from end to end, thus quickening that sense of solidarity which is the essence of Pan-Islamism. We also saw that Islam, as a whole, declined to obey the summons to a fake Holy War, preferring to await the outcome of a death grapple between the Western Powers in which Islam was not directly concerned.

The close of the war offered what seemed to be a golden opportunity for Pan-Islamism on a grand scale. The Versailles

Peace Conference was just such a revelation of European intentions as the Pan-Islamic leaders had been waiting for in order to perfect their plans and enlist the moral enthusiasm of their followers. At Versailles the European Powers showed that they had no intention of relaxing their hold upon the Moslem East.

By a number of secret treaties negotiated during the war, the Ottoman Empire had been partitioned among the Allies, and those secret pacts formed the basis of the Versailles settlement. Furthermore, Egypt had been declared a British protectorate early in the war, which the Versailles Conference had barely adjourned before England announced an "agreement" with Persia which made that country another British protectorate in fact if not in name. The upshot was, as already stated, that the Moslem East was subjected to Western political domination as never before.

But there was another side to the shield. During the war years Allied statesmen had officially proclaimed that the war was being fought to establish a new world-order based on such principles as the rights of small nations and the liberty of all peoples. These pronouncements had been treasured and memorized throughout the East.

When, therefore, the Moslem world saw a peace settlement based, not upon those high-sounding professions but upon the secret treaties, it was fired with a moral indignation and sense of outraged justice which knew no bounds.

So ominous were the storm-signals that even before the close of the Versailles conference many European students of Eastern affairs expressed grave alarm.

For instance, early in 1919, a leading Italian authority on Moslem matters[13] warned: "The war's convulsion has shaken Islamic and Oriental civilization to its foundations. The entire Eastern world is in ferment. Everywhere the hidden fire of anti-European hatred is burning. Risings in Morocco, riots in Algiers, discontent in Tripoli, so-called nationalist attempts in Egypt, Arabia, and Libya are all different manifestations of the same deep feeling, and have as their object the rebellion of the Oriental world against European civilization."

13 Leone Cztani, Duke of Sermoneta.

That was no exaggeration of the explosive temper which then prevailed. Indeed, the ensuing years saw a long series of revolts, from Central Asia to Morocco, some of which succeeded.[14] Afghanistan and Persia threw off British tutelage, while Egypt won technical independence. The great revolt in the Riff mountains of Morocco was suppressed only by the full weight of France's ponderous military machine, brought into action after Spanish armies had been humiliatingly beaten by the tactical skill of Abd-el-Krim.

Far and away the greatest Moslem victory, however, was that won by the Turks under Mustapha Kemal. And it is precisely the nature of this Turkish triumph which rendered a general Pan-Islamic movement thenceforth impracticable; because the Turks went nationalist in the most uncompromising way.[15] Turkey's decision tipped the scales against Pan-Islamism. Today, nationalism predominates throughout the Moslem East. Only in Arabia and North Africa do nationalist and Pan-Islamic factors tend to combine in ways which offer highly interesting future possibilities.

The European Powers victorious in the Great War had condemned to death both the Ottoman Empire and the Turkish people. The Versailles Conference did more than shear away the empire's non-Turkish provinces; it partitioned Asia Minor, the Turkish homeland, as well. The Allies felt that they might do this with impunity. The Turks were bled white—literally beaten to the dust. Constantinople was in Allied hands and large Allied armies remained nearby. Few persons thought that the Turks would even try to make trouble.

The map-makers of Versailles overlooked two items: the spirit of the Turkish people and the patriotic genius of Mustapha Kemal, a Turkish general then not widely known. These neglected factors, however, were destined to play a decisive role. The Turks have always been a ruling race. To them, therefore, the prospect of foreign domination was intolerable. The climax came when Turkish protests caused the Allies to send in Greek forces to enforce their decision. That was the last straw! Galvanized into a last-ditch fight,

---

14 For a detailed survey of these nationalist movements, see the author's previously mentioned book, *The New World of Islam*, especially Chapters V and VI.

15 Those immediate post-war movements are surveyed in the author's *New World of Islam*.

the Turks rallied around Mustapha Kemal, who, improvising an army out of next to nothing, smashed the well-equipped Greek forces, marched right up to the Allied lines about Constantinople, and curtly told the Allies to get out. Then ensued one of the most amazing back-downs in modern times. Despite their overwhelming material superiority, the Allies simply did not have the stomach to face Turkish determination, together with the nasty repercussions which their crushing of the Turks would surely produce on an already exasperated Moslem world.[16]

An English diplomat vividly depicts the situation. Says George Young: "Anyone who, like myself, went through the crisis at Constantinople, when the rows of British dreadnoughts, the regiments of British Guards, British machine-guns, airplanes, and all the modern mechanisms of war were about to abandon the imperial prize of the world because the half-armed, half-starved levies of the Turkish Nationalists were threatening their positions, can understand the moral force of a mass-movement of nationalism."[17] So the Allies presently agreed to evacuate Constantinople, the abortive partition-treaty was scrapped, and by a new treaty Turkey acquired a freedom from foreign control such as the old Ottoman Empire had not known for generations.

Thus did New Turkey arise, phoenix-like, from the Ottoman ashes. And it was all due to nationalism; to the tremendous power, of Western origin, which Mustapha Kemal had invoked. Well, that was just the power that could regenerate Turkey throughout. The more of it, the better! Such was the lesson drawn by the Turkish people.

And though they soon realized that nationalism implied Westernization, they did not shrink from the logical consequences. This is why Mustapha Kemal and his colleagues have, in a single decade, transformed every phase of Turkish life; why the Turkish people have adopted things Western all the way from our alphabet to our hats and caps.

---

16 The author will frankly admit that when he wrote his *New World of Islam*, early in a 1921, he deemed a general Pan-Islamic movement highly probable. At that time, of course, the epoch-making triumph of Mustapha Kemal had not yet taken place.

17 George Young, 'The Near East Goes West," *Yale Review*, March, 1929.

Present-day Turkey is technically a modern nation-state on the most approved Western pattern. If the reality still lags behind the form, the gap is closing with every succeeding year. And there seems to be scant likelihood of a reaction to the old ways. Turkey has definitely "gone Western."

It has also "gone Turkish"—one hundred per cent Turkish. There was no repining over the loss of Balkan or Arabic possessions. Good riddance to rebellious provinces whose forcible retention had sapped the vigor of the true Turkish stock. However, what remained must be made doubly secure. And there was, in Turkish eyes, just one way of doing it—to get rid of all non-Turkish elements.

The Nationalists had not forgotten the sad failure of the Young-Turks to create a composite "Ottoman" patriotism. Neither did they forget war-time Armenian intrigues with the Russians and the warm welcome which the native Greeks of Asia Minor had recently given the incoming Hellenic troops. The Armenians were a minor matter; wholesale massacres during the Great War had tragically solved that problem.

More difficult were the blocks of Greek population in various parts of Asia Minor, settled there for ages and totaling fully 1,500,000 souls. Yet out they had to go, deported to Greece in exchange for Moslem minorities under Greek rule.

It was a major operation, seemingly harsh and cruel; but it has apparently justified itself. That antagonism, compounded of nationalism, race, and religion, had apparently become too envenomed to be compromised or glossed over. At any rate, the deed is done—and Turco-Greek relations are now excellent.

Although Turkey has become ultra-nationalistic and is fast becoming Westernized, it still remains basically Moslem. Though Islam's old-time predominance is a thing of the past, "this does not imply the end of Islam any more than enlightenment and rationalism implied the end of religion in Europe."[18]

Present-day Turkey is nationalized and secularized, but it has not been de-Islamised.

---

18 Hans Kohn, "Ten Years of the Turkish Republic," *Foreign Affairs*. October, 1933.

The brilliant success of transformed Turkey has made it the model for its eastern neighbors, Persia and Afghanistan. Both countries, now free from Western control, are following Turkey's example, though at a slower pace and thus far with less gratifying results. The Arabic lands to the southward, however, are in no such fortunate posture. They are still under French or British rule, camouflaged as "Mandates" of the League of Nations. Furthermore, this belt of subject Arab-speaking people lies between Turkey and Independent Arabia, where a political experiment is being worked out markedly different from the wholly nationalist Turkish solution.

Arabia is again astir with militant unrest. Once more a commanding personality combined with a fanatical religious revival girds the sons of the desert to united action. Here the dynamic is, not nationalism, but Islam. Also the present movement is a sequel to the stirring Wahabi epic of long ago. Lastly, behind the play of politics and the clash of arms, we glimpse a great "human interest" story; a tale incredible as the *Arabian Nights—yet* thoroughly up-to-date and strictly true.

We saw how Wahabism, thrown back into the desert, became thenceforth a purely spiritual force, so far as the outer world was concerned. In Arabia itself, the Wahabi Confederacy gradually weakened. Its ruling House of Saud temporarily ceased to produce strong men, and that spelled disintegration. A rival house arose—that of Ibn Rashid which ultimately captured Riyadh, the Saudi capital. Yet already the spark of commanding genius had reappeared in the person of a little boy, Abdalaziz ibn Saud, who with his father escaped the wrath of the conqueror and fled into exile at the court of a friendly princelet on the Persian Gulf. That boy was destined to become the present ruler of Arabia, one of the great figures of our time.

Abdalaziz ibn Saud, Emperor of the Desert, is every inch a king. Physically a giant, his mind and spirit likewise tower above other men. His life-story is romance personified. The scion of a royal house fallen from its former high estate, Abdalaziz grew up, a tall, gangling lad, reserved and shy, nursing dreams confided only to a doting aunt who, sensing his latent talents, continually told him: "You must be a great man!"

Barely grown, the young eaglet determined to try his wings. Learning that his people groaned beneath the oppressor's yoke, he set forth secretly at the head of forty chosen comrades, vowed to victory or death. His goal was none other than Riyadh, his ancestral capital, a city of 20,000 souls, well garrisoned by the henchmen of Rashid. By a surprise attack amazing in its rashness, Abdalaziz and his handful of daredevils penetrated the citadel. There, in single combat, the young leader decapitated the foreign governor with a blow of his scimitar. There at the city rose, they annihilated the Rashidi garrison, and acclaimed the House of Saud once more.

That epic duel took place early on a January morning of the year 1901. And ever since then Saud has been expanding his realm. Step by step he has trodden the path to empire. Never a miscalculation. Patiently he prepares the ground; then, when the time is ripe, he garners the fruits by a lightning stroke. His recent taming of the ruler of Yemen through an extraordinary combination of force and conciliation means that throughout Arabia no real opponent remains. Henceforth, the road is clear to still wider fields. For Ibn Saud's vision ranges far; as far as men of Arab blood and speech, who stretch from Mesopotamia clear across North Africa to Morocco, the Moslem "Land of the West."

Furthermore, here is no vulgar conqueror, avid of mere personal power and glory. Ibn Saud is a man devoted to a great ideal, itself a legacy from his famous ancestor two centuries ago. Indeed, much of Saud's success is due to a similar compact made early in his career. Shortly after his recapture of Riyadh there appeared before him a notable religious leader, ready to pledge his loyalty as "The Sharp Sword of Saud." This man was one Feisal ibn Dawish, the head of a fanatic Wahabi order known as the *Ikhwan* or "Brethren." Wearing the white turban of the Prophet in token of their boundless devotion, these austere puritans were chosen instruments to a skillful hand.

The historic combination had again occurred. A great prince and a militant zealot having once more joined forces, history would be almost bound to repeat itself. In fact, it did so, and on familiar lines. Traditional tactics were successfully employed. The new Wahabi state methodically expanded by rigid discipline, systematic propagandist infiltration, and occasional smashing strokes. Wild tribes were subdued. The rival House of Rashid was broken. The Desert Empire bloomed again.

As soon as Inner Arabia was reasonably unified, Ibn Saud began to test out its borders. The obvious opponent was again the Turk. Though more decrepit than ever, the Ottoman Empire held the Holy Cities on the Red Sea littoral, together with certain provinces on the Persian Gulf. Early in 1914, Ibn Saud struck at the latter, expelled the weak Turkish garrisons, and added them to his domains. The Sultan was preparing to retake his lost provinces when these obscure bickering were lost in the gigantic upheaval of the World War.

Saud's attitude toward that struggle was inevitable. In his eyes the Turks were not merely hereditary foes but also religious backsliders of a most reprehensible kind. When Turkey joined the Central Powers, therefore, Saud became Britain's ally—and profited accordingly. Yet this alliance had its limitations. However desirable as a provider of gold and munitions, the English were kafir—unbelievers, who had already subjected many Moslem lands to their infidel yoke. With such people, true friendship was impossible.

The English likewise had misgivings. British diplomacy aimed to dominate the Near East, once the Ottoman Empire was shattered. Downing Street knew a lot about Saud and realized that he would never lend himself to its designs. There was, however, another Arab potentate who seemed more amenable. This was the Shereef of Mecca. A grandee of noble lineage, the Shereef displayed typical Meccan traits—avarice and canny opportunism. In short, he knew on which side his bread was buttered and was unlikely to let self-interest be swayed by religious scruples.

British diplomacy accordingly groomed the Shereef as its favorite. The results of the Versailles settlement converted the Shereef into King of the Hedjaz, with his oldest son, Feisal, King of Irak (Mesopotamia), and a younger son, Abdullah, ruler of Transjordania, a dependency of Britain's Palestine Mandate. It looked as though Ibn Saud was safely bottled up in his deserts by a Shereefian "sanitary cordon" backed by Britain's imperial favor.

Anyhow, that was what the Shereef and his sons devoutly hoped. Yet they could not sleep quite sound o' nights so long as Saud's power remained intact. Therefore Shereefian diplomacy began to tamper with the Bedouin tribes, and presently the Hedjazi King ventured upon a direct trial of strength. Asserting claims to a certain frontier district, the Shereefian monarch despatched a formidable expedition consisting of 2500 regular troops well provided with artillery and machine-guns, and supported by 10,000 irregular light horse.

This invasion came as a complete surprise. Saud's border Emit sent word to Riyadh for help, meanwhile mobilizing the local tribesmen for defense. These, however, consisted largely of *Ikhwan.* The Brethren simply could not be held in leash. They yearned for martyrdom; thirsted for the blood of those misbelieving Meccan dogs. So the Emir (himself a Brother) resolved to give immediate battle despite the fact that his force numbered barely 1800 men. Laying an ambuscade, the Brethren, armed only with rifles and daggers, launched themselves suddenly upon the Shereefian army. In a trice it was all over. The Hedjaz soldiery were massacred to a man, the light horse scattered to the winds, and Saud's reinforcements were met by their victorious comrades laden with spoil.

After that decisive show-down, Saud's next move was only a matter of time. In the winter of 1925 he overwhelmed the Hedjaz and sent the Shereef flying into exile. The Holy Cities were once more in Wahabi hands. Again a great cleansing of the Augean stables took place. Brigandage, graft, and immorality were put down. The hosts of pilgrims from all parts of the Moslem world were assured absolute security and fair-dealing. Only the grossly superstitious were aggrieved, since idolatrous practices were forbidden. The Prophet's tomb at Medina, for instance, is now guarded by *ikhwan,* and any pilgrim whose respects savor too strongly of saint-worship is promptly prodded off by the butts of their long spears.

South of the Hedjaz lies Yemen, a fertile land with a relatively dense population. Yemen had long been a thorn in Saud's side. Most of its inhabitants are Shiah heretics who venerate their ruler, Yahyia, as an *Imam* or saint. Ignorant and fanatical, Imain Yahyia had always been fiercely jealous of Saud and encouraged reactionary or factious elements opposed to Saud's policy of progressive unification.

Obviously, Yahyia had to be dealt with. Saud first tried diplomacy, but forbearance proved useless. So, early in 1934, Saud launched one of his characteristic thunder strokes. With paralyzing suddenness and tactical skill, his columns swept into Yemen. The ensuing clash was war in the modern sense. For all his medievalism, the Imam had built up an army well drilled and equally well equipped, while Saud's forces possessed field guns, tanks, and other up-to-date military gadgets, including airplanes. The tremendous fighting spirit of Saud's troops again proved to be the decisive factor. After a short, sharp campaign, the Imam was thrown back on his fortress-capital of Sanaa, and the world awaited tidings of its capture after a more or less desperate resistance.

The world, however, was in for a big surprise. Though complete military victory lay within his grasp, Saud deliberately stayed his hand. Yemen was merely part of a very much larger whole. What Saud had in mind was, not the annexation of a new province, but the bringing of Yemen and its Imam in line with his grand strategy for a united Arabism.

That he had powerful backers in this far-sighted policy was shown by the opportune appearance of a delegation comprising the most important Arab nationalist leaders in Syria, Palestine, and Egypt, who sought to mediate between the combatants. Whether or not this intervention was prearranged, it certainly suited Saud. Accordingly, he offered the Imam extremely liberal terms, renouncing all conquered territory in return for the Imam's pledge to live henceforth in friendly co-operation.

The text of this unusual treaty, signed at Taif in June, 1934, makes interesting reading. Its preamble states that it is a "pact of Moslem and Arab brotherhood, to promote the unity of the Arab nation, to enhance its position, and to maintain its dignity and independence." Both parties declare that "their nations are one, and agree to consider each other's interests as their own." The foreign policy of both states is to be so harmonized that they will act as a unit in all larger matters. Practically, this means that Yemen will be a protectorate of Ibn Saud, enjoying full local self-government but dependable in case of foreign complications. The effective unification of the Arabian peninsula is thus complete.[19]

19 Technically, that word is not quite accurate. At the extreme southwestern tip of the Arabian peninsula stands the British outpost of Aden, guarding the narrow straits from the Red Sea into the Indian Ocean, while in the southeastern corner

The Treaty of Taif is a revelation both of Saud's consummate statecraft and of the portentous echoes evoked by his ideal of a Greater Arabia. To appreciate its significance, look at the map. Just north of Free Arabia lie Irak, Palestine, and Syria. These regions, with their almost solidly Arabic populations, are chronically restive under British or French rule. The same is true of British-controlled Egypt, while on the far horizon lie Italian-dominated Libya and the French possessions clear west to Morocco. Wherever Arab blood, speech, and culture exists, combined with Moslem fervor, the fame of Ibn Saud resounds.

Meanwhile, Abdalaziz consolidates his empire, for Oriental ends yet largely by Occidental means. This busy monarch leads a life strangely, almost grotesquely, compounded of East and West. He divides his time between the Holy Cities and his desert capital of Riyadh—a remote spot which few Western eyes have seen. There, above the crenellated walls of a city embowered in palm groves, rises a palace that might have housed Haroun-al-Rashid, with such familiar appurtenances as a well-stocked harem guarded by emasculated black slaves. Yet that same Oriental palace blazes with electric lights and tinkles with telephone bells, while the date palms are dwarfed by the masts of a powerful wireless station keeping its master in constant touch with the outer world. And when Saud goes forth, be does so, not on prancing steed or swaying camel, but in a luxurious limousine followed by a long retinue of motor-cars ranging from sprightly flivvers[20] to lumbering trucks filled with soldiers and supplies.

Such is the story of this Master of the Desert. Here, where the present merges with the future, we must leave him on his path to empire. The outcome is known only to Allah, the All-Wise, the Inscrutable!

The story of Saud is of more than local significance. It illustrates one of the two distinct trends in the Moslem world today. Looking at Turkey, we are apt to think that the Moslem East is re-shaping

of Arabia lies the Sultanate of Oman, a British dependency. Oman is, however, cut off from the rest of Arabia by waterless deserts, while the British at Aden could not venture large-scale aggressive action against Saud. Therefore, to all intents and purposes, Saud's mastery over Arabia is complete.

20 A cheap car or aircraft, especially one in bad condition.

itself exclusively on Western models; that nationalism has definitely triumphed over the Pan-Islamic ideal. That seems to be true of Turkey, and in lesser degree of Persia and Afghanistan. In the Arabic lands, however, Islam still predominates, albeit nationalistic tendencies likewise exist. The probable outcome appears to be, not a conflict between the two factors, but rather their fusion in a composite sentiment which may be termed either Pan-Islamic Nationalism or Pan-Arabism with a strongly Islamic flavor. The latter will presumably prevail in the Arab-speaking parts of Asia, together with Egypt, which, though geographically in Africa, is intimately connected with the neighboring Asiatic Arab regions. Over the rest of North Africa, however, Pan-Islamic Nationalism is the more likely course of political evolution. The term itself may sound rather paradoxical, yet it would seem best to suit the special conditions which there prevail.

Owing to the huge barrier of the Sahara Desert, North Africa has always been so sharply sundered from the equatorial regions to the southward that it does not effectively form part of the "Dark Continent." Despite a slow trickle of Negro blood through the centuries, brought across the desert mostly by slave-caravans, North Africa is racially not negroid. Everywhere west of Egypt the population is basically Berber—a "dark-white" stock similar to the brunet elements in Spain, Italy, and elsewhere on the European shores of the Mediterranean. The Berbers remind one temperamentally of the Balkan Albanians: they are extremely tenacious of their language and customs, and they have an innate sense of common kinship, but they are inveterate clansmen, having always been split up into many small tribes, sometimes combining in loose confederacies yet never developing a true national consciousness.

Alongside the Berbers we find everywhere a varying proportion of Arabs. The Arabs have colonized North Africa ever since the Moslem conquest twelve centuries ago. They converted the Berbers to Islam and Arabic culture, but they never made North Africa part and parcel of the Arabic world as they did Syria and Mesopotamia, and in somewhat lesser degree Egypt. The two races have never fully fused. Despite more than a thousand years of Arab tutelage, the Berbers' manner of life remains distinct. They have largely kept their language, and there has been no general intermarriage. Pure-blooded Arabs abound, often in large tribal groups; but they are still, in a way, foreigners.

With such factors of discord, North Africa's political life has always been troubled. The most stable region has been Morocco, though even there the Sultan's authority never really extended to the mountain tribes. As for the so-called "Barbary States" (Algiers, Tunis, and Tripoli), they were little more than port-cities along the coast, the hinterland enjoying practically complete tribal independence.

Over this confused turmoil spread the tide of French conquest, beginning with the capture of Algiers in 1830 and ending with the military occupation of Morocco today. France brought peace, order, and material prosperity; but here, as in other Eastern lands, Western tutelage created a new sort of unity among the natives through their common dislike of the European conqueror and a common aspiration towards independence. Accordingly, the past generation has witnessed the appearance of "Young Algerian" and "Young Tunisian" movements headed by French-educated leaders who have imbibed Western ideas of self-government and nationalism.

However, it is interesting to note that their goal is not the creation of distinct Algerian and Tunisian nations, but rather the forging of a larger North African nationality strongly Islamic in tone. For of course, these leaders, even those most externally Westernized, are deeply affected by Sennussi teaching and other Pan-Islamic influences. "All over North Africa there is a new sense of Islamic unity. Islam may be a waning force in Asia, but so far as North Africa is concerned, the exact opposite has taken place. There Islam has entered upon a revivalist period."[21]

All this portends a stubborn clash between an aroused North African nationalism and the imperial power of France. We have already glimpsed the French dream of African empire.[22] That grandiose hope will fade like a mirage of the desert unless North Africa be securely held. And France's hold will be sure only when a majority of the population is truly French in spirit, if not in blood.

21 "North African Unity," *The Round Table,* September, 1929, pp. 717–22.

22 Part I, Chapter V, entitled "France and the Black Power."

To that vital end France has wrought tirelessly for a hundred years, and much has been accomplished. Today, French North Africa contains well over a million residents of European blood, in large part perhaps of Spanish or Italian descent, yet mostly loyal French citizens. Within the bounds of the Christian, European community, Gallicization has succeeded.

Yet the combined European elements form only a small minority beside the natives. Even in Algeria, the French stronghold, the European community numbers less than twenty per cent of the total population. And every attempt to convert or disrupt the solid native block has thus far failed. A generation ago there was much talk of playing upon the traditional differences between Arabs and Berbers, thereby weaning the latter away from their co-religionists and over to French civilization.

Today such schemes have been tacitly abandoned. Instead, well-informed Frenchmen recognize, even when they do not publicly admit, that Arab and Berber are being welded together as never before by the new nationalist urge, compounded as it is of Islamic fervor and antagonism to foreign rule.

To be sure, France's military might is so great that armed rebellion is at present not even remotely possible. Yet the fanatic fury which smolders in North African breasts now and then emits a lurid glow, fleeting but infinitely ominous. What an anti-European rising would be like was horribly revealed by the recent Moslem riots in Algeria against the local Jews. The atrocities then committed by the rioters are ample warning that the Christian community might suffer a similar fate. And, on the other hand, France would stick at nothing rather than endure the collapse of her African Empire and witness the massacre of a million French citizens settled just across the Mediterranean. Here, indeed, rises the specter of an eventual death-grapple, truceless and merciless on both sides.

Naturally, the topic is rarely mentioned in the French press, the gruesome subject being well-nigh taboo. Yet qualified foreign observers do not like the look of things even in Algeria, where French rule is most solidly based. Indeed, it is precisely in Algeria that the very weight of French dominion has provoked the strongest and best-organized nationalist movement, headed, as in Egypt, 'by wealthy native notables and supported by the educated middle class as well as by the ignorant masses.

More than a decade ago, an English investigator reported: "Public security in the Algerian provinces is not as good as in Egypt. The local French officials are unable to cope with the situation. In Oran, nine-tenths of the crime goes unpunished. The French colonists are selling their land in disgust, and their places are being taken by Berbers, thus hastening the decline of French influence and prestige."[23]

Quite recently, a like inquiry yielded similar conclusions. The gulf of mutual repulsion between Europeans and natives (contemptuously referred to in French colonial slang as *bicots)* is both wide and deep. In Algeria, certainly, the French are not looked up to as a superior race.

"The native often fears the French official, but rarely respects him. It is noteworthy that in Algeria there is no title of respect used by natives when addressing Europeans, such as *Sahib* in India or *Tuan* in the Far East. The ordinary Algerian hardly troubles to say *Monsieur* to a European, and will often *tutoyer* him . . . Naturally, the French do not trust the natives. When the natives (who outnumber the Europeans in Algeria almost six to one) ask for the right to elect their own representatives to sit in Paris, they are told they can do so by becoming French citizens. In practice, however, that is rarely done, because the required conditions savor of apostasy to a Mohammedan . . . There is bound to be a bar between the native and the Frenchman. Between them is the difference between Christianity and Islam—between East and West. The basic methods of thinking and feeling and living for the mass of the natives have not been radically changed or modified by French rule."[24]

Strange though it may seem, it is in Morocco, France's latest conquest, that French prestige is highest and native opposition least organized. The reason appears to be that Morocco is as yet a protectorate rather than a colony, skillfully governed by exceptionally able French officials. Also, local authority is still largely in the hands of great feudal chieftains who may be reconciled to French

23 H. E. Wortham, "France and Islam," *The Outlook* (London), April 22, *1922.*

24 B. K. F., "The French Attitude to Color," *The Spectator*, July 4, 1931.

overlordship so long as their power over their own retainers is not notably curtailed.

Yet the Moors are proverbially the proudest and fiercest of all the North Africans, while the recent exploits of Abdel-Krim show both their innate love of freedom and their tremendous fighting-power. Can France keep Morocco permanently in leash when North Africa is astir with the new nationalistic ferment? It may be so, but the logic of events points otherwise. And a truly nationalistic North Africa, in turn, spells an eventual struggle grim and implacable almost beyond calculation.

PART III
AFRICA IN SOLUTION

AFRICA IN SOLUTION

AFRICA is the great waxing factor in world-affairs. What the New World of the Americas was four centuries ago, that Africa is today—a practically virgin field, as plastic in the hands of its possessors as it is rich in untapped resources. Thrice the size of Europe, Africa is today everywhere[1] under European control. That control is virtually unchallenged save in the northern belt between the Mediterranean Sea and the Saharan or Libyan deserts; and North Africa, as we saw, has little in common with the rest of the continent.

The real *Africa* is the huge land-block stretching from the confines of the desert belt southward through the tropics until its lower tip enters the south temperate zone. Here lies incalculable wealth awaiting exploitation. Here likewise are native stocks so backward and ill-organized that they can offer scant resistance to European plans and projects. This Africa is as clay on the potter's wheel, ready to be molded into virtually any shape which may be desired. Disagreement among the potters can alone mar the pattern or break the mold. Against Europe's concerted will, Black Africa must play an essentially passive role.

There is the vital distinction between Africa and the Orient. Asia, for all its discordant turmoil, is the home of peoples whose past achievements have endowed them with distinctive civilizations and with a strong self-consciousness now sharply re-awakened. This intense Asiatic revival spells the rapid decline of Western

1 Although Abyssinia and Liberia are technically independent, that independence is due mainly to European consent. Neither state could maintain its sovereignty against the will of the European colonial Powers.

colonial empire throughout the East. But as Europe is thus forced to give ground in Asia, it must inevitably be driven to strengthen its hold over Africa and intensify those economic developments which have become necessary to its economic well-being. Despite the rapid progress recently made, Europe's exploitation of Africa has only begun.

Upon Africa, indeed, Europe's gaze is increasingly focused. In the eyes of far-sighted Europeans an efficiently developed Africa offers a solution to many of their economic problems. Says H. G. Wells, for example: "Africa is economically necessary to European civilization as the chief source of vegetable oils and fats and various other products of no great value to the native population. European civilization can scarcely get along without those natural resources of Africa. Now here we are up against a problem entirely different from the problem that arises in the case of India and China, which is that of a politically powerless but essentially civilized population which can be trusted to modernize itself and come into line with existing efficient Powers if it is only protected from oppressive disintegrating forces while it adjusts itself.[2] Africa is quite incapable of anything of the sort. Negro Africa is mainly still in a state of tribal barbarism . . . If continuing access to the resources of Africa is to be maintained; if a return to the Arab raider and general chaos and massacres is to be avoided, it is clear that, in some form, control of the central parts of Africa by the modern civilized world must continue."[3]

In similar vein, Count Coudenhove-Kalergi writes: "Although Soviet Russia separates Europe from Asia and the Atlantic Ocean sunders Europe from America, the Mediterranean links Europe and Africa more than it divides them. Africa has become our nearest neighbor, and its destiny is part-and-parcel of our destiny. The more Europe departs from Asiatic and American politics, the more she is thrown back on Africa. Through the emancipation of America and of Asia, she has lost her Latin-American markets to the United States and her East Asiatic markets to Japan. Africa thus

---

2 That is, of course, Mr. Wells's opinion. Our survey of India and China suggests that his verdict may be rather simplistic.

3 H. G. Wells, "Europe's Control of Africa," *Manchester Guardian Weekly*, January 6, 1922.

represents the future basis of European production and the future market for European goods . . . The transformation of Africa into a great European plantation would improve the whole economic condition of our continent and would raise the standard of living among all its peoples."[4]

The larger aspects of the situation are thus sketched by an English authority on African affairs: "Africa is the continent of the twentieth century . . . If we examine the position of Africa on a map, we cannot fail to be struck by its central situation with regard to the rest of the world. It is essentially the central continent. Africa occupies a key-position on the earth. It now occupies, economically, the key-position in the industrial life of European civilization.

Although vast political and economic upheavals in the Far East will perhaps change the relations between the white races and the teeming peoples of Asia; though a bomb cast into the center of the Pacific Ocean may produce repercussions throughout the civilized world, it is in Africa that the great economic advance of the future will take place . . . Within a century, a new world will have been created between the Mediterranean and the Cape of Good Hope—a world roughly and laboriously hewn out of the stubborn rock of African inertia for the benefit of the industrial nations."[5]

The surprising thing is that Africa's vital role in European eyes is so recent. Half a century ago Africa was still literally *The Dark Continent.* Its secrets were only just being disclosed by a few bold explorers, and the European public could still be edified by fantastic tales like *She* or *King Solomon's Mines.* Even a generation ago Europe's political control over the vast interior was nominal, while the "opening up" of Africa and its systematic development are mainly the work of the last two decades.

Why, until yesterday, did Europe neglect so marvelous a realm of opportunity, lying almost at its door? In part, it was due to Europe's preoccupation with more distant portions of the world. But why, in the first place, had regions far afield been chosen in preference to one so much closer at hand? The answer is that "the lay of

4 Count Richard Coudenhove-Kalergi, "Europe Turns to Africa," *Pester Lloyd* (Budapest); translated in *The Living Age,* February 1, 1930.

5 Evans Lewin, "Africa in the Twentieth Century," *Yale Review,* October, 1927.

the land," together with an evil coastal climate, caused Africa to present a forbidding and discouraging aspect to all approaching its shores—especially on its Western sea-front.

Since modern Africa is a thing dating only from yesterday, we should cast a brief backward glance at the Dark Continent as it was before the White Man came.

By its very make-up, Africa was predestined to seclusion. A transverse band of desert stretching from sea to sea shuts the bulk of the continent away from Europe and Asia. Elsewhere, Africa bounds lonely oceans with a fringe of fever-haunted swamp and jungle through which there are no natural portals to the hinterland, because near the mouths of even its mightiest rivers are dangerous rapids blocking navigation. The interior of Africa is a series of plateaus, some much higher than others, yet all raised considerably above the narrow coastal strips which lie between them and the sea.

Since these unfavorable circumstances are most pronounced on its Atlantic side, Africa was well-nigh impenetrable to Europeans; indeed, before the days of railroads and river steamers, there was no special incentive to penetrate the unknown interior when large-scale transportation was impossible. Therefore, though the West Coast was known to Phoenicians and Carthaginians, and though Portuguese navigators were scouting southward five centuries ago, the white man was ever a bird of passage, trading casually with the coastal natives for gold-dust, ivory, and slaves.

Africa south of the Sahara is Black Man's Land. Here the Negro has dwelt for countless ages. Naturally, his history has been one of almost complete isolation. Cut off from the Mediterranean world to the northward by deserts which he had no means of crossing, and bounded elsewhere by oceans that he had no skill in navigating, the black man vegetated in savage obscurity, his homeland being well named the Dark Continent.

Until the white tide began breaking over his sea-fronts, the Negro's isolation had been interrupted only by brown men landing on his eastern coasts or coming up the valley of the Nile. In fact, it is not unlikely that, had Europe not overrun Africa, most of the Dark Continent would have fallen under Arab sway and become part of the Islamic world. The Negro tribes were unable to stem the

Arab advance. Indeed, after a short struggle, they usually turned Moslem and thenceforth made common cause with the Arab or Arabized invaders against their still pagan brethren. Even today, though subject to European control and limited to purely peaceful methods, Moslem propaganda goes on and Islam's frontier pushes steadily southward through the heart of Black Africa.

Yet, whether subject to brown or white rule, and however affected by conversion to Islam or Christianity, the black man remains essentially himself. We should therefore seek to evaluate the Negro's temperament, ideas, and social life in order to understand his relation to the immense changes occurring in his homeland today.

The black race, scattered broadcast over Africa as it has been for ages, is naturally not of a piece. Excluding mixed breeds due to infusions of Arab, Berber, and Hamite[6] blood, and not counting remnants of very old dwarf races like the Congo pygmies and the now almost extinct Hottentots and Bushmen of the far south, the distinctively Negro peoples differ widely amongst themselves. There are notable contrasts between the semi-pastoral Bantu of South Africa and the West African Bush Negroes; between the settled agriculturists of East Africa and the low-grade tribes of the Congo rain-forest.

Nevertheless, beneath all these variations there exist basic likenesses of thought and feeling as well as of general physical type. From the first glance we see that, in the Negro, we encounter a being very different from the other branches of mankind. The Negro's outstanding quality is great animal vitality. In this he easily surpasses all other races. To it he owes his intense emotionalism.

---

6 The Hamitic race inhabits the northeastern corner of the African continent. This stock forms the substratum of the present highly mixed population of Egypt, while it predominates in Abyssinia and among the adjacent Galla and Somali peoples. Although, owing to wholesale importations of black slaves, the modern Hamites are much more negroid than are the Arabo-Berbers of North Africa, they are still both physically and temperamentally very different from true Negroes. As a converse to the partial negrification of the Hamites, the Negro tribes of East and East-Central Africa contain a good deal of Hamitic blood, due to Hamitic conquests and slave-raids during many centuries. However, the Hamites were not as aggressive and never ranged as widely as did the Arabs and their Berber colleagues.

To it is also due his extreme fecundity, the Negro being the quickest of breeders.

This abounding vitality shows in many other ways, such as the Negro's ability to survive harsh conditions of slavery under which other races have soon succumbed. It likewise enabled him to endure the strain of an exceedingly trying climate and the ravages of tropical disease Again, native political conditions took a heavy toll, divided as the Negroes always were into many tribes, *warring* savagely amongst themselves and widely addicted to cannibalism. Then, too, the native religions were unusually sanguinary, demanding prodigal human sacrifices. The killings ordained by Negro wizards and witch-doctors sometimes attained unbelievable proportions. These various factors combined to cause a wastage of life which in other races would have resulted in a stationary or declining population. The Negro's biological weakness and strength can alike be summarized by saying that, for a struggle against other races "involving actual conflict, the Negro race is one of the most poorly equipped on earth; but for the ability to propagate under untoward circumstances it is apparently one of the best."[7]

Yet this vitality, though triumphant over great physical and climatic hardships, seems deficient in other respects, especially on the psychological side. Morel points out that "the African dies from unhappiness more readily, perhaps, than any other human, being." Steady, disciplined labor and lack of sociability "depress the African. He loses hold on existence. His capacity to resist disease weakens. His procreating powers decline. He becomes spiritless, melancholy, collapsible. It is a question primarily of psychology. The tropical African is essentially a creature of moods; a child of joy and a child of sorrow; a being of strong emotions which must find an outlet. He likes to dance, to linger chatting over camp fires, to vary his life according to the seasons . . . The African is intensely sociable. He droops under prolonged restraint, while solitary confinement quickly kills."[8]

This psychic weakness is perhaps the Negro's most serious handicap in the adjustments to Western civilization with which he is inexorably and increasingly, faced. The traditional life of

7 S. J. Holmes, *Studies in Evolution and Eugenics,* p. *230* (New *York,* 1923).

8 E. D. Morel, *The Black Man's Burden,* pp. 58–59 (London and New York, 1920).

these primitive beings is in most respects the very opposite of civilized existence with its order, regularity, and emphasis on individual responsibility. The African has everywhere led a group-life, restricted yet intense. His tribal unit is all-in-all to him. A South African student of native ways summarizes the fundamental character of genuinely Negro societies throughout Africa when he writes of the Kaffirs: "They are thoroughgoing collectivists. Their very babes are socialists . . . Socialistic ideals affect almost every conception of the Kaffirs, giving color and form even to their ideas about such widely different things as justice and witchcraft . . . Amongst the Kaffirs, the person of the individual belongs in theory to the chief. He is not his own, for he is the chief's man . . . The individual consciousness is not fully developed, though the clan-consciousness is amazingly strong. The individual amongst the Kaffirs to a large extent confuses—we might even say *fuses*—himself with his clan; therefore he has not that strong sense of personal property and 'rights' that obtains amongst people who have become acutely conscious of their own individuality. In a Kaffir kraal there is not only no incentive but no room for individual initiative. The consequence of this is that the entire tribe reaches—for it aims at—a low, dull level of mediocrity, in which no one is behind or in front of the mass."[9]

This primitive communism both expresses the African temperament which created it and intensifies the Negro's natural bent by preventing such individual initiative as he may latently possess from ever showing itself. In his native state, the African neither needs nor wants anything above a low level of primitive satisfactions.

Once that easy goal is attained, he vegetates in an almost animal contentment, well described by an English writer, who says: "The native's aspirations are bounded by his needs, which are: wives sufficient to provide in their youth a family to look after him in his old age and to till land enough to feed himself and his belongings. Middle age finds him living that absolutely idle existence which is the highest bliss to the untutored native mind, and in the afternoons he is drunk on beer brewed by his wives."[10]

9 Dudley Kidd, *Kaffir Socialism,* pp. 3–40 (London, 1901).

10 Quali, "The Native in British East Africa," *Contemporary Review,* April, 1918.

These tribal groups are as primitive economically as they are socially. Almost everywhere they are inefficient and semi-nomadic. The villages of the bush and forest Negroes are impermanent affairs. As soon as a crude agriculture has exhausted the fertility of garden-patches originally cleared by burning, the tribe abandons its flimsy huts and moves to some new spot, where the cycle is repeated. The tribes of the unforested plateaus are even more nomadic and equally inefficient. Lack of proper breeding-methods results in scrub herds of cattle poor in quality and always tending by excessive numbers to destroy nearby pasturage, so that these pastoral peoples must be forever on the move. Even the Bantu or Kaffir tribes of South Africa, which combine cattle-raising with agriculture, do both ineffectively and suffer intermittently from famine.

This chronic nomadism in large part explains the fierce tribal wars which were always going on before the white man came. Tribes seeking elbow-room inevitably collided with those already in possession of coveted lands. The result was a battle to the death in which the vanquished were often literally as well as figuratively "eaten up."[11] This method was occasionally systematized, as among the Zulus, who made themselves such redoubtable warriors that under their great war-chief, Tchaka, they exterminated all the tribes around them to the tune of at least a million lives.

The African's restricted group-consciousness prevented the most extensive conquests from ever resulting in a higher level of political development. Beaten tribes were slaughtered; almost never were they incorporated. Thus the tribal stage was never surmounted into confederacies or large unified states.[12] This political backwardness is of course basically due to the African nature. On these matters Reinsch remarks: "Low social organization and consequent lack of efficient social action form the most striking characteristic of the Negro race . . . A lack of social fellow-feeling, an absence of every vestige of patriotism, is shown by the readiness with which Negroes allow themselves to be used to fight against their neighbors. The

11 The habitual African term used to describe the fate of beaten tribes.

12 We are here speaking of full-blooded Negroes. The powerful states which have at times arisen in the Sudan and in Nigeria are due primarily to Islamic inspiration, and the ruling classes have always been more or less impregnated with Arab, Berber, or Hamitic blood.

Arab slave-raiders never lack men to fight their battles; for, though their Hamite troops may refuse to attack the bands of another trader, the Negroes are always ready for the savage onset, even upon men of very nearly their own flesh and blood. The terrible custom of cannibalism, too, can be explained only by taking into account this absence of a feeling of common humanity."[13]

Such was the Dark Continent at the white man's coming, and such it had been for uncounted ages. Black Africa had apparently reached a political, economic, and social level ranging from utter savagery to, at most, barbarism; and, of and by himself, the African showed no signs of rising above that level.

We need not tarry to consider the much-discussed question as to whether or not the Negro is capable of creating a civilization of his own. He *never has* done it, so far as history shows; certainly, no purely Negro civilization has existed in recent times.

Therefore, it was a race primitive and backward wherever it had not been quickened by Islamic influences that confronted the inpouring tide of Western, white civilization. Before discussing its effects upon the Negro, let us first survey the invasion itself.

Europe's mastering of the Dark Continent is almost wholly the work of the last fifty years. True, some three centuries ago, Dutch settlers took root on Africa's southern tip, the Cape of Good Hope, and from that small beginning has grown a vigorous white nationality which today dominates South Africa. Yet the African south, with its temperate climate and its large white population, stands in many ways apart from the rest of the continent. The huge bulk of tropical Africa is of much greater importance in world-affairs. And here, white penetration is so recent that it has barely outgrown the pioneering stage.

A handful of intrepid spirits wrested from the Dark Continent its long-guarded secrets. Dauntless explorers like Livingstone and Stanley; devoted missionaries, Catholic and Protestant; mighty hunters; a sprinkling of commercial adventurers on the pattern of Trader Horn—such were the bold pioneers who brought back wondrous tidings to the white world. The world listened; grew

---

13 Paul S. Reinsch, "The Negro Race and European Civilization," *American Journal of Sociology*, September, 1905.

interested—and the "scramble for Africa" began. Starting about 1880, a scant two decades saw Black Africa dotted with European flags, pegging out rival claims. Britain and France emerged from the scramble far and away the big winners. Germany acquired several worth-while African parcels, only to lose them in the Great War. Little Belgium got the vast Congo heart of Africa by a lucky fluke. Even Portugal managed to expand her old coastal frontages into two large land-blocks. That was about the story. Today, with Germany out of the picture, and with Belgium and Portugal necessarily playing minor roles, Britain and France are the dominant, positive factors in shaping the Africa of the future.

The amazing transformation wrought in a few decades is aptly summarized by Evans Lewin. "Fifty years ago," he writes, "few would have anticipated that Africa would be covered by a network of railways opening new countries, bringing civilization to inaccessible wilds, and completely changing the relations of black and white; that the precarious tenure of a few coastal ports, frequently fever-stricken or shut off from the interior by swamps and forests, would tighten into an unassailable grasp of the central lands."

After surveying commercial and industrial centers already well-developed, he goes on to sketch this remarkable glimpse into the future: "Northward of the rich mineralized region of Katanga is the Great Rift divide . . . as yet undeveloped owing to lack of railway communication. This section, however, is soon destined to become a place of intense industrial activity; for towards it will be almost inevitably attracted several converging railway routes, just as through Katanga itself will pass similar transcontinental routes. It lies in the heart of Africa . . . the future economic hub of the whole continent.

"Entirely undeveloped today, save for a few isolated settlements, this extensive territory may be compared only with the Great Lakes region of North America. Its waterways, joining together vast territories such as Katanga, Tanganyika plateau, and the Congo and Nile basins, will eventually afford (with railway links) an almost unrivaled means of inter-communication."[14]

---

14 Lewin, *op. cit.*

All this shows how firmly Europe has bound Africa to itself Europe needs that almost untapped mineral wealth Europe likewise needs those varied tropical products—cotton, rubber, coffee, cocoa, palm oil, ground nuts, to mention merely those of chief importance. And Europe will presumably grow still more dependent upon African raw materials as her Asiatic sources of supply threaten to become insecure.

What is the character of this tremendous economic development? Some critics call it "imperialistic exploitation" of hapless natives. Yet that is a one-sided, and even more an out-of-date judgment. It is perfectly true that, formerly, terrible abuses existed like those in the Congo rubber concessions and on the Portuguese cocoa plantations. Today, however, large-scale brutal exploitation of the natives is virtually over, because every colonial Power in Africa now recognizes that it is bad business as well as bad ethics; because, on balance, such practices do not pay.

Europe can develop tropical Africa only with the aid of black labor. Now, taken as a whole, tropical Africa is under-populated, considering the vast undertakings which are in prospect. Therefore, an assured supply of healthy, contented black labor is, and will be, a prime necessity. We do not have to stress this point, because it is generally realized, and every colonial government in tropical Africa is acting accordingly. That does not mean that everything is as it should be. There are doubtless plenty of stupid or corrupt officials, together with shortsighted planters and concessionaires grasping after quick profits regardless of ultimate consequences.

Yet however numerous such abuses may still be, they are incidental to rather than typical of the current trend towards juster and sounder methods formulated according to the dictates of truly enlightened policies.

Every sensible colonist knows that brutal tyranny and grinding exploitation break the native's spirit, kill his working incentive, and very likely mean a declining population with a consequent disastrous labor-shortage.

Therefore, over and above official action, colonial public opinion becomes less and less tolerant of abuses which bring in their wake such dire economic penalties.

Should even this not suffice, a second powerful motive springing from enlightened self-interest likewise counsels good treatment of the natives. This is due to the fact that Europe regards tropical Africa not only as an indispensable source of raw materials but also as a market for its manufactures which is capable of indefinite expansion in proportion to the economic well-being of the native populations.

Already Africa takes vast quantities of European textiles and many other goods of the cheaper grades. These are all bought by the natives. How did they get the money? Obviously in wages earned in European employ or in cash paid them for produce grown or gathered by themselves, as with the cocoa and palm-oil of West Africa, where the natives work on their own account rather than upon plantations. In each case, however, the commercial results are the same: for the first time in their history, native populations which formerly lived at a bare subsistence level have money to spend for new wants and desires. And this, in turn, means that every European trading interest will do its best to promote the natives' prosperity and will object to seeing them ground down to starvation wages which would cripple their buying power.

No; the real question in tropical Africa is, not how to stop abuses, but how, with the best will in the world, to prevent the sudden impact of Western civilization from so disrupting the native social order and so demoralizing the native individually that these primitive populations will degenerate in every way. That is the great problem which must somehow be handled if tropical Africa is to know genuine progress and prosperity.

In viewing the African's relation to Western civilization we should be careful to avoid both cynicism and sentimentality, sticking to realities and remembering that, by and large, the present situation was unavoidable and the consequences inevitable.

On this point a South African writer has penned certain lines so full of good common sense that we cannot do better than quote him. Says Dudley Kidd: "It is fatally easy to set up in the mind some unreal image of an oppressed and voiceless black man, who is too gentle and peaceable, and withal too guileless, to provoke hostilities except under the most provoking oppression of some wicked white men. This mental image affords a splendid occasion for giving expression to those most pleasurable and luxurious of all emotions, indignation and pity . . . The question then ceases to be a *native,* and becomes a *white,* problem. Under the influence of prejudice or passion, the native, who is the subject of the contention, is lost sight of . . . The argument becomes practically independent of the actual Kaffir of the kraal, and would not be modified much if the aborigines of South Africa were Siamese, Red Indians, or even Martians. *The Native Problem is the problem of the native.* This is so obvious when once stated that one would be ashamed to say it unless it were so constantly forgotten. Before we can understand the bearings of the Native Problem we must study native customs and thought. We shall never get any nearer a solution of the problem by concentrating . . . on political panaceas for imaginary and non-existent needs; for it is the Kaffir, and not our emotion, that is the determining factor in the problem."[15]

In short: Look at the native as he *is—and also as he was.* Our glimpse of Africa before the white man came showed its deplorable and apparently hopeless condition. Despite the hectic thrills of tribal battles, witch-findings, and dance-orgies, the life of the average native was in exact accord with old Thomas Hobbes' famous phrase: "nasty, brutish, and short."

If the African managed to escape the ever-lurking perils of famine and tropical disease, he stood an excellent chance of being killed by his own chief for some triviality, killed and eaten by tribal foes, tortured by some half-insane witch-doctor, or (worst of all) captured by slave-raiders. Indeed, had not European rule put a stop to this scourge, Arab and Abyssinian slave-hunters might by this time have ravaged and depopulated the whole of equatorial Africa. The Negroes had nowhere shown the ability to stand up to the invaders. Thus white rule, with all its attendant ills, has certainly not robbed the Africans of an idyllic past to which it would be well for them to return. Indeed, the peace, order, justice, hygiene, economic betterment, and opportunity for individual initiative brought about by white rule are appreciated by the natives themselves, who do not want to give up these new benefits. Yet those good things must be dearly paid for.

15 Kidd, op. *cit.,* pp. 10–11.

We here encounter the chief difference between African and Asiatic adjustments to the impact of the West. The Oriental peoples have, for the most part, high cultural and spiritual values of their own, which have ennobled their historic pasts and give them solid foundations on which to rebuild in course of time. The African Negro, on the other hand, evolved no native civilization. He therefore possesses no notable spiritual or cultural[16] values. Kidd's characterization of the South African Bantu applies broadly to the other Negro folk.

"The Kaffirs," he writes, "are certainly an unprogressive race . . . They have developed no national unity, being split up into rival clans and tribes; they have developed no lofty religion, being satisfied with a crude and but slightly ethical ancestor-worship, combined with a modified form of totemism and a belief in magic and fetishism; they have developed no philosophy, accepting the crudest hedonism, and giving up the problem of existence as not worth seriously troubling about; they have evolved no lofty ideals of any sort, being frankly content with abundance of cattle, beer, and women."[17]

We have seen that the unmodified African way of life has everywhere been a primitive communism, narrowly yet intensely centered in the tribe. This social system inhibited larger loyalties or wider sympathies, and stunted individual development; yet it *was* a social order, effectively disciplining the individual by the force of custom and taboo. This gave the Negro a group-morality, in default of that individual morality possessed by other races which have created high ethical codes.

Now that primitive social order may have sufficed so long as the African dwelt in isolation; but it could not long resist the impact of the West, because it is wholly incompatible with Western civilization. Yet its sudden loss must spell at least temporary mental and moral chaos for individuals thus suddenly deprived of traditional disciplines, with virtually nothing to take their place.

There lies the deeper crisis through which Africa is passing today. And it obviously has no logical connection with misgovernment or

16 We are here using the word in its broad sense. Certain Negro peoples have developed local arts and crafts which are well worth fostering and preserving.
17 Kidd, *op. cit.*, p.51.

economic exploitation. White abuses may intensify bad conditions, but conditions would be bad enough even though white rule were vastly more enlightened and just. A primitive race is being compelled to adjust itself to radically novel circumstances for which it is quite unprepared. Whether or not it will succeed still remains to be proved.

Meanwhile, the ordeal will be, at best, a grueling one. "Disease, Drink, and Clothing form Civilization's trinity of evil, in so far as the physical well-being of most savage races is concerned. European diseases kill far more savages than European rifles."[18] Everywhere it is the same melancholy story.

The natives of East Africa rank relatively high in ability and intelligence, yet the undermining of their tribal order has brought most of them into a sad plight, thus tellingly analyzed: "The native's future now hangs in the balance. If he continues as at present, it will be as a drag on the civilized progress of the country. His methods of life are a bar to a healthy, increasing birth-rate . . . His life is a chaotic medley of customs that are good and customs utterly deleterious. Though the advent of European civilization has produced benefits which he cannot fail to recognize, it has thrown into his life, amongst other things, a currency system to which he finds it hard to adjust his native life and ideas, and which bids fair to prove his undoing in the end . . . The weakness of his existence causes a spread of its evil influences. His Sons acquire an increasing desire for strong drink and an increasing aptitude for collecting easy money. His women discover that there are easier methods of living than that which circumscribes their existence by motherhood when young and by menial tasks when old. And so he *drifts,* his tribal life gradually dissolving, whilst nothing has as yet been instituted to replace it."[19]

In South Africa, a similar breakdown of group-mores has produced identical effects. Says Kidd: "We brought about the dawn of economic individualism. We gave the Kaffirs an example—that most potent kind of lesson—of a new kind of liberty, which some of them, naturally, thought excellent. The natives grew reluctant to part with individual gains. We taught them the value of thrift and

18 *Ibid.*, p. 201.
19 Quali, *op. cit.*

personal property; we created new wants and urged the natives to labor for us in return for wages—which, of course, was an entirely new thing to them, for in olden days they only worked so as to provide for their actual needs. Traders persuaded the natives to bring them skins, or grain, or wool, or other produce; and so we introduced a new economic era. Previously there had been but little division of labor, and no production of commodities. The people did not distinguish between use-values and exchange-values; but under our tuition they began to see the value of growing things, not for purposes of consumption, but for utility of exchange. We taught them the use of money.

"We thus brought in the era of economic individualism; and, since a Kaffir loses self-control when plunged into an entirely new environment, we sapped the very foundation of the spirit that had hitherto constituted the motive-power in clan-life. If by these means we have not utterly undermined the entire structure of the Clan-System, it is difficult to see what we have done."[20]

Thus far, be it noted, we have considered only the first stage of the readjusting process, when the Negro remains at home. Where he goes forth from his kraal into the white man's settlements and is thus exposed to the full impact of strange new forces, the results are even more disturbing. The hordes of black men, drawn from countless tribes, who come to sell their labor at mine-compounds, on plantations, or in domestic service, are a frowzy and bewildered lot. Mrs. Millin, that keen yet sympathetic portrayer of the South African scene, depicts the sordidness of black humanity in its "grub-form preceding civilization" when she shows us "a swarm of dirty, dusty-haired natives, dressed in the discarded clothing of the European—the filthy, unsightly rags that not the most degraded of white men would wear. There are circumstances under which dirt and tatters are held to be picturesque. Yet not even an artist of today would wish to express his realism in the drabness of dirt of a group of natives waiting outside a pass-office."[21]

These black men come nearly always with the intention of saving enough from their wages to go back home, buy a wife and a few head of cattle, and thereby realize the native ideal of "the good

20 Kidd, *Op Cit.*, p. 45.

21 Sarah Gertrude Millin, *The South Africans*, pp. 241–42 (New York, 1927).

life." Most of them do return to their native kraals. Yet contact with Westernism even in its most superficial aspects has changed them—and usually changed them for the worse. "If they have been to Johannesburg they will probably have brought back with them a great variety of things, including spats, watches, chains, old neckties, shirts, bunches of useless keys, 'swear words,' the love of spirits, conceit, disease, and sometimes militant Atheism; all of which things they take to as if to the manner born. Not that it is only at Johannesburg they get these questionable things: they pick up dirt by instinct, and in all conscience were full enough up with conceit, lust, and desire for drink, before they left their kraals. But naturally at Johannesburg they are free from what little restraint exists in the tribe, and the virulent germs of their nature find a suitable medium for a quick 'culture.'"[22]

Furthermore, these disorganized individuals tend to infect their stay-at-home neighbors, and thus to disrupt the entire kraal. In time, that disruption may become complete, so that we have the melancholy spectacle of "tribes that are degenerating, tribes that have emancipated themselves from allegiance to their own chiefs or ideals, that have no land or possessions, that have yielded their own traditions anti have acquired very little from white civilization with which to replace the loss. That, for the Kaffir himself, is the chief tragedy—the irretrievable, uncompensated loss. When he came sweeping down the east coast from the North three centuries ago, all South Africa seemed to be his province. He was bold and virile and prolific . . . Today the children of the race of Tchaka, . . . all the black people who were once friends or enemies to one another and who challenged the march of civilization, they are all the charges, the servants, the dependents, the victims, the problems of the white man."[23]

A considerable proportion of the black laboring population do not return to their native kraals, but go definitely over to the urban life of the West. Most of these transplanted savages root precariously on the fringes of our economic and social life. A few graduate from squalid "nigger-towns" into relative comfort in the Western sense, and likewise acquire a modicum of white ways and ideas.

22 Dudley Kidd, *The Essential Kaffir* p. 26 (London, 1904).

23 Millin, *op. cit.*, pp. 223–26.

Yet even among this elite, adaptation takes a heavy toll. Says Morel: "The Europeanized African of the West Coast towns, who wears European clothes, and whose women don corsets, stockings, and fashionable foot gear, is far less long-lived than his ancestors, and has far fewer children. As a class, the educated West African is a perishing one: a class which, at heart, is profoundly unhappy."[24]

In precisely the same vein, Mrs. Millin paints a truly striking word-picture of the "civilized" black town-dwellers in South Africa. "They have," she writes, "their social sets and social standards. They live in brick houses with streets at their doors . . . They have English or Dutch Christian names, and call one another Mr. or Mrs.—Mrs. Selebane, Mrs. Itumeleng, Mr. Oliphant, .. . They sing hymns, giving them an odd Kaffir quality in the singing—wildness penetrates the meek notes of the music. They go to school. They learn the piano. They play tennis. They love letter-writing. 'I take this short delightful—' they begin in English, although they converse in Dutch or Sesuto . . . Indeed, such people are, on the whole, a decent, honest, respectable, law-abiding community; but not—given the opportunity—as clean as the domesticated Zulus, nor as healthy or agreeable to look at. They die easily of many diseases—and chiefly of syphilis."[25]

Our survey of current trends among the natives in Britain's African colonies is not cheering. Yet conditions in British Africa are, by-and-large, better than elsewhere—ahead of conditions in the Belgian Congo, and certainly vastly superior to those in Portuguese Africa. France's record with the natives comes second only to England's.

France has, on the whole, governed well, though its imperialistic policy and its large-scale conscription of black soldiers bear hard upon the natives in certain ways.

Furthermore, attempts to hasten the spread of the French language and French ideas, while they may produce a few really cultured individuals, hasten the destruction of tribal consciousness and local traditions, thus intensifying the chaos of the transition period. The British, on the contrary, usually try to preserve the best

---

24 Morel, *op. cit.*, p.160.

25 Millin, *op. cit.*, pp. 246–48.

features in the native way of life; they certainly have no desire to turn Negroes into British Africans as France aims at transforming Negroes into *Français de couleur.*

The strength and weakness of French rule in Africa are alike revealed in that extraordinary book, *Batouala,* which won the Prix Goncourt and became an international sensation when it appeared, about a decade ago. Its author, René Maran, is a full-blooded Negro who is also an official in the French colonial service.

M. Maran has certainly absorbed French culture, and evidently feels himself a patriotic black Frenchman—*un vrai Français dc couleur.* Nevertheless, the tempo and motif of *Batouala* are decidedly un-French; un-European. The story, concerned with the life and death of a petty Negro chief, is "an African idyll; hot, savage, violent, ugly; having rhythm and having vitality, but a rhythm and a life that are not ours. All through seems to run the pulsation of that drumming which is articulate language for the African bush, but for European ears mere frenzy.

"The life depicted has nothing in common with ours but the sun and the moon. Through this sole link is conveyed what we can recognize as beauty; yet at the same time we are made to feel that it is not our sun or our moon . . . The book is not solely a work of art; it is also an indictment . . . against the methods of colonial rule and the type of men employed in it. .. . The present policy may exterminate the native Africans; it cannot make Frenchmen of them." It is interesting to note that, though thoroughly loyal to France, M. Maran inveighs bitterly against the mass-conscription of black man-power for prospective use on European battlefields. "He is in revolt against the idea of sending these unfortunate people to be butchered in defense of a civilization to which they do not belong; which is to them of no value."[26]

Batouala is the most widely known of several important books on French Africa and its problems.[27] That they happen to be

26 This characterization, together with those of the other two books which follow in the text, are taken from an extensive survey of recent French literature in this field by Stephen Gwynne, "Literary Studies of Greater France," *Edinburgh Review,* October, 1926.

27 These are all adequately summarized and interpreted by Stephen Gwynne's survey, previously cited.

novels does not detract from their significance, because the French habitually discuss topics of great popular interest in fictional form.

A most enlightening volume of this series is *Koffi,* by Gaston Joseph, "for whose authority on detail M. Angoulvent, sometime Governor-General of the colonies, goes warrant. This *roman vrai d'un noir* describes, according to him, a truly typical career . . . In truth, Koffi, the black boy who wanted to be like a Frenchman, might be cited as an awful example. A naked little Pagan living in an inland village of the Ivory Coast, he was fired by the conversation and appearance of a somewhat older youngster who returned from town to swagger about in European clothes and talk about the hops and gaieties."

So Koffi went to town, and "while he was cook in a civilian household, attended the meetings of *La Jeunesse Intellectuelle,* where he listened with admiration to speeches in the equivalent of Baboo English. His knowledge of French, however imperfect, enabled him when acting as interpreter for a capable and wise magistrate to help on the work of civilization. Finally, when the chief of his tribe died, Koffi contrived to be chosen as his successor.

"Then the trouble began. On the moral side, Koffi's conversion had been genuine. Where the chiefs before him had given judgments based on custom and on a superstitious tradition, the *Français de couleur* decided according to equity, following the example of his late master. Furthermore, he never called in the aid of fetish diviners. Naturally he had the fetish men up in arms. They succeeded in giving him a dose of poison, enough to frighten him and send him for advice to his mother—against the opinion of his Europeanized wife. The mother passed him on to a witch, and between the two all the fetish belief was revived in his mind.

"Still, he continued to be the advocate in his tribe of white men's ideas. His fellow tribesmen come to him and complain of increased taxes for which they get nothing. Koffi tells them they get protection which gives them peace; they get free dispensaries, and schools where their children can be taught what the parents never knew. We learn thus what the good French official desires to fix in the native mind. Special stress is laid on the value of roads, and of vehicles for transport to replace human porterage. But though Koffi can argue he cannot enforce, and when his people strike on their taxes, he must take their part. His worries bring on drunkenness; he loses all authority, and in the end is arrested and banished to the *far-off* French Congo.

"It is pleasant to learn that he achieved peace and prosperity there by manufacturing and selling an aphrodisiac, until he died of drink. Still, considered as an apostate, his career was not a success; and M. Angoulvent, admitting it as typical, can only declare his faith that all die unsuccessful Koffis, all the *Français tie couleur* who end by being indifferent Africans, go like fallen leaves 'to form a rich humus out of which will one day spring the Tree of Life and the Tree of Knowledge.'"

Equally significant, from a different angle, is Robert Randau's novel, *Le Chef des Porte-Plume—an* extremely realistic study of French officialdom in tropical Africa.

Batouala stressed the prevalence of drunkenness among French officials, and "M. Randau's picture is surcharged with alcoholism.

"But that is only one count in what may fairly be called his indictment of French human nature, as exhibited under tropical conditions. Like M. Claude Farrère in *Les Civilisés,* a book dealing with colonial life at Saigon, French Indo-China, M. Randau holds that the Frenchman is apt to run wild sexually in the tropics . . . He makes it very plain that West Africa is no country for the white man, still less for the white woman . . .

"I do not propose to go into the scenes of this extremely disagreeable novel which describes how a Governor-General and his associates behave when off duty. On duty they are, M. Randau implies, as different as Jack at sea from Jack ashore.

"But I must quote one passage in which Governor Ledolmer, the principal character in the story, asks himself why Frenchmen should risk their lives in West Africa, where their race can never be acclimatized, and can only atrophy through crossing bloods: 'What are we here for? To make the fortune of a few dozen more or less honest traders? To teach the Negroes Rousseau's paradoxes about human goodness and the Social Contract? These folks were used to simple ideas and beliefs; we upset their psychology—to what end? Are they some day to create republics like Liberia, or the South

American states? We shall have spent ourselves only to bring about the triumph of race-hatred. The half-civilized townspeople have their mouths full of the Principles of *1789;* they make only one inference from them—that you must push out the European. And what pains me most is that, among them, no man of mark arises, no thinker, writer, or artist; the tropics never produce anything that counts in the scale of human thought.' . . . This point of view needs an answer, which M. Randau puts in the mouth of a younger man. It is this: 'The African blacks hold the great reserves of raw materials. At this moment their best blood is being shed with ours against the *Boche.* Therefore we need them; therefore they will commit themselves to our path; and for us to guide them in it is only the last item in the menu of our policy.'

"That puts it plain enough. France's need (not her impulse to take up the White Man's Burden) is decisive; she needs Africa and Africans; therefore she will guide them on their own way—perhaps without too rigid application of the doctrines of 1789."

Factors such as those just described explain in large measure the profound disintegration, psychological as well as social, today prevalent among the black populations under French rule. These acutely disturbed conditions, in turn, account for the heavy loss of life in many districts, which in some cases implies a literal dying-out of the inhabitants.

A decade ago, for instance, the well-known English traveler, Frederick Migeod, after two journeys across equatorial Africa, reported a deplorable situation in the French Congo area.

Whole tribes were moving in from the hinterland to the coastal region near the mouth of the Congo, where, lacking the will to live, they frankly voiced their desire to die out.

"The Gaboon area," said Migeod, "is becoming a vast graveyard for the dying races of Central Africa . . . It is indeed the most amazing case of racial suicide on a huge scale that the world has ever seen. I passed among tribes where the women refuse to bear children, and in another generation, if the present ideas prevail, they will have simply ceased to exist. I heard of a tribe further north where the chief has absolutely forbidden marriage, with this same idea.

"So pronounced is this lack of will to live that many tribes have been compelled by the French authorities to grow enough food to keep themselves alive, and the arts of pottery and the making of agricultural implements have quite died out.

"I believe that this desire to die dates from the introduction of the liquor traffic among the natives, now happily stopped, and the spread of certain diseases by newcomers from Europe and other parts of Africa. But certainly there is nothing more extraordinary than this drift of peoples into the Gaboon, which they have apparently decided to make the grave of their races."[28]

More recently, an official report of Doctor Boye, Chief of Health Service, notes the continuance of these conditions in French Equatorial Africa, and in French West Africa as well. He states that "tribes formerly prosperous and vigorous are today on the verge of extinction." A provincial governor in French Congo reports that in districts where, only fifteen years ago, population was dense, there are today "only skeletons of villages."

Conditions in French West Africa are somewhat better, but even there the natives' health is bad—on the average, only one recruit out of six is fit for military service. The two chief scourges are syphilis and malaria—both prime causes of infant mortality. But tuberculosis is also rampant, spread by soldiers returned from European service and also associated with the growing use of alcoholic liquors. Furthermore, there is much evidence of deliberate restriction of births through wholesale abortion.

The weight of evidence thus indicates that the transition period through which Africa is passing bears harder upon the French colonies than upon those under British rule.

In our survey of tropical Africa we saw that enlightened self-interest tended to impel the whites to further the wellbeing of the natives and to encourage the increase of the Negro populations. Since the natural wealth of the African tropics can be developed by the whites only with the aid of abundant black labor, because climate prohibits white settlement, there is here no basic economic conflict between the races.

---

28 Interview in London by *The New York Times's* representative, cabled under date of May 16, 1921.

The sole *seeming* exceptions to this rule are a few highland areas in East Africa, where elevation overcomes heat sufficiently to produce cool uplands which are climatically "white man's country," in the sense that whites can live there healthfully and raise thriving families of children. The best-known of these highlands is in Kenya Colony, British East Africa, though there are similar highlands in Tanganyika, Nyasaland, and the Kivu district of the Belgian Congo. Accordingly, they are all becoming the home of a resident white population which, though as yet small, is growing at a fairly rapid rate.

These white settlements are often referred to as "problems" involving a fundamental clash between black and white, with repercussions that may envenom racial relations throughout tropical Africa. When we look at the facts, however, such statements seem either quite unfounded or, at most, grossly exaggerated.

In the first place, those highland districts are all relatively small—indeed, insignificant, compared to the immense bulk of tropical Africa. Again, climate makes it impossible for them ever to support a *solidly* white population. The reason is that, no matter how high and cool an upland near the equator may be, the actinic rays of the sun, being unaffected by altitude, are just as dangerous to the average white man there as they would be in the hot lowlands nearby.

Therefore, occupations involving prolonged exposure to the sun, and especially agricultural field-work, cannot be successfully conducted by whites.[29] As a matter of fact, most of the white settlers in the highlands of equatorial Africa are large-scale farmers or ranchers, and such persons need plenty of black labor. Thus, the prosperity of the highland settlements should be an economic benefit to blacks and whites alike.

The larger realities of the situation are ably set forth by a British colonial official whom long experience renders an authority on such matters. Says Sir Daniel Hall:

---

29 Seeming exceptions to this, as in Queensland, Australia, are largely explained by the fact that such regions lie on the very edges of the tropics adjacent to the temperate zones, where the actinic power of the sun is much less than near the equator. Of course, humidity and temperature also play an important part, but the actinic rays seem to be the decisive factor.

"Much has been heard of the necessity for a common native policy in East Africa. Further, it seems to be thought that such a policy would be easy of realization did not Kenya with its white settlers stand in the way. But Kenya is only one of the territories where one has to reckon with the white settler, the man who is not merely conducting an agricultural or mineral exploitation but who is making a home.

"Again, it is difficult to see how any common denominator can be found between native peoples like the Baganda, with their comparatively advanced systems of government and land-holding, or the tribes in the Bukoba province of Tanganyika (who go about in motor cars or at least on cycles), and many tribes which are still in the nomadic pastoral stage. When one gets closer to the problem in Kenya, which in its diversity may almost be regarded as an epitome of all East African conditions, it is clear that the native problem is not one but several; and, moreover, that its political aspect is negligible in comparison with the economic and social difficulties. At home one is led to think of Kenya as a source of conflict between white man and native; near at hand, the anxious question for the Administration is how to maintain the conditions under which the native can continue his accustomed life, even with all the relief he obtains by working for the white man."[30]

Thus the much-touted "Kenya Question" turns out to be not only quite different from what certain critics would have us believe, but also is in itself merely a small part of a very much larger whole. And in none of its phases is any genuine economic conflict between the races discernible. The problem of tropical Africa retains its basic unity.[31]

---

30 Sir Daniel Hall, "The Native Question in Kenya," *Nineteenth Century and After,* January, 1930.

31 Neither here nor in our discussion of South African affairs will we treat specifically the Indian factor. Had it not been checked by drastic restriction or downright prohibition, the immigration of East Indians would have given rise to problems of extreme gravity, alike in East and in South Africa. Because of such restrictive measures, however, the Indian element, while it will long continue to be locally vexatious, should apparently not seriously complicate the basic problem of the relations of black and white. In a general survey such as that undertaken in this book, many minor issues, however interesting, must be omitted, in order to maintain due balance and proportion.

Far different, however, is the situation in South Africa. There we do find a very real clash between black and white; a complex antagonism which causes race-tension already grave and bound to become graver still as time goes on.

Africa thrusts massively down from the Tropics well into the south temperate zone. Near the southernmost curve of its blunted tip, a bold promontory juts out into the sea. This is the Cape of Good Hope, named by Portuguese discoverers rounding the Dark Continent on their epoch-making voyage to India four centuries ago. Thenceforth the Cape with its sheltered harbor served as a way-station to ship-masters of various nationalities en route to the East, yet for a long time no flag was raised over a spot which offered little to men whose gaze was fixed on the fabled Indies. Not until 1652 did the Dutch make a permanent settlement, called Cape Town, chiefly so that their East India-men might have an assured supply of fresh meat and green stuff midway in their long voyages.

Once established, however, the Dutch settlers found the Cape a pleasant place, with a temperate climate, good soil, and adequate rainfall. But those conditions were strictly local. A short distance inland terraced mountains rose, tier on tier, to a vast plateau which swept grandly northeastward into the unknown—as a matter of fact, for fully a thousand miles. This was the high veldt, "a great bare land, sharply picked out in gold and black by the sun."[32]

In those old days, South Africa was not merely bare but also singularly empty of human life. Over its illimitable distances ranged bands of Bushmen—little yellow-skinned nomad hunters with wizened monkey-faces. Slightly higher in the human scale, yet very primitive, was another breed, the Hottentots. That was all. The tall Bantu Negroes had not appeared on the scene. Early navigators first encountered those big, fierce black men far up the east coast, around Delagoa Bay.

The white man was thus the first to stake out a claim. Had he come rapidly and in great numbers, he might have made South Africa wholly white. For it is climatically white man's land. All South Africa lies below the tropics. Even when one goes northward and the sun gets unduly strong, its heat is tempered by altitude. The

32 Millin, op. *cit.,* p. 51.

aborigines certainly were no hindrance to white settlement. The wild little Bushmen were bound to vanish like smoke before the coming of any strong race.

As for the Hottentots, they were equally foredoomed. Also, they did not make efficient slaves, so that subtle danger to the white racial future was absent. The way was open for the whites to enter and utterly possess the land.

But this the white man did not do. He entered slowly and spread tardily. Furthermore, be presently brought in Javanese from the Dutch Indies and Negroes from other parts of Africa, to till the soil and do domestic service. True, these imported slaves were not many, yet they were enough to fix the servile tradition upon South Africa and thereby keep the white settlers a master-class disdaining the more menial occupations.

A few far-sighted individuals saw the danger and urged the bringing in of white rather than colored labor. The words of one of these objectors have a prophetic ring.

Said Van Imhoff, a member of the Dutch Governor's Council: "Having imported slaves, every common or ordinary European becomes a gentleman and prefers to be served rather than to serve. We have, in addition, the fact that the majority of farmers in this colony are not farmers in the real sense of the word, but plantation owners, and many of them consider it a shame to work with their own hands." However, such warnings were disregarded, and colored labor, cheaper and more docile, became the rule.

As time passed and the fertile coastal valleys became comfortably filled, the rapidly multiplying Cape Dutch scaled the mountain-passes and emerged upon the high veldt. There was bred the South African Boer—sun-tanned and lean, bold and stubborn, simple and God-fearing, easy-going and conservative.

Hunters, ranchers, or dry-farmers, the Boers spread steadily inland until, more than a century after the Dutch founded Cape Town, up-thrusting white frontiersmen met the black Bantu wave rolling down from the north. And then the real trouble began: that great racial clash "predestined on the day the first Dutchman landed at the Cape, and the first Bantu turned his dark face to the south."[33]

33 *Ibid.*, p. 267.

Thenceforth the hinterland was red with war. Despite long rifles unerringly aimed, the Boer pioneers were hard-pressed by those surging black hosts that seemed to have no end. Had not the Kaffirs fought each other as fiercely as they fought the whites, the Boer frontier might have been driven back to the coast. Then into this confused welter of strife came a new factor. South Africa passed from Dutch to English rule. British settlers arrived; British soldiers took up the struggle against the blacks; British law and order began to be imposed upon Boer and Kaffir alike.

Yet this last was almost equally distasteful to both, especially when slavery was formally abolished throughout the British Empire in the year 1833. In Boer eyes, this was an intolerable upsetting of a way of life bequeathed them by their fathers, which they did not propose to abandon. So presently the boldest and most embittered of the Cape Dutch hitched their oxen to great covered-wagons; piled in their goods, their womenfolk, their numerous children; and, with their cattle and their black servitors, set forth into the free, uncharted wilderness to the northward. That was the Great Trek.

It was a true migration. Steadily, casually, the *voortrekkers* wandered on; now settling in likely spots, now beating oil the onslaughts of savage black hordes from behind the shelter of their covered-wagons, drawn up in *laager* or hollow square—just like their remote migrating Teutonic ancestors, and just as their distant American blood-kin were doing at that very moment against Redskins on Far Western plains. Usually, good marksmanship picked off the encircling blacks like antelopes or broke Kaffir charges by withering blasts of rifle-fire. If not—then those beleaguered Boers died utterly, the men fighting to the last, the women killing themselves and their children to avert a fate in their eyes worse than death—the shame unthinkable of falling into black hands.

For those transplanted Dutchmen, like all Nordic peoples, were keenly race-conscious and had an especial aversion to taking up black blood. They have never blinked the issue. The Boer Fundamental Law *(Grondwet)* explicitly declares: *There shall be no equality between black and white.* From that the South African

Dutch never have, and never will, budge one iota. They may be killed out some day, but they will not compromise on the principle of race-integrity. Furthermore, an overwhelming majority of the British settlers agree absolutely with the Boers on this vital point. Therefore South Africa today has a "color-bar" just as strict as the American "color-line."

Indeed, the South Africans are even more acutely conscious of the color problem than Americans are outside our "Deep South," because in South Africa the whites are everywhere a minority. Taking the Union as a whole, the white element numbers slightly less than one-fourth of the total population.[34] The presence of a large and increasingly restive black majority is fast healing the historic breach between Boer and Briton which came to a bloody climax in the war of a generation ago. So, though bitter memories still linger and crop out in political bickerings, the younger generation is acquiring a common South African patriotism, and another decade or two will presumably see a firmly welded white *Afrikander* nationality.

That is the white side of the picture. The black side is more complex. To begin with, the Bantu rank among the most warlike and virile of the Negro stocks.[35]

Despite the prevalence of new diseases among the town-dwelling Negroes and the degeneracy of certain badly disorganized tribes, the black population shows no signs of dying out. Indeed, where they have been shielded from the full impact of our civilization, as in the native protectorates, they have bred with enormous rapidity. In Basutoland, for instance, under the fostering care of British officials guiding native rulers who have maintained tribal discipline, the population has apparently increased five-or six-fold within a century, so that Basutoland is today over-peopled. Incidentally, it should be noted that laws against selling or giving liquor to natives are so strictly enforced in South Africa that the natives have been

---

34 The latest census reports for the Union of South Africa gives Whites, 1,676,000; Colored, 5,409,000. Of the colored total, 165,000 are Asiatics, mostly from India, and 545,000 mixed-bloods or other races. There are therefore 4,697,000 of unmixed Bantu (Kaffir) stock.

35 The Bantu do not, however, seem to be as intelligent as certain other Negro peoples, such as the Baganda of East Africa.

protected against the alcoholism which has elsewhere proved so destructive to Negroes. The Kaffir still brews his native beer, but it is so low in alcoholic content that, though it gets him pleasantly mulled, it seems to do him little harm.

The South African natives should be visualized as living under all sorts of conditions, ranging from kraal-dwellers barely touched by white influences right up to those "high-society" black folk portrayed by Mrs. Millin, who live in almost European fashion. Then there are certain mixed-blood communities with a special consciousness of their own. The most striking of these groups is that of the so-called "Cape Boys," centering at Cape Town and vicinity. The Cape Boys are, in very truth, "a peculiar people." They are partly descended from the slaves of Dutch colonial times; so in them are Hottentot, Javanese, Malay, white, and Bantu strains, with presumably a spice of Bushman for good measure. These amazing mongrels despise the blacks and hate the whites who refuse them the social equality for which they secretly yearn. Quite numerous in Cape Colony, they have long been recognized as a grave source of potential trouble. In fact, all the mixed-bloods, together with the more Europeanized blacks, chafe against the color-bar, especially as manifested in certain "Jim-Crow" regulations on railways and other public conveyances.

Yet social friction in South Africa is not yet so intense as might off-hand be imagined. To the great mass of "raw Kaffirs," racial discriminations mean next to nothing and are usually taken as a matter of course. Most of the race-antagonism that now exists is due to economic reasons. South Africa's economic life is run on a distinctly racial basis. All unskilled labor is black; semi-skilled workers are either black or colored,[36] while all skilled workers and business or professional men are white.

These economic lines are rigidly drawn. The poorest white man will not touch "Kaffir's work," while a clever black mechanic is not allowed to take a "white man's job." Since both races are increasing at a fairly rapid rate,[37] economic pressure gets more

36 That is the term often used in South Africa to distinguish what we term mulattoes from full-blooded Negroes.

37 And at about the same rate. According to the last census, the whites gained 19.06 per cent; the colored 15.16 per cent. Some of the white increase was,

and more intense. Were there no color-bar, the natives, with their much lower living-standards and wage-scales, would tend to oust whites from many occupations. Even as it is, there are many "Poor Whites," unable to get jobs, who have become chronic paupers. Furthermore, such economic conditions prevent large-scale European immigration. Had the Negro not been present, South Africa would undoubtedly have had a rapid influx from Europe during the past century which might easily have given the Union a white population several times as great as it is today.

With race-tension inevitably growing, and with the whites unable to increase their relative numerical strength, the situation becomes steadily more ominous and white ascendancy less secure. Of this the whites are only too well aware, so they are now striving to buttress their position and at least partially safeguard their future by a policy of racial segregation.

The whole of the Union is eventually to be marked off into white and Negro districts within which the two races shall separately dwell, though black labor may sojourn temporarily in the white areas, as officially specified. "The idea is that the black man ought to be detached from the white man's share of South Africa, and allowed to develop on his own land and along his own lines. The white man shall not enter the black man's sphere except mildly, to give a guiding hand. The black man shall not enter the white man's sphere except, humbly, to give a helping hand."

This, of course, "is not a new thing. A hundred years ago missionaries advocated some form of it. The early Transvaalers were in favor of an almost absolute cleavage of black from white . . .The Basutos are, in a measure, self-governing, and there are not more than three white men to a thousand natives in Basutoland. So are Bechuanaland and Swaziland native reserves under the Colonial Office, and there are, besides, in all the Union provinces, native reserves and locations. We have then already a modified form of segregation."[38] Yet the systematic, thorough-going segregation now in prospect will bear hard upon the natives, especially the semi-Europeanized elements, who look down on the uncivilized Kaffirs

---

however, due to immigration, while the native increase was due entirely to births. Thus statistically corrected, the natural increases are almost identical.

38 Millin, op. *cit.*, pp. 377–79.

and wish neither to live among them nor be identified with them. As the segregating process goes on, it must inevitably intensify native unrest.

However most Afrikanders believe that thus only can white ascendancy, perhaps white existence itself, be perpetuated. The alternative is vividly expressed in General Smuts's grim warning that white South Africa must have a care "lest one day little brown children play among the ruins of the Union Government Buildings."

No man, indeed, has better voiced the Afrikander viewpoint than did this eminent Boer leader in an address delivered nearly twenty years ago. "In South Africa," he said, "we are not simply in a white man's country. It has been our ideal to make it a white man's country, but it is not a white man's country yet.

"There are certain axioms which have been laid down in regard to the black and white races. One is that there must be no intermixture of blood. All previous civilizations on the African continent have failed—perhaps because that principle was never recognized. The superior civilizing race was lost in the quicksands of African blood. Our forefathers, both English and Dutch, have been strong on this point, with the result that the white blood has remained pure in South Africa, and it has become axiomatic there that it is a dishonorable thing and contrary to our whole tradition that there shall be any mixture of white and black blood.

"Instead of mixing up black and white all over the country, we are now trying to keep them as far apart as possible in government. In that way we are striving to lay down a policy which may take hundreds of years to work out but which in the end may be a solution of our native problem; and the result will be that in the long run you will have all over South Africa large areas inhabited entirely by blacks, where the blacks are looking after themselves according to their own ways of life and forms of government. In suitable parts you will have your white communities . . .

"It is useless to run black and white at the same momentum and to subject them to the same political machinery. White and black are different not only in color but almost in soul."[39]

---

39 This address was reprinted in the *Journal of the African Society* (London) July, 1917.

Despite its attendant difficulties and dangers, this policy of progressive segregation represents the bare minimum which white South Africa believes necessary to its salvation. For many Afrikanders, however, segregation does not suffice.

They see in it merely a palliative; not a cure. South Africa, they assert, must be made racially what it is climatically—white man's country. With iron logic, they argue that European ascendancy cannot lastingly endure in a land one-quarter white and three-quarters black.

Therefore, they conclude, while both populations are relatively small, the blacks must be *transported* to those vast regions of tropical Africa which are still under-peopled and where the blacks of the Union can accordingly be found suitable homes.

Afrikanders have been discussing this transportation project for many years, and though it is still generally deemed impracticable, they discuss it more and more frequently as time goes on. One thing is certain: Afrikanders will attempt to do whatever they have fully made up their minds must be done in order to preserve white ascendancy and integrity.

Meanwhile, this small but vigorous Afrikander people is looking beyond its borders, realizing that its own local problems are logically involved with the general course of events in the Dark Continent. As a South African writer recently remarked: "It already begins to feel that everything African concerns it more or less, and the sources of the Nile itself no longer seem so far away. Are not Europeans settled so far north as Kenya turning a hopeful eye to the Union? . . . Prominent Transvaal politicians propose that a kind of inverted Dixie Line should be drawn by international agreement, separating the color-bar states of White Africa from the color-blind states of Black Africa to the north . . .

"Doubtless, settlers from those parts could easily find accommodation south of this Dixie Line; on the other hand, encouragement of every kind would be given to native tribes wishing to shift towards the north . . . Then, looking still further north, the advocates of this policy hope for a buffer belt of equatorial territories, from the Cameroons to Abyssinia, neutralized and controlled by the League of Nations, segregating the militarized

French West African colonies."[40] Thus white South Africa plans and ponders—alert, watchful, irrevocably determined on certain things.

Stand off and look at Africa as a whole. What do we see? In long perspective we glimpse three major situations, each differing profoundly from the others.

French North Africa, the long coastal-belt between the Mediterranean and the Sahara, portends grave trouble. There, fully 10,000,000 Arabs and Berbers are being welded by a blend of religious fervor, cultural pride, and hatred of alien rulers into a strange sort of nationalism with highly explosive possibilities. Should this new spirit ripen, France might not be able to hold North Africa, or could regain it only after a frightful struggle in which the native population would have been crushed and in large part destroyed.

South of the Sahara no such situation exists. Throughout tropical Africa we see little except a huge welter of primitive societies and crude ways of life crumbling under the impact of our civilization as though touched by a powerful dissolvent acid. The dominant white man is, of course, not beloved, yet neither is he greatly hated. Rather is he feared, admired—and copied.

Negro risings may occur, but these will be due less to racial antagonism than to the disturbing effects of economic and political measures framed by the white rulers. Only in French West Africa is there the possibility of a concerted, large-scale native revolt; and that would take place, not because the French are white, but because conscription, prolonged and general, had infuriated whole populations and also taught them to fight in French fashion. Yet even this possibility seems remote. On the whole, tropical Africa will presumably continue to dissolve socially and be reconstructed economically by European capital and initiative.

South of the Zambezi the sky darkens and, as in the far north, storm-clouds lower. Yet these cloud-masses are neither so dense nor so indicative of a mighty tempest to come. The two situations are

---

40 A South African Pen, "Africa from the South," *The Round Table, December 1930.*

decidedly unlike. Even if we disregard the racial factor and, in this instance, put Negroes on the same plane with Arabs and Berbers, the South African blacks possess no commensurate spiritual and cultural driving-power. And those intangibles count enormously; they are apt to make all the difference between a vain uprising no matter how wild and bloody, and a successful upheaval. It is true that the Bantu are mostly good fighters; that amongst them there is today general unrest, widespread discontent, and a deal of bitter hatred against the white Afrikanders. All this portends trouble—probably plenty of trouble in years to come. By looking only at this phase of the situation we could easily paint a most alarming picture of what may be in store.

Yet it would be a picture drawn badly out of scale. The larger viewpoint shows some 5,000,000 savages or semi-savages, scattered over vast territories, not merely ill-armed but unequipped with spiritual or cultural weapons, and above all exposed to the same disintegrating effects of a higher alien civilization which are sending the black peoples of tropical Africa economically and socially into the melting-pot. To think that, in a conceivably near future, the Kaffirs could forge the moral strength and unity needed to best such tough adversaries as Boer and Briton, is little short of absurd. Thus the nightmare of a mighty black revolution hurling the white man back into the sea whence he came appears as the figment of an over-wrought or jaundiced imagination.

In South Africa, as elsewhere on the Dark Continent, our civilization and our race will go forward, destroying and creating, until the outlines of a transformed Africa shall eventually be disclosed.

EPILOGUE

CUSTOM ordains that a survey should have a definite conclusion. The human mind instinctively craves solutions; it wants diagnosis of its ills to end with a recipe for their cure. If this is not done, we tend to be disappointed; to experience a certain sense of frustration. This is normal and natural. Yet it is unavoidable in any adequate survey of our present-day world, reeling under the impact of strange, titanic forces; rolling swiftly toward a future essentially unpredictable and hence unknown.

The outstanding feature of the contemporary world-situation is that it appears to be as unprecedented as it is complex. Never before has one civilization prevailed over the entire earth. All mankind, with its wide distinctions of temperament and tradition, is faced with the necessity of adapting itself to a way of life evolved by a single branch of the human species.

Can our distinctively Western civilization be successfully transplanted and generalized? We have seen how diverse are the reactions of various races and how manifold the attendant complications. Clearly, no one formula will serve nor will a simple answer suffice. Definite trends may appear in given situations, and those trends can be evaluated. But any attempt to generalize from conditions so unlike one another as those today observable among American Indians, Asiatics, and Africans defies a common denominator.

Adaptations to Western civilization throughout the world will inevitably vary with human variation. This means that mankind has entered upon a transition period whose outcome is uncertain. Mere adoption of Western technics and method does not spell complete Westernization; neither does it necessarily imply that Westernism will everywhere be successfully assimilated. Westernism's deeper effects upon alien peoples, now becoming visible, are too profound to give any unqualified assurance as to the outcome. Time alone can determine where, when, and in what measure harmonious blends will come to pass.

Indeed, it is not yet certain that Western man will accommodate himself to the predominantly mechanistic civilization he has created. The unbalanced character of contemporary Western life is only too plain. To be sure, there are hopeful indications that Western man is preparing to redress this lack of balance; that a more spiritual and cultural age is dawning for our modern world. Yet hope is not certainty. There have been false dawns.

However unpredictable the future, the present is ours to better and so to shape that a brighter morrow may come. In order to do this we must know precisely where we stand and what are the problems confronting us. That is why this book has been written. It tries to see the present-day world as a whole, to glimpse its outstanding aspects, and to comprehend their interrelations.

Eschewing prophecy and avoiding simplistic solutions, the author has confined himself to the task (difficult enough in itself!) of interpreting current conditions and suggesting methods of action. Perhaps this survey, admittedly inadequate and possibly faulty, may stimulate other minds more understanding and better equipped to grapple with the dilemmas that beset our troubled times.

Index

D

E

F

G

Q

R

S

T

U

V

W

Y

Z

Lightning Source UK Ltd.
Milton Keynes UK
UKHW022355020720
365921UK00002B/111

9 781646 066445